Psyched for Torah

Cultivating Character and Well-Being Through the Weekly Parsha

RABBI DR. MORDECHAI SCHIFFMAN

KODESH PRESS

PSYCHED FOR TORAH:

Cultivating Character and Well-Being Through the Weekly Parsha

© Mark Schiffman 2022

Hardcover ISBN: 978-1-947857-77-3

Paperback ISBN: 978-1-947857-76-6

PUBLISHED AND DISTRIBUTED EXCLUSIVELY BY

Kodesh Press LLC

New York, NY

www.kodeshpress.com

kodeshpress@gmail.com

Set in Arno Pro by Raphaël Freeman MISTD, Renana Typesetting

Printed in the United States of America

Contents

Jake & Karen Abilevitz

In memory of Karen's father

DR. SEYMOUR BEN-ZVI

שמעון דב בן שמואל אריה ע״ה

Sorah & Shlomo Acoca

Susan & Ira Cohen

Carin & Ben Dachs

Varda & Jeff Grodko

Zachary Grodko

Linda & Aaron Kinsberg

Gali & Yehuda Kohen

Jacklyn & Etai Lahav

Disha & Benjamin Schiffman

Andrea & David Sanders

Nava Sanders

Loren & Harry Schiffman

Carol & Dr. Julian Seewald

Malka & Doron Simon

Esther & Rabbi Etan Tokayer

Rachel & Chaim Weinstein

Preface

I have two distinct memories from high school of being asked what I wanted to be when I grow up. In one instance, I answered a rabbi. In the other, a psychologist. Years later, unable to make up my mind, I decided to be both.

In truth, I view my career pursuits as an integrated whole. My overarching mission statement is to help people (including myself) become the best versions of themselves, so they can lead meaningful lives. In my experience, the best way to accomplish this goal is by integrating the wisdom and lessons from the Torah and the modern discoveries from the field of psychology. Combined, they create an ideal space for personal, communal, and spiritual flourishing.

If I could analyze my high school mind, when I answered "psychologist," my view of psychology was limited. When we think about psychology, many of us imagine a therapist's couch. In fact, when I would later poll students in my introductory psychology courses, I learned that the reason many signed up to study psychology was to find out more about how therapy works. They were usually surprised to discover that the topics of mental illness and psychological therapies comprised only two of the fourteen units.

If I could analyze my post-college mind, at the end of my years in *semichah* at Rabbi Isaac Elchanan Theological Seminary (RIETS), when deciding what career I should pursue, the aspect of psychology which excited me the most was not the clinical, therapeutic aspect, but rather, the field of positive psychology. I was introduced to this field – and, critically, how it could overlap with Torah – when I was privileged to take a few courses at Azrieli Graduate School of Jewish Education and at RIETS with Dr. David Pelcovitz, whose positive influences over my life are immeasurable.

Dr. Martin Seligman, founder of the field of positive psychology, argued that for too long psychology had utilized a deficit model. The assumption had been that there was something wrong with people and we must fix it. Little focus was placed on happiness, well-being, or flourishing. If you imagine that people could function on a scale of −10 to +10, Dr. Seligman argued that psychology put too much emphasis on helping people who were at −7 improve to −2. He felt that the field should also focus on finding ways to help someone who is a +2 move to becoming a +7.

As a rabbinic intern at Kinsgway Jewish Center, I committed to giving a series of *shiurim* on the connections between positive psychology and Jewish thought. The endeavor of preparing and delivering those *shiurim* further aroused my passion for the integration of Torah and psychology. I was lucky enough to remain at Kingsway Jewish Center as the assistant rabbi while simultaneously pursuing a doctorate in psychology at St. John's University. I am incredibly grateful for the support I have received from the Kingsway leadership (the presidium, Yitz Elman & Jeff Grodko, current and past chairmen, Dr. Julian Seewald, Alice Loubaton, Rafi Lazerowitz, and so many other dedicated board and committee members) and membership (too many to list!) for encouraging and reinforcing my interest in the intersection of Torah and psychology, as well as coming together to provide financial backing for this project. A special thank you to Karen & Jake Abilevitz, who sponsored the original Lox & Learn series where I delivered those first *shiurim* on positive psychology and Judaism, and for their continued support throughout the years.

At St. John's, I continued to investigate elements of positive psychology, while also learning about training in other areas of psychology. Besides for learning the depths of psychological testing, learning disabilities, personality, developmental, and social psychology, I was given the opportunity to train as a therapist. I am incredibly grateful for the supervision I received at the Albert Ellis Institute, where I studied the intricacies of Rational Emotive Behavior Therapy under the tutelage of my mentor Dr. Raymond DiGiuseppe, as we well as Drs. Kristen Doyle and Michael Hickey. My clinical training was supplemented with the expert mentoring of Drs. Martin Galla and Yael Muskat of Yeshiva University's Counseling Center, where I was privileged to work for several years, with superb and dedicated colleagues. Besides for influencing my thinking and writing as it relates to the contents of this book, their guidance has made me into the therapist I am today and afforded me the ability to open my own private practice.

My interest in positive psychology was supplemented by a keen desire to also help alleviate the pain and suffering of those who suffer from anxiety, depression, anger, and other clinical disorders. I learned that it was possible to help people move from −7 to −2 *and* from +2 to +7. My dissertation melded the two perspectives together, focusing on the positive psychology of gratitude, but supplementing it with theories and concepts related to the irrational beliefs associated with unhealthy emotions.

This book quotes from many different subfields of psychology. Some concepts are therapeutic in nature, others focus on positive psychology, strengths, and well-being. Yet other sub-disciplines – including educational, social, personality, cognitive, and developmental psychology – will be utilized. Some of the psychologists quoted are household names, but many more aren't well known. Some ideas and studies are well-entrenched and documented through replication; others are more recent and still need to be corroborated through follow up research. The studies cited, as well as some additional relevant resources are listed at the end of the book.

The Torah concepts elucidated are built on the words of the early and later commentaries. I quote from an eclectic group of Torah personalities. Some insights have been gleaned from close reads of the *pesukim* themselves, while others from creative midrashic analysis. While this book draws on a broad range of sources, there are several works that have consistently provided sharp psychological insights on the *parsha*. These include Rabbi Jonathan Sacks' *Covenant and Conversation*, Rabbi Dr. Abraham J. Twerski's *Twerski on Chumash*, Rabbi Zelig Pliskin's *Growth through Torah*, and Rabbi Dr. Tzvi Hersh Weinreb's *The Person in the Parsha*.

While the topics covered are vast and varied, the unifying theme is that the ideas are meant to help us understand ourselves better, and motivate us to become the best versions of ourselves that we can be. Recurring themes include building self-awareness, cultivating happiness and spirituality, building and maintaining relationships, understanding and managing emotions, and improving character traits like grit, self-control, humility, kindness, empathy, and gratitude.

To express my own gratitude to all who have influenced me and helped directly or indirectly with my development and the eventual printing of this book would be an impossible endeavor. While not mentioning everyone by name, I am grateful to all family friends, teachers, *rabbanim*, social workers, school psychologists, and administrators who helped throughout my elementary school days at Yeshiva Derech HaTorah, particularly Rabbi Yisroel

Grossberg and Yehuda Goldstein, and my high school years at Yeshiva of Flatbush: Rabbis Joseph Beyda, Selim Dweck, *zt"l*, Jonathan Kroll, Ronald Levy, and Yitzchok Rosenblum, as well as Mica Bloom, Shelly Kaplowitz, Howard Rothbort, Jill Sanders and Dr. Rochelle Dweck, stand out amongst many important others. I am especially thankful to my *rabbanim* at Yeshivat Netiv Aryeh who inspired and guided my personal growth and taught me the necessary skills to pursue a career as a serious analyzer of Jewish text, especially Rabbis Aharon Bina, Nir Chanochi, Eytan Coren, Ally Ehrman, Chaim Eisenstein, Yitzchok Korn, Rafi Roness, and Yoel Yehoshua.

My time as an undergraduate at Yeshiva College, where I majored in psychology and was able to pursue my Torah studies with intensity, was incredibly meaningful. I am grateful for all the professors, and *rabbanim* who impacted me during that time. Special thank you to RIETS Rosh Yeshiva, Rabbi Mayer Twersky, whose *shiur* I attended for four years, and to Rabbi Dr. Eliezer Schnall for being an exemplary model of Torah U'Madda in the realm of psychology, and for graciously bringing me in on several important projects in the field, including co-authoring chapters in academic textbooks.

In addition, my time at RIETS – training in the study of text and Jewish law, as well as the practical side of rabbinics – helped solidify my commitment to becoming a rabbi. While I was influenced by all *rabbanim* and teachers, I am particularly grateful to those I was privileged to develop a close relationship with, including Roshei Yeshiva, Rabbis Dovid Hirsch and Baruch Simon, as well as the now dean of RIETS, Rabbi Menachem Penner, and Rabbis Hayyim Angel, Dr. Nachman Cohen, and Dr. J.J. Schacter.

As mentioned, my time at Azrieli aided the evolution of my interest in Torah and psychology, but also helped open my eyes to the nuances of effective teaching and communication. I am grateful to all of my professors at Azrieli, now colleagues, for their influence on me and all they do for the field of Jewish education, including Drs. Chaim Feuerman, *zt"l*, Scott Goldberg, Moshe Krakowski, David Pelcovitz, Laya Salomon, David Schnall, Karen Shawn, Moshe Sokolow, and Ilana Turetsky. Special thank you to the Dean of Azrieli, Dr. Rona Novick, for her continued wisdom and guidance in my career development.

Thank you to Ari Hirsch of the *Jewish Vues* for encouraging me to start writing weekly on psychology and the *parsha*, as well as to Shlomo Greenwald of *The Jewish Press* and Rabbi Nechemia Coopersmith at Aish

.com for serving as publishers of my Psyched for Torah column over the years. It is those essays that are collected here for publication. My deepest appreciation to my dear friend from Kingsway, Etai Lahav, who I cajoled into volunteering to edit my weekly essays. He somehow carved out time during his busy work schedule to send back a revised and edited copy, sometimes within minutes, so I could make the publishing deadline. On the latest round of edits, getting the manuscript ready for publication, thank you to Nava Finkelman and Rabbi Alec Goldstein from Kodesh Press for their insightful questions, comments, and important changes.

My greatest professional and personal debt of gratitude goes to Rabbi Etan Tokayer, the head rabbi of Kingsway Jewish Center, who believed in my potential enough to bring me in as an inexperienced rabbinic intern, and who took a gamble on me when I explored the possibility of being an assistant rabbi at the *shul* while I pursued my doctorate. He has always been effusively supportive of both my rabbinic and psychological careers, as well as my attempts to bring the two disciplines together in *shiurim* or *derashot*. My personal growth, as well as the growth of the *shul*, are due to his leadership, vision, and continued support.

And then comes family. My parents, step-parents, and in-laws, Harry and Loren Schiffman, Linda and Aaron Kinsberg, and Andrea and David Sanders, as well as my brother and sister-in-law, Ben and Dishy Schiffman, have always served as role-models of what it means to dedicate yourself to helping others, whether through education, volunteering, or community work. They have been supportive of me throughout each step of my personal and professional life. It has been very meaningful throughout my career, to have my parents, step-parents, and in-laws consistently attend my *derashot* and *shiurim*, serving as cheerleaders. It is comforting to know that at least one person in the audience will be smiling.

To my wife, Meira. If it wasn't for your continued dedication, I would not have had the luxury to spend so many years pursuing different degrees. You have always been my biggest supporter. And with your devotion and infectious smile, I hope that together, with God's help, we can imbue the values embedded in this book into our beautiful and wonderful children.

I consider myself blessed in that looking back over my life I can see God's influence in shaping my trajectory. Besides for gifting me physical and emotional health, the right blend of supportive mentors, meaningful jobs, and a loving family, there have been countless fortuitous opportunities, chance encounters, and coincidental quirks, that pronounce God's loving hand, guiding me throughout. It is to Him, that I am eternally grateful.

Mordechai Schiffman
Brooklyn, New York
January 2022

Parshat Bereishit

The Original Marshmallow Test

Imagine you are presented with a puffy and fluffy, delicious, sweet-smelling marshmallow. You are told that you have a choice. You can either eat this marshmallow now, or, if you can muster the self-restraint and hold off eating it for a while, you will eventually get a second marshmallow to enjoy along with the first. What would you do? Eat one now, or constrain yourself to double your fortune?

Social psychologist Walter Mischel initially conducted this famed Marshmallow Study back in the 1960s with preschool aged children. He then tracked them for years afterwards. The children who demonstrated self-control by waiting until the researcher returned to the room had higher standardized achievement tests, lower body mass index (BMI), decreased substance abuse, and lower rates of divorce later in life, as compared to those who took the first marshmallow right away. Those who exhibit self-control are generally more successful, healthier, and have better relationships than those who choose instant gratification.

Rabbi Dr. Tzvi Hersh Weinreb (*The Person in the Parsha*, p. 7–10) notes that we can sum up the story of Adam and Chava in the Garden of Eden in contemporary psychological terms by saying that they failed the first marshmallow test. God told Adam not to eat from the Tree of Knowledge. Yet the snake's incitement and the aesthetic enticement of the fruit led to Chava's, and then to Adam's, failure to exercise self-control.

This reading is appealing from the basic sense of the verses and has basis in the commentaries. For instance, when the verse informs us that Chava took the fruit and ate it (Bereishit 3:6), the Netziv (Rabbi Naftali Tzvi Yehudah Berlin) explains that "she was not able to strengthen herself over the desire."

Still, just looking at this episode as a test in self-control overlooks another essential element and an important character in the story, namely, God.

In an updated version of Dr. Mischel's study, published in the journal *Psychological Science*, researchers explored other variables besides sheer self-control that may contribute to a child's success in the equivalent of the marshmallow test. They were particularly interested in finding out to what extent a child's ability to delay gratification was dependent on "reputation management," meaning to what extent the child was concerned about what other people would think of them. Researchers divided children into three groups: (A) children who were told that the teacher would find out what choice was made, (B) children who were told that their peers would find out, and (C) children who weren't told anything about who would find out. When children believed the teacher would find out, they exercised greater self-control than the other two groups, and children who believed their peers would find out exhibited greater self-control than those who believed their choice would not be disclosed.

The story of Adam and Chava is not just a failure in self-control; it is also a failure in reputation management. They fell short in their ability to be concerned with what God commanded. They ignored the fact that He would find out the results of the experiment.

If we are looking for self-control strategies that could help us along our own journey to overcome our struggles with delaying gratification, we would be wise to keep in mind reputation management. Be it food, drink, procrastination, or other temptations, if we truly care what God thinks of us and believe that He knows the results of the test, perhaps we would do a better job at not eating whatever our metaphoric marshmallow may be.

Healthy & Unhealthy Emotions

We all try to avoid negative emotions. We don't want to feel sad, nervous, or frustrated, so we ignore, escape, or repress. Yet negative emotions are often functional. They provide important feedback about how we relate to ourselves, others, and our environment. If understood and utilized properly, negative emotions can help us become more successful and meaningful people. However, when unhealthy, negative emotions can distance us from our goals. Depression, anxiety, and anger can be overly distressing and impede our productivity and growth. Navigating the line between healthy and unhealthy emotions is essential, yet often difficult.

After God did not pay any attention to Kayin's offering, we are told that Kayin was "very distressed" (va-yichar le-Kayin me'od) and "his face fell" (va-yiplu panav) (Bereishit 4:5). This verse is clearly describing two psychological factors, but it is unclear what each phrase means. Sforno interprets "distressed" as referring to jealousy that his brother's offering was accepted, and "his face fell" as feeling shame for his own offering having been rejected. Other commentators suggest the former phrase refers to anger, and the latter to depression.

Rabbi Yerucham Levovitz (Daat Torah, pp. 26–27) sidesteps the question as to which emotions were experienced, and instead he focuses on the different functions the two emotions serve. After we fail, it is natural and healthy to feel a negative emotion, such as sadness, frustration, or remorse. This functional negative emotion – represented in the verse as Kayin being "distressed" – can motivate us to improve our ways for the future. While this "distress" can be positive, it then transforms into an unhealthy emotion of "his face fell."

This, Rabbi Levovitz argues, is the way of the evil inclination. It doesn't just want to knock us down; it wants us to stay down. Instead of the negative emotion leading to improvement, it leads to despondency.

In fact, when God addresses Kayin afterwards, He informs him that if he chooses to improve his ways, all will be forgiven, but if he doesn't, then sin crouches at the door, ready to pounce again. It is here, Ramban contends, that Kayin is introduced to the concept of repentance. Sforno adds that God is telling Kayin that it is pointless to brood over the past; rather, one should correct one's behavior for the future. Our emotional response to sin should be functional. It should lead us away from future sin and toward improved behavior. If we respond to sin in an emotionally unhealthy way, it will just lead to more sin.

One strategy for keeping our emotional response to sin healthy is to not let the sin corrode our sense of self. As the Midrash states, "Praiseworthy is the person who is higher than his sins, and not that his sins are higher than he is" (*Bereishit Rabbah* 22:11). We must keep our core identity above our sins, and not permit our sins to define who we are. As Rabbi Shimon tells us in *Pirkei Avot* (2:13), "Do not be wicked in your own eyes." If we identify ourselves as wicked, evil, or sinful, it will lead to an unhealthy emotion and destructive response.

From the story of Kayin, we learn the need to respond to failure and sin in a functional, and even positive, way. We can do this by acknowledging the sin and feeling an appropriate amount of negative emotion about the past. If we relate to our failures internally in a healthy fashion, that will enable us to refocus our energy on fixing what went wrong and improving ourselves for the future.

Parshat Noach

Living Mercifully

There is a fascinating debate amongst Jewish thinkers as to whether our motivation for being giving people should be because it is a religious imperative or because it is just the right thing to do. Recent research suggests another possible motivation and while perhaps it should not be our primary intention, it is a solid incentive. Giving people, studies show, tend to have increased mental health and longer life expectancy. Some studies link being a caregiver, whether for a family member or for others, with living longer. Others indicate that people who consistently volunteer outlive similarly aged peers that don't. There are even studies that link owning and taking care of pets with a longer life span.

When Noach is commanded to gather the animals, he is given two seemingly contradictory instructions. On the one hand he is told that he should bring the animals to the ark (*tavi el ha-teivah*, 6:19), and on the other, he is told that the animals will come to him (*yavo'u eilecha*, 6:20). Rabbeinu Bachya clarifies that the intent is that Noach will not have to go and retrieve the animals from their natural habitats, since all the animals will approach Noach on their own. Once they arrived near the ark, Noach was tasked with bringing them inside. Yet, we are left wondering: If God would provide a miracle that ensured that the animals all came to Noach on their own, then why make him responsible for bringing them into the ark? Why not just finish the miracle and have the animals board the ark on their own?

Rabbi Moshe Alshich provides a powerful explanation. If viewed from a perspective of strict judgement (*"din"*), Noach did not merit being saved either. The only way he would survive is if God dealt with him with mercy (*"rachamim"*). To earn God's mercy, Noach needed to demonstrate his own acts of mercy. He needed to perform acts of kindness and generosity to warrant being saved. God could have just brought the animals into the ark, but Noach needed the opportunity to interact with the animals and demonstrate his ability to be compassionate. Therefore, the animals came on their own, but Noach needed to physically escort them into the ark.

The stated purpose in the *pesukim* of this whole enterprise is in order "*le-hachayot*" – to make live. The verb is intransitive, meaning that it does not explicitly state who is made to live through Noach's actions. Radak explains that it refers to the animals. Noach was responsible for the physical health of the animals and needed to provide food for them daily in order that they live. Alshich, building off his thesis that Noach needed to exhibit his ability to act mercifully in order to survive, explains that *le-hachayot* can also refer to Noach himself. By becoming the caretaker of the animals, Noach himself would be granted a longer life.

In a world flooded with verbal violence and hostility, we would do well to learn a lesson from Noach. Just as Noach learned to be compassionate, merciful, and generous to all beings, so too, we should learn to be compassionate, merciful, and generous to all beings. By helping others, we ourselves are transformed. By doing so, may we merit God's mercy and be granted the benefits documented in the psychological studies: living long, happy, and healthy lives.

The Right Kind of Praise

"Amazing job!" "Incredible accomplishment!" "Awesome performance!" Praise is an essential element of healthy relationships, whether at home, in school, or at work. Yet, there is a dark side to praise when it is done inappropriately. Dr. Eddie Brummelman notes that parents often deliver inflated praise to their children, thinking that it will boost their self-esteem. Yet his research demonstrates that inflated praise can backfire in one of two ways. If a child has low self-esteem, inflated praise may lead the child to have even lower self-esteem, since the child might say to himself, "If you think this is so amazing, you obviously don't have such high expectations of me." Alternatively, for some children, embellished praise can lead to narcissistic thoughts, like "Wow, I really am the best!" Praise is essential, but it is essential for praise to be tempered, not extravagant.

While the Torah says that Noach was "righteous" (Bereishit 6:9), what we are not so sure about is how righteous he was, due to the modifying phrase "in his generation." The Talmud quotes a debate as to how to understand the nuance of this statement (*Sanhedrin* 108b). Rabbi Yochanan says that he was righteous only as compared to his own debauched generation, but he would not have been considered righteous in a different generation. In contrast, Reish Lakish argues that the fact that he was able to stay righteous, despite his generation's depravity, proves that he obviously would have been righteous if those around him were virtuous.

While this debate is fascinating on its own, there is a powerful message embedded within Rashi's comments on it. A close reading of Rashi's gloss reveals two major differences between the Talmudic presentation and his formulation. First, Rashi reverses the order in which the Talmud quotes the opinions. The Talmud quotes Rabbi Yochanan's negative opinion first, while Rashi quotes the more positive opinion of Reish Lakish first. This choice may allude to the importance of prioritizing praise over critique. Second, Rashi doesn't quote the opinions by name. He writes that "some of our Sages explain it to his credit" and "others explain it to his discredit." Notice how in explaining the praise he attributes the opinion to the Sages, while the negative opinion he just attributes to "others." Rabbi Ephraim Shapiro (quoted by Dr. Ari Ciment in *Pirkei Dr. Ari*, p. 13) suggests that Rashi is hinting to the fact that while sometimes being critical is warranted, providing a positive spin is a more praiseworthy act. That is why the opinion that praises Noach is attributed to "Sages," while the one that discredits Noach is just mentioned in the name of others.

The Torah describes Noach as righteous and *tamim*, and commentaries differ on the exact meaning of the word *tamim*. Explanations cover a wide variety of attributes: flawless, perfect, humble, beloved, simple, whole, intelligent, virtuous, authentic, and pious (see *Otzar Mefarshei HaTorah*, p. 208). When God subsequently speaks to Noach directly, He tells him to go into the ark, "For you alone have I found righteous before Me in this generation" (Bereishit 7:1). Here, Noach is only referred to as righteous, without the second appellation of *tamim*. Picking up on this subtlety, Rashi, quoting the Talmud (*Eruvin* 18b), concludes that "only a part of a man's good qualities should be enumerated in his presence."

Commenting on this statement, Rabbi Akiva Adler emphasizes the importance of praise within education. Parents and teachers should make a habit of praising their children and students often (*Ikvei Eliyahu*, p. 15). Yet the praise should not be overly lavish or extravagant. It may be true that Noach was both righteous and *tamim*, but when praising him directly, God only mentioned his righteousness. Embellished and inflated praise, even if warranted, can backfire. Praise is essential, but it is essential to strike the proper balance between the positive benefits of healthy praise and the destructiveness of inflated praise.

Parshat Lech Lecha

Spiritual Gratitude

If my friend is gracious enough to give me a twenty-dollar bill as a present, my gratitude would appropriately be directed at him. Yet, if I happen to find a twenty-dollar bill on the street, to whom should I direct my gratitude?

For those who aren't particularly spiritual or religious, finding money on the street may engender positive emotions, but gratitude would likely be absent, as there is nobody to thank. For those who are religious, however, such fortunate experiences could lend themselves to being grateful to God. Dr. David Rosmarin hypothesized that since religious individuals have more opportunities to feel and express gratitude, they consequentially are able to reap the positive benefits associated with gratitude – such as increased feelings of happiness and life-satisfaction – above and beyond the advantages associated with gratitude in general.

Taking the twenty-dollar bill example one step further, we can add an additional layer of reflection. From a religious perspective, even if my friend gives me a gift, my gratitude to him should be supplemented with an additional gratitude towards God. Meaning, every benefit accrued socially should also be attributed to God's providence and beneficence. The question becomes, who to thank first: your friend or God?

After Avram helped the five kings defeat the four kings, Malki-Tzedek, king of Shalem, who was also the "priest of God Most High," brings out bread and water for Avram and his soldiers (Bereishit 14:18). As an expression of gratitude, Malki-Tzedek blesses Avram to "God Most High, Creator of heaven and earth" (14:19) and afterwards blesses God, "Who has delivered your foes into your hand" (14:20). The Gemara (*Nedarim* 32b) critiques his priorities. He should have blessed God before he blessed Avram, as first one blesses the Master and only afterwards the servant. As a result of his error, God removes the privilege of priesthood from Malki-Tzedek and bestows it upon Avram instead.

Ibn Ezra provides an alternative approach and suggests that Malki-Tzedek's order of blessing is appropriate: First he should bless Avram, acknowledging that he saved the captives, and only afterwards bless God, who aided Avram in his quest. Rabbi Joseph B. Soloveitchik adds a fascinating approach to explain Malki-Tzedek's reasoning: God, as it were, requires man's assistance in revealing His presence in the world. Avram's job was to spread God's message in a world where He was obscured by idol-worship. It is specifically through Avram's success that God would be blessed. The blessing to Avram also functioned as a blessing to God.

While the different approaches may disagree on who should be blessed first, the resonating message is important in either case. There is a purposefully blurred line between gratitude towards people and gratitude to God. When others do us a kindness, we should not limit our gratitude to the interpersonal realm. We must expand our expression of gratitude to God as well. The person doing the *chesed* is acting as an emissary of God, making His name great and revealed in this world. In addition, we must acknowledge that it is God's providence that allowed for the kindness to happen.

By incorporating a Divine element into all of our interpersonal gratitude experiences, may we merit additional spiritual and psychological well-being, above and beyond what is generally associated with being grateful people.

Resolving Conflicts

Without effective intervention, conflict escalates quickly. Whether at work, at home, or with friends, if a fight isn't nipped in the bud, the consequences can leave a long-lasting negative impact. Some people simply avoid conflict instead of directly dealing with it. They pretend the conflict doesn't exist, even though it is still there under the surface, primed to erupt. Other people shut down and withdraw completely (what Dr. John Gottman calls "stonewalling"), a response which prevents resolution and makes the problem worse. Still other people fall into a cycle of perpetual arguments over an extended period of time, leading to increased tension as the arguments repeat indefinitely.

After living successfully with each other for years, a conflict (*riv*) began to fester amongst Avram and Lot's herdsmen (Bereishit 13:7). Noticing the problem, Avram approaches Lot and says, "Please let there not be strife [*merivah*] between me and you, between my herdsmen and yours, for we are brothers" (13:8). Rabbi Moshe Alshich suggests that there is a fundamental difference between the word used for conflict in the first verse (*riv*) and in the second (*merivah*). A *riv* is a small disagreement; a *merivah* is when the disagreement spirals into a much bigger issue. Noticing the *riv*, Avram quickly takes action to prevent it from becoming a more destructive *merivah*.

Alshich references the verse in Proverbs that compares the beginning of strife to the release of water (17:14). The Talmud (*Sanhedrin* 7a), in the name of Rav Huna, elaborates on the metaphor and suggests that a quarrel is compared to a puncture in a hose, which causes water to burst out. If the hole is not repaired quickly, it will widen to the point where it can no longer be fixed. Similarly, if a dispute isn't resolved immediately, the damage can be irreversible.

Noticing that there was no way to effectively stay together, Avram then suggests a "win-win" solution, where both parties could expand and grow in their own direction, ending the conflict while still on good terms. A close reading of the verses based on the commentary of Rabbi Yitzchak Arama, and aided by contemporary research related to conflict resolution, leads to some important strategies to help resolve disputes.

First, Avram, being in the position of power, could have brazenly demanded that Lot leave. Yet Avram uses what Dr. John Gottman calls a "soft start up." He starts very peacefully and politely, using calm and inviting language: "Please let there not be [*al na tehi*] strife...." Second, Avram states the issue without placing the blame on Lot. Avram takes partial responsibility, even mentioning himself and his herdsmen in relation to the conflict before mentioning Lot and his herdsmen. Third, in order to avoid an adversarial mentality of "me vs. you," Avram reminds him of their closeness and strong relationship (*anashim achim anachnu*). Finally, Avram empowers Lot with the autonomy to choose which direction he wanted to go. Avram was willing to defer to accommodate Lot to avoid building tensions.

Avram serves as a role model for us, both by teaching us to resolve conflicts, rather than letting them fester, and by teaching us the best ways to settle them. By using a soft start up, not blaming, taking responsibility, focusing on the shared relationship, and compromising, Avram was able to move forward with Lot on good terms, setting the stage for the next phase of their shared story. As arguments arise in our own lives, we can apply these same strategies to help resolve the conflicts in an effective manner.

Parshat Vayeira

Healed by Kindness

A common and logical response to the experience of intense or chronic pain is to decrease activity and focus on the self. However, research indicates that people in pain who focus outside of themselves by, for example, volunteering, reap benefits such as a decrease in both physical pain and negative emotional symptoms, such as depression. The same is true when it comes to aging. As people age, they tend to focus on their own needs and decrease their activity, while research suggests that even (or especially) for the elderly, volunteering is correlated with improved well-being, lower mortality rates, and a decrease in general functional decline. In one fascinating study, researchers measured how quickly older adults walked and climbed stairs both before and after a year's worth of volunteering, and found that those who volunteered had improved walking and stair climbing speeds.

The Torah portrays the scene of Avraham welcoming the angels (who were disguised as unidentified nomads) by providing a detailed account of how Avraham prepared and executed the mitzvah of *hachnasat orchim*. In fact, Radak suggests that the primary purpose of the entire story is to provide us with a paradigm for how to perform acts of kindness. Even a cursory reading of the *pesukim* leaves the reader in awe of the speed with which Avraham exhibited hospitality. When performing each task, Avraham doesn't just walk; he runs. The preparations are done with zest and vitality. His actions are even more impressive, as Ramban points out, since he was old, and weakened from the pain of his recent *brit milah*, and because he had a household full of servants who could have done the work on his behalf. Avraham teaches us the importance of doing the mitzvah with alacrity (*zerizut*), and making sure to do most of the mitzvah on one's own (*mitzvah bo yoter mi-beshlucho*).

In his elucidation of Avraham's behavior in the story, Alshich prefaces his analysis by explaining that there are several reasons a guest may feel uncomfortable accepting an invitation. Primarily, guests do not want to impose on their hosts. This could be related to the financial burden incurred by hosting, or to the time and energy necessary to clean the house and tend to the guests' needs. In addition, the guests themselves may be in a rush and do not want to get caught up in a long layover at the host's home.

To perform acts of *chesed* properly, we need a degree of social intelligence so we can behave in a way that is more beneficial to those around us. Avraham uses strategic language when speaking to allay the fears his guests might be experiencing. He tells them that he has people who can help, so it will not be such a burden, and that they can stay under the tree, so they do not have to worry about intruding inside the house. He also tells them that he will just bring out a little water and a slice of bread so that they do not feel that they are imposing, but then brings out an entire meal so they can be satiated. Finally, Avraham himself moves so quickly, so the guests would not feel uncomfortable in case they were rushing to leave.

Rabbi Eliezer Ashkenazi (*Maasei Ha-Shem*) mentions the Midrash wherein one of the angels came on a mission to heal Avraham. While the *pesukim* do not explicitly indicate when or how that occurred, Rabbi Ashkenazi suggests that the healing was a blessing that came as a direct consequence of the *chesed* that Avraham performed. By commencing and performing an act of kindness, his pain decreased, and his speed, alacrity, and vitality improved. Avraham – old, frail, and pained – was healed.

May we all learn from Avraham, the paradigm of *chesed*, and personally commit to passionately perform acts of kindness, with nuanced social awareness and sensitivity. Even when we are tired, down, weak, or frail, when we visit the sick, comfort the mourner, host guests, or perform other acts of kindness, it will add energy and vigor to our lives. By so doing, may we merit living long lives infused with health, happiness, and vitality.

Worst Things First

Do you ever have a task that you must do but really don't want to? Do you procrastinate and push it off to the last minute? This usually leads to missed deadlines and lost opportunities. Even if you successfully completed the task, the dread of working on it, or the guilt of not working on it, hovers like a tempestuous cloud throughout the process.

To avoid the anxiety of procrastination, social psychologist Dr. Ian Newby-Clark suggests that we put the "worst things first." First focus on the item that you don't want to do the most and get that off your to-do list. By prioritizing what we don't want to do and getting it done early, we avoid the looming emotion of impending dread that would otherwise build over the course of the day. This can also help generate positive momentum for later tasks.

Avraham is a paradigm of alacrity and productivity. Being a pillar of kindness, we are awed but not shocked at how swiftly he tends to the needs of his guests. Despite the fact that he was healing from his *brit milah*, the verses reiterate how he "ran" and "quickly" cared for them. The Sages also learn from this scene that the righteous say little but do much (*Bava Metzia* 87a).

Rabbi Yerucham Levovitz (*Daat Torah*, pp. 117–118) suggests that when the Sages praise those that say little but do much, they aren't simply commending those who follow through on their word. Rather, they are emphasizing the importance of not spending time talking about accomplishing. Discussing, deliberating, and debating about action is essentially procrastination. The righteous don't talk about what they are going to do; they just do it. They "talk" through their actions.

It is one thing to be prompt, proactive, and productive when you are doing what you love, but it is an entirely different challenge when the required task is one that you dread. After seeing Yishmael behave inappropriately, Sarah tells Avraham that she does not want Yishmael to be associated with Yitzchak. Avraham is terribly pained by the fact that Sarah wanted him to send away Yishmael (see Bereishit 21:11 and Rashi). Despite Avraham's reservations, God tells him to listen to Sarah.

While Avraham was always going to obey God's command, he also loved Yishmael deeply, which made this a very difficult test for him. Despite this, we are told *va-yashkem Avraham ba-boker* – Avraham woke up early in the morning to send away Yishmael (Bereishit 21:14). Rabbi Yisrael

Meir Kagan highlights that despite the difficulty, Avraham acted with alacrity to complete his task (*Chafetz Chaim al HaTorah*, p. 62). He didn't procrastinate; he did the worst – or hardest – thing first.

We can learn from Avraham not to spend too much time talking about doing, but being proactively productive. Avraham serves as role model in this area, not just for things that he valued or enjoyed, like acts of kindness, but also for how to accomplish and follow through when the task is necessary but distressing, as he did in the case of Yishmael. We all have important things that we try to push off because they seem too distressful or daunting. For some it is studying or maybe a work assignment, for others laundry or paperwork. However, by doing the worst things first, we avoid prolonging the negative cloud, ensuring that we don't fall into the enticing trap of procrastination.

Parshat Chayei Sarah

Smart Chesed

What does it take to be a person who embodies *chesed*? We tend to associate kindness with both emotions and behaviors. I feel empathy towards someone, and I help them through action. Yet there is an essential element to *chesed* that often gets overlooked: thinking. Dr. Nancy Eisenberg, a psychologist who studies the importance of prosocial behavior (what we might call *chesed*), argues that helping others requires several essential cognitive processes. First, we need to perceive the needs of another by interpreting the situation and making inferences about what they are thinking or feeling. Second, we need to evaluate the most beneficial course of action. Finally, we have to formulate and carry out a plan to help them. In short, she contends, the action of prosocial behavior first requires perception, reasoning, problem-solving, and decision-making.

It should come as no surprise that when looking for a wife for Yitzchak, Avraham's servant, whom Chazal identify as Eliezer, focuses his test on the trait of *chesed*. After all, his master, Avraham, epitomizes *chesed*. As we noted in the previous parsha's essay, "Healed by Kindness," based on Rabbi Moshe Alshich, an essential component of Avraham's *chesed* was his ability to use his social intelligence to anticipate his guests' concerns, in order to help them in the best way possible. We can hypothesize that as part of his search for someone with the trait of *chesed*, Eliezer would test how well Yitzchak's potential match could think in those terms.

On a simple level, the *pesukim* indicate that Rivka demonstrates *chesed* by offering water to both the servant and the camels. Malbim highlights and adds that Eliezer doesn't just ask Rivka to give him water: he says *hatti na chadech ve-eshteh* – he asks that she tip the jug for him, as opposed to him taking the jug from her and drinking himself. She could have angrily responded, "Take it yourself, I am not going to pour it into your mouth!"

But that is not how she reacts. She responds with wisdom, sensitivity, and perspective. She thinks to herself: Why is he asking me to pour for him? Perhaps there is something wrong with his hands so he is not able to draw water for himself. And if he can't draw water for himself, he must not be able to draw water for his camels either! That is why she responds positively to his request and goes above and beyond what he asks for and provides for the camels as well. She is able to dig deeper and hypothesize about the potential problem. Eliezer's test isn't just about *chesed*, it's about smart *chesed*.

Rabbi Yosef Dov Soloveitchik, in his commentary *Beit HaLevi*, also frames Eliezer's test as requiring Rivka to demonstrate intelligence and sensitivity in the context of *chesed*. The test, he argues, was not whether she would give him water, since it would not be so special to help a thirsty traveler. Rather, the test was what she would do with the water left in the jug after he drinks his fill. The first option would be to take the water back to her house and give it to her family, as she had originally planned before he asked her for it. The problem with this is that to Rivka, this person is a random nomad. It would not be sanitary to allow him to drink from the barrel and then have her family drink the rest. The second option was to spill the leftover water out. The problem with this option is that it may insult the person she was helping. Stuck with two bad options, she comes up with a third option – to give the water to the camels! This way nobody drinks tainted water, nobody gets insulted, the camels get to drink, and she eases the workload of the nomad. She demonstrates that she likes to help others, in a way that is healthy, sensitive, and smart.

Chesed isn't just about doing *something*, but about doing things intelligently. Truly understanding the depths of what someone needs is essential for effective helping. Uncovering what was not asked is often more important than identifying what was. In order to make sound and sensitive decisions, we must first think through the various options and potential consequences. This may include knowing the right times to visit or call people, inquiring and accommodating special dietary needs, or thinking through how to be discreet so that helping others doesn't become embarrassing.

While each situation provides its own nuances, may we learn to generalize from Avraham and Rivka's examples, and not just do *chesed*, but to do smart *chesed*.

Intellect & Emotion

This essay was published in memory of Rabbi Jonathan Sacks, zt"l, the week of his passing in November 2020.

Rabbi Jonathan Sacks, *zt"l*, was a master at employing modern psychological research to shed light on concepts from the Torah. His writings often read like an Intro to Psychology textbook, not just quoting household names like Freud and Frankl, but also referencing pioneering developmental, behavioral, social, cognitive, and positive psychologists. He wrote about the psychology of happiness, gratitude, emotional intelligence, mindset, altruism, evil, conformity, shame, and grief, among others. His affinity to the ideas of Cognitive Behavioral Therapy and one of its founders, Aaron Beck, is apparent in many of his works. Perhaps one of his favorite ideas emerges from neuroscientist Antonio Damasio, whose work helped shift how we view the relationship between intellect and emotion. This work may also help us better understand an important part of Rabbi Sacks' legacy.

Based on various philosophical traditions, there is a common misconception that rationality is totally divorced from emotion. Damasio argues that this supposed dichotomy between thinking and feeling is false. For example, Damasio noticed that patients who incurred lesions to their ventromedial prefrontal cortex were able to rationally analyze choices, but they were unable to come to conclusive decisions because they were unable to feel emotion. Damasio outlines his neuroscientific research in his book *Descartes' Error*, where he contends that our brains make decisions by integrating both emotional and rational components. Our thinking requires feeling.

Rabbi Sacks utilized Damasio's research as a springboard to highlight Judaism's connection between intellect and emotion. For instance, he invoked Damasio's research to explain the importance of the non-rational *chukim* (*Chukat* 5777), the connection between the two goats sacrificed on Yom Kippur (*Acharei Mot* 5779), and perhaps most importantly, to accentuate the importance of cultivating the affective domain, primarily through music and song, to guide us in our religious decision making (*Vayelech* 5775). While, to my knowledge, he does not make the following connection in his writings, I would add that we can identify this idea in Avraham's reaction to Sarah's death.

After hearing about her death, "Avraham came to eulogize Sarah and to weep for her" (Bereishit 23:2). Notice that there are two components of his response: a eulogy (*hesped*) and weeping (*bechi*). Rabbi Joseph B. Soloveitchik distinguishes between weeping, which is an emotional response of "spontaneous, overwhelming and uncontrollable grief," and eulogy, which is "rooted in logical judgement" and serves as a clear analysis of the disastrous event and its consequences" (*Out of the Whirlwind*, p. 31).

Several commentators deal with the fact that the logical order of weeping and eulogizing seems to be reversed. The psychological expectation, as well as the indication from other verses (see Bereishit 50:3–4) and the Talmud (*Moed Katan* 27b), is that weeping precedes the eulogy. Doesn't the emotional response come before the rational one? Why does Avraham first eulogize, and only then weep?

Perhaps the answer goes back to Damasio's research. The question assumes that logic and feeling are two distinct processes, but for Avraham, the two may have been integrated. His logic and emotions blended together, where his thinking impacted his feelings and his feelings impacted his thinking. Perhaps this is how Avraham was able to transition from loss to rebuilding so quickly. Avraham did not suppress the emotion, nor get stuck in it. He was able to move forward and plan for the future, by securing land, finding a wife for Yitzchak, and having more children.

Rabbi Sacks himself epitomized this integration. His towering intellect was infused with input from his moral emotions. His religious and philosophic rationality was suffused with spiritual sentiments. Using his own terminology, he was both "Halakhic Man" and "Aggadic Woman"; he was both the priestly voice of analyzing, and the prophetic voice of justice and compassion. He was someone who preached eloquently, but more importantly, demonstrated what he preached through his personality. To continue this aspect of his multifaceted legacy, we are charged to develop both our intellect and our emotions, as well as learn how to use both in the service of God and humanity.

Parshat Toldot

The Space to Grow

Murray Bowen was one of the pioneers in the field of family therapy. He noted that families have a system of psychological interconnectedness. For instance, when one member of a family becomes anxious, this tends to have an emotional snowball effect on the other members of the family. In order to maintain psychological health and wellness, individuals need to not become too affected by the thoughts, emotions, and actions of other members of their family. Rather, each individual should experience and balance both intimacy with, and independence from, others in the family, a state known as "differentiation of the self."

In his essay in *Covenant & Conversation*, "On Clones and Identity," Rabbi Jonathan Sacks noted that Yitzchak was the least individuated of the patriarchs. Not much is reported about Yitzchak's life, but we do know that he seems to repeat many of the events and actions of Avraham. They both leave their land and enter the land of the Plishtim because of a famine. They both tell Avimelech that their wives are their sisters. To accentuate the parallel, the Torah tells us that Yitzchak re-digs the same wells as Avraham, and gives them the same names. There seems to be a lack of differentiation of self on Yitzchak's part.

Apparently, there was insufficient water from Avraham's wells that Yitzchak re-dug, so Yitzchak moved towards individuation and initiative by digging a new well. Yet the Torah tells us that his first attempt was fraught with difficulty. The people of Gerar claimed that the water from the well belonged to them, which led to an argument. Consequently, Yitzchak named that well "Esek" because of the strife that ensued. Yitzchak's second attempt to dig a well also led to controversy with the people of Gerar, so he called it "Sitnah" because of the hatred and enmity it engendered. Finally, Yitzchak's third attempt to dig was free from dispute. Yitzchak calls this well "Rechovot," which connotes peace, freedom, and space. With this, Yitzchak is able to create a physical location for himself, as well as carve out his own personal place in his family narrative.

What is unclear, however, is why the third attempt was successful, while the first two were not. The Chafetz Chaim suggests that the Torah is teaching us a lesson in grit and perseverance: if at first you don't succeed, try and try again. Rabbi Norman Lamm suggests another approach in the name of his uncle, Rabbi Joseph Baumol. We can detect a fundamental textual difference between the first two diggings and the third. For the first two, the *pesukim* highlight that it was Yitzchak's servants who dug the wells – *va-yachperu avdei Yitzchak* (Bereishit 26:19, 21). Yet, for the third well it says *va-yachpor be'er acheret* (Bereishit 26:22). Yitzchak – not his servants – dug the third well.

While there is a place for delegation, there are actions in life that must be performed by the individual if they are to be successful. Avraham served as an important role model, but this time Yitzchak had to differentiate himself and forge his own path. This journey could not be proxied out to others. It was something Yitzchak needed to experience himself. *He* needed to dig the new well, not his servants. Once he took responsibility and acted on his own accord, he was able to merit Rechovot – the space to grow on his own.

The message for us is clear as well. While it is important to learn from and be connected to the family figures who helped develop us, at a certain point the process of differentiation is essential. Taking the initiative, and finding our own path, will help us flourish and develop into the people we were meant to become.

The Truth About Honesty

Be honest for a moment. How often do you lie? Immanuel Kant viewed honesty as a categorical imperative, meaning that he thought that it was never acceptable to lie. Before him, theologians such as Augustine and Aquinas argued that any form of lying is a sin. In Jewish thought, the Midrash tells us that the seal of God is stamped with truth (*Shir HaShirim Rabbah* 1:9). One of the ten commandments is to not bear false witness (Shemot 20:13), and there are additional prohibitions against being dishonest in business or generally misleading others (Devarim 25:13–15). We think lying is bad, and we advocate for honesty. Yet if we examine the stories of our forefathers, particularly those of Yaakov, lying seems to occupy a significant part of the narrative.

Yaakov, with Rivka's assistance, dresses up like Esav and brings food to Yitzchak, in order to receive the blessings which Yitzchak wanted to give to Esav. When Yitzchak asks him "Who are you, my son?" Yaakov responds, "I am Esav your firstborn." Rashi defends this lie by suggesting that it could be read as two separate statements: "I am" the one who is bringing you food, and, parenthetically, "Esav is your firstborn." While perhaps that minimizes the verbal untruth to some degree, it does not eliminate the fact that the whole act is one of deception. How are we to understand the dishonesty of Yaakov and Rivka, especially when juxtaposed with the demands for honesty in other parts of the Torah?

Rabbi Dr. Yehudah Brandes (*Torat Imecha*) suggests that the question is only a formidable one from a theoretical perspective. Only someone who sits in an ivory tower, and talks and thinks in abstract ideas, can entertain the possibility that lying is never acceptable. The Torah is meant to be learned and lived in the real world, a world that is filled with paradoxes, contradictions, ethical conundrums, and dialectical tensions. Truth is not the ultimate value within a Torah framework, and it needs to be considered alongside other values, such as peace and emotional sensitivity to the feelings of others. The Torah does not expect people to stick to the truth to the point where they will be taken advantage of by others. This is why Avraham lies to both Pharaoh and Avimelech, telling them that Sarah is not his wife, but his sister.

Israeli-born psychologist Dan Ariely presented the keynote address at the Association for Psychological Science annual convention in 2016, and outlined the research he had conducted on lying. To start his presentation,

Ariely framed his discussion by quoting *Chumash*. When God said to Sarah that she was going to have a child, she responded incredulously, "How can I have a child when my husband is so old?" When God repeats what Sarah said to Avraham, God lies! He tells Avraham that Sarah questioned how she would have a child if *she* is so old. Ariely, echoing the Talmud, concludes that the moral of the story is that it is permissible to lie for the sake of marital peace. Maurice Schweitzer, Ariely's collaborator and professor at Wharton School of the University of Pennsylvania, argues that it is incorrect to conceive of lying as inherently immoral. Rather he argues that we should separate dishonesty from selfishness. We could be benevolently dishonest ("this food tastes great!") and selfishly honest ("never serve this again"). Through his research he concludes that "When we tell people, 'Never lie to me,' what we really mean is, 'Don't be selfish.'"

As a general rule, lying is unethical, but there are times where other values, such as compassion, peace, modesty, or humility, may override the virtue of honesty (see *Bava Metzia* 23b–24a).

Obviously, this approach opens up a Pandora's box. The subjective judgement about when it is acceptable and even appropriate to lie can be improperly used to justify unethical behavior. While this is definitely a real danger, the way to deal with this issue is not to pretend that lying is always wrong. Rather, as Rabbi Brandes recommends, it is to learn and to teach how to weigh moral dilemmas through the prism of Jewish ethics, exploring the sources, carefully weighing the values relevant to each situation, being aware of common self-deceptions, and consulting with wise and God-fearing teachers and mentors.

Parshat Vayeitzei

Believing in Our Abilities

One of the best predictors of success is the belief that our actions can bring about the desired results. Believing in our ability to accomplish something specific will help boost our motivation and make it more likely that we will succeed in attaining that goal. This power of believing in our own abilities, referred to as "self-efficacy" in the psychological literature, was first formulated by Albert Bandura. Bandura understood self-efficacy to be domain specific, meaning that we have different beliefs regarding the different types of ability in question. For example, I may have high self-efficacy for writing but low self-efficacy for calculus. Later researchers suggested that there can also be a general self-efficacy that is not domain specific. This means that I can have a general belief in my ability to accomplish tasks and overcome barriers, regardless of what type of task it may be.

As Yaakov makes his way to Charan he dreams of angels ascending and descending on a ladder that reaches the Heavens (Bereishit 28:12). Through this vision, he realizes that God was present in that place (*Achein, yesh Hashem bamakom hazeh*), of which he seemed previously unaware (*ve-anochi lo yadati*) (Bereishit 28:16). Rabbi Shimshon of Ostropoli, perhaps bothered by the assumption that Yaakov did not perceive God's presence before the dream, rereads this *pasuk* with a message related to self-efficacy. To fully understand his point, we first need some background.

In his vision of God's throne, Yechezkel (10:14) describes seeing four faces: a cherub, a lion, an eagle, and a human. The Gemara in *Chullin* (91b) elaborates on Yaakov's dream and suggests that the angels were going up and down, looking at the picture of the human face by the throne and comparing it to Yaakov's face. Seeing the resemblance, they became jealous of his presence on the throne and wanted to harm him, so God had to protect Yaakov.

Rabbi Shimshon of Ostropoli suggests that Yaakov was previously aware that there were creatures that could reach elevated spiritual heights. He knew that the cherub, lion, and eagle had their place by God's throne, but he was not aware that his image was there as well. It was not until the dream, when he saw the angels comparing the image on the throne with his face, that he realized his true potential. In a brilliantly creative rereading of the *pasuk*, Rabbi Shimshon suggests that Yaakov's word choice alludes to self-efficacy. He already knew the spiritual potential of "*achein*," in Hebrew spelled *aleph – chof – nun*, representing the lion (*aryeh*), cherub, and eagle (*nesher*). Yet, until this dream, he was unaware of the spiritual potential of *anochi*, literally "myself," spelled *aleph – nun – chof – yud*, representing, the three images from "*achein*" with the addition of the *yud* – for Yaakov.

This new-found self-efficacy was not domain specific. It was not just limited to spiritual pursuits. Yaakov's new attitude pervaded all his interactions, as is clear from the very next episode regarding the shepherds by the well. In a powerful *drasha* ("The Stone on the Well – Boulder or Pebble?"), Rabbi Norman Lamm contrasts the attitude of the shepherds with that of Yaakov. When Yaakov asked the shepherds why they do not water their herds, they respond that there is a giant stone covering the well and until more people come to help push it off: *lo nuchal* – they just can't do it (Bereishit 29:8). They don't believe in their ability, so they don't even try. Yaakov, believing in his ability to accomplish, walks over to the stone and succeeds in removing it from the well. He believes in his ability to effect change, puts in the effort, and succeeds.

How many areas of life – spiritual or otherwise – do we write off as being too hard or not within our abilities? Perhaps if we learn this lesson from Yaakov, we can work on boosting our self-efficacy by realizing our potential, putting in the effort, and increasing our chances of success and accomplishment.

Making Time Fly

While every minute has sixty seconds and every hour has sixty minutes, our perception of time can change, making some minutes feel like hours and some hours feel like minutes. In a fascinating experiment, Leah Campbell and Richard Bryant (in their creatively titled article, *How Time Flies: A Study of Novice Skydivers*) studied how first-time skydivers perceived time in relation to their first jump. Divers who felt afraid estimated the experience as taking longer than it did in reality, while divers who felt excited felt that the event took less time than it actually did. Time drags on when we are afraid, and really does fly when we are having fun. Philip Gable and Bryan Poole (as summed up in *their* creatively titled paper, *Time Flies When You're Having Approach-Motivated Fun*) present an important caveat. Just being content or satisfied doesn't necessarily make time seem fast. Another determining factor in making time fly, in addition to it being fun, is that it is spent while pursuing an important goal.

Yaakov loved Rachel very deeply, and offered to work seven years for her father, Lavan, so that he could marry her (Bereishit 29:18). How would you predict the passage of time would feel if you had to wait seven years before marrying the person you loved? Presumably, for most of us, those seven years would drag on and feel like "forever." Interestingly, we are given a glimpse into Yaakov's subjective perception of time. We are told that the years "seemed to him but a few days" (*ke-yamim achadim*) because of his love for her (Bereishit 29:20). Why did those years seem to fly by for Yaakov, but for most of us working in pursuit of a long-term goal, seven years would feel like an eternity?

Rabbi Moshe Alshich (*Torat Moshe*) is convinced that Yaakov's love and longing for Rachel in fact made "every day feel like a thousand years," a painful and agonizing wait. He contends that it was only afterwards, in retrospect, that the power of his love and connection to Rachel made him forget the excruciating anguish of the wait time.

Other commentaries disagree. They assume that Yaakov perceived the seven years to pass quickly, not just in retrospect, but even while he was experiencing it in real time. Abarbanel suggests that Yaakov's love for Rachel was so great that he thought that seven years was a bargain; he would have been ready and willing to spend even more time in pursuit of her. Consequently, the time frame did not seem daunting for him, and he went through it with a positive mindset. Similarly, Shadal (Samuel David

Luzzatto) suggests that his love for Rachel infused each day with peace, enjoyment, and hope. It is pain, discomfort, and negative emotions that make time seem longer, but peace and positive emotions make time fly by.

Chatam Sofer approaches this issue from a goal-oriented, as opposed to an emotional, perspective. He contends that only someone who is waiting for time to pass would feel that time moves slowly. However, to Yaakov's credit, despite his great love for Rachel, he was able to treat each day with the proper reverence, taking advantage of his time, acting productively, and being mindful of each day's tasks. Rabbi Aharon Kotler (*Mishnat Rebbi Aharon*, 3:176) takes the concept one step further: Not only did Yaakov not squander his time, he used the time to actively work towards a goal. He knew that he still needed to develop himself personally and spiritually in order to build a family and fulfill the destiny that was outlined in his dream, and used this time to continue to cultivate his strengths.

Combining these approaches, we learn from Yaakov two essential ingredients for leading a purposeful and engaged life: planning and implementing meaningful goals while simultaneously savoring the experience of positive emotions. If we feel distressed over having to wait for something, we should create an important and reachable goal, and start actively working towards accomplishing it. The pursuit of the goal, along with the positive emotions that come as a consequence, will help make the time fly.

Parshat Vayishlach

Who Is in Control?

Do you believe that your life's events are determined by external factors, or by your own efforts? In the 1950s, psychologist Julian Rotter began exploring how people related to such questions and developed a construct called "locus of control." People who have an internal locus of control believe that the events of their lives are generally determined by their own abilities and actions, while those with an external locus of control believe their fate is determined by factors beyond their control. People with an internal locus of control generally take more responsibility and feel more agency in their decisions. Consequently, an internal locus of control is associated with higher achievement in school and at work. In contrast, those with an external locus of control tend to be more passive, blame others, and experience more stress and depression.

One could argue, that for most of his life, Yaakov had an external locus of control. His fate seemed to be determined by blessings, curses, the instructions and rules of others, and the events of his past. In a transformative experience, "Yaakov was left alone" from his family (*"Va-yivater Yaakov levado,"* Bereishit 32:25), wrestles with an unnamed man, and emerges victorious. One way to read this episode is as a cautionary tale. The Slonimer Rebbe, for instance, suggests that the Torah is highlighting the hazards of isolation (*Netivot Shalom*, pp. 226–228). When one is alone and cut off from others, there is a strong threat of danger. When an individual is connected to friends, family, and community, the risk of harm is decreased. Solitude is a risk factor for physical, psychological, and spiritual harm, and that is why Yaakov was attacked while alone.

Alternatively, the episode can be read in a more optimistic light. The Midrash (*Bereishit Rabbah* 77:1) notes that both Yaakov and God are described as *levado* – being alone. Yaakov is *Va-yivater Yaakov levado*, while God is *Va-nisgav Hashem levado* (Yeshayahu 2:11). This indicates that there is a positive aspect to being *levado*. Instead of translating *levado* as "alone," Rabbi Menachem Mendel Kasher (*Torah Sheleima*) quotes two alternative interpretations. The first is that *levado* indicates a distinctiveness and particularity. Just like Avraham is an *Ivri* and the Jewish people are "a nation that dwells alone" (Bamidbar 23:9), so too Yaakov fits the paradigm of being positively and singularly designated. The second possibility is that *levado* implies singularity and uniqueness of character. Yaakov's merit and strength were unparalleled by others.

Like the Slonimer Rebbe, Rabbi Yerucham Levovitz (*Daat Torah*, pp. 205–206) understands *levado* as meaning "alone." But unlike the Slonimer Rebbe who assumes being alone was destructive, Rabbi Levovitz takes the more optimistic view of the episode and assumes that being alone is constructive! How can aloneness be interpreted in a positive light? Rabbi Levovitz explains that God's aloneness symbolizes that He is entirely self-sufficient. He does not need the help of others to accomplish anything. Yaakov is also *levado*, meaning he has reached a state of self-sufficiency. He did not need to rely on others, embodying an entirely internal locus of control.

This, Rabbi Levovitz explains, is the meaning behind Ben Zoma's set of four questions and answers in *Pirkei Avot* (4:1): "Who is wise? He who learns from everyone … Who is strong? He who conquers his will … Who is rich? He who is happy with his lot … Who is respected? He who respects others … " Ben Zoma's underlying message is that the development of these four traits is not dependent on others, but definitionally, must come from within. Wisdom is not dependent on waiting for others to teach us, but must come from a desire and love of learning that seeks to gain knowledge from everything. Strength is not a comparison of how physically strong we are as compared to others, but is said to be self-control, measured and performed internally. Wealth is not dependent on how much money we have, but is instead the subjective feeling of satisfaction irrespective of material possessions. Finally, even respect, which we would think must originate from others, is also within our control. By respecting others, we gain control of our own respect.

While being isolated and alone is not healthy, being overly dependent on others for our success is also not ideal – and can even be counter-productive.

Like Yaakov, who followed God's model of being self-sufficient, we too would do well to develop an internal locus of control by taking responsibility and thus actively enhancing our physical, psychological, and spiritual health.

Healthy Anxiety

Anxiety is a normal, healthy emotion that we all experience. Anxiety disorders, however, are not. Where do we draw the line between healthy and
disordered anxiety? Dr. David Myers defines a psychological disorder as
being deviant (different from the norm), distressful (to self and/or others),
and dysfunctional. This last point is especially important in distinguishing
healthy versus unhealthy anxiety. If the anxiety is based on a real threat
and motivates us to prepare effectively for that threat, then it is probably
healthy. However, anxiety is probably disordered under the following circumstances: it causes us to avoid, instead of confront, whatever is causing
it; the anxiety interferes with trying to solve the problem that initiated it;
it negatively impacts other important values or goals, such as our relationships with others.

Yaakov experiences his share of anxiety, perhaps setting the stage for
his Jewish descendants throughout the millennia. His last interaction with
his brother Esav left Yaakov fleeing for his life. As he is about to engage
with Esav again, Yaakov is unsure how Esav will react. Did Esav move on
and forgive, or does he still want to kill Yaakov for stealing the blessings?
Yaakov sends envoys with an appeasing message, and finds out that Esav is
coming to greet him with 400 men. When Yaakov hears this, we are told
that "Yaakov was very frightened [va-yira Yaakov meod] and distressed
[va-yeitzer lo]" (Bereishit 32:8). The fact that Yaakov was afraid for his life
is self-evident from the context. However, the verse adds that he was also
distressed, causing commentators to speculate about a host of secondary
triggers that may have contributed to Yaakov's anxiety.

Rashi suggests that he was "frightened" of being killed by Esav and
was "distressed" that he may have to kill Esav. Even though killing Esav in
self-defense would be morally justified, it does not mitigate the anxiety
beforehand nor necessarily the trauma afterwards (had it played out
that way). Others suggest that he was "frightened" for his own life, but
was "distressed" about the welfare of his family or the loss of his property
(Rabbi Shmuel ben Chofni). Alternatively, he may have been anxious as he
was uncertain of Esav's intentions. Yes, he was "frightened" that Esav was
coming to kill him, but if he knew that for sure, at least he could prepare
militarily. However, it was also possible that Esav was coming in peace.
Consequently, he was reticent to show military strength, which could
accidentally provoke Esav (Bechor Shor).

An additional layer that complicates Yaakov's emotional experience is the fact that God previously promised that He would protect him. If so, then why was Yaakov afraid in the first place? The Talmud answers that Yaakov was afraid that his sins may have caused an annulment of God's promise. Particularly, his lack of being able to honor his parents while he was away for so many years (see Chizkuni), in stark contrast to Esav's virtue in this realm, may have swayed the merits in Esav's favor (see *Bereishit Rabbah* 76:2). Taking a different approach, other commentators suggest that Yaakov's "distress" was actually a direct result of being "frightened." Since God promised him security, in his mind, he shouldn't have been anxious (*Daat Zekeinim*). He was anxious about the fact that he was anxious!

Despite being both "frightened" and "distressed," and despite the plethora of anxiety-provoking stimuli, Yaakov's emotional experience was healthy. As Abarbanel points out, Yaakov clearly believed in God's promise, otherwise he would have hid or avoided going back home. Yaakov trusted in God, and his anxiety was a normal emotional reaction. Knowing things rationally doesn't cause our anxiety to disappear. The essential question is not whether we feel any anxiety, but whether we act according to our goals and values, despite the anxiety.

Yaakov serves as a paradigm for how to deal with anxiety. Despite feeling anxious he took charge of the situation, and functionally prepared for several different possibilities. He planned the diplomatic route of gifts and appeasement, set up his camp for fighting should that have proved necessary, and engaged in heartfelt prayer (Rashi, 32:9). We would do well to learn from his example when we are anxious, effectively preparing for different realistic outcomes, and praying to God for help and guidance through our challenges.

Parshat Vayeishev

Influence Techniques

When Yosef's brothers decided to kill him and throw him into a pit, Reuven realized that he needed to intervene to save Yosef's life. Reuven's explicit intention was to return Yosef to Yaakov. But what would he say or do to convince the brothers not to kill Yosef? Their decision seemed unanimous and definitive. The Midrash (*Ruth Rabbah* 5:6) states that if Reuven would have known that his decision would be recorded for history, he would have picked Yosef up on his shoulders and escorted him back to his father. But is this realistic? Would the brothers have allowed Reuven to just walk away with Yosef after they had condemned him to death?

Dr. Robert Cialdini is known for his research on influence and persuasion. He spent three years as an "undercover" researcher training at used car dealerships, telemarketing firms, and fundraising organizations, in order to observe, analyze, and categorize principles of effective persuasion. An analysis of Reuven's methods for influencing and persuading his brothers reveals several strategies that Dr. Cialdini outlines in his research.

In the introduction to his bestselling book *Influence: The Psychology of Persuasion*, Dr. Cialdini writes that the first and foremost principle of persuasion is tapping into the other person's self-interest by convincing them that their decision will be to their advantage. This is so fundamental and obvious, he writes, that he doesn't even count it as one of his six principles of influence. This, Rabbeinu Bachya argues, is Reuven's strategy in convincing his brothers not to kill Yosef (Bereishit 37:21–22). He doesn't just say "let's not hit him" because that would leave open the possibility that Reuven was motivated by his own feelings of empathy and self-interest. Rather, he adds the word *nefesh*, in order to emphasize that they all have the common goal of not becoming murderers.

Another powerful method of influence is to convince the others that they have something in common, for example, by identifying as members of a group with similar interests. Rabbi Yosef Bechor Shor identifies this strategy within Reuven's word-choice. Reuven does not speak *at* them, saying "don't kill him." Rather, he purposefully includes himself in the group with the intention of increasing his influence by saying, "let *us* not kill him." Rabbeinu Bachya suggests that this strategy is also apparent in another strategic word-choice. Instead of saying "don't spill *his* blood," he just says, "don't spill blood." This subtle tactic indicates to the brothers that Reuven identifies with their hatred of Yosef, and that he is not concerned about Yosef's blood per se.

Dr. Cialdini writes that there is a single word which dramatically boosts the power of influence: *Because*. In one study by Dr. Ellen Langer, when people making copies at a photocopy machine were asked by a stranger "Excuse me, I have 5 pages, may I use the Xerox machine?" – 60 percent of the people complied. When the stranger added "because I am in a rush," 94 percent complied. Even more fascinating, when the stranger just added the obvious explanation of "because I have to make copies," there was still a 93 percent compliance rate. By just adding any explanation, influence is increased. Abarbanel sees this strategy in Reuven's argument as well. At first, all Reuven says is "let us not kill him" (37:21). Apparently, the brothers were not yet convinced, so Reuven adds in the next *pasuk*, "let us not spill his blood, let us throw him into a pit" (37:22). Abarbanel explains that after the brothers did not respond to his general statement of "let us not kill him," Reuven now provides the "because." Let us not kill him *because* it is terrible to spill innocent blood directly.

By analyzing the *pesukim* in depth, we get a glimpse into the genius of Reuven's strategy for stopping his brothers from committing murder. He used the subtle persuasion techniques of self-interest, group identification, and providing an explanation in order to diffuse the threatening situation and save Yosef's life. While we hopefully will not find ourselves in such life-and-death persuasion scenarios, the techniques mentioned can be useful in helping to inspire others. Anybody in a position of influence has a responsibility to use his or her influence for increasing the good in the world, but should also make sure to use good influence techniques to best help bring about the good. Learning from Reuven, with the help of Dr. Cialdini, can start us on the right path.

Jewish Mindfulness

Mindfulness has become a buzzword, and for good reason. Practicing mindfulness has been shown to help with psychological and physical health. It plays a central role in several effective therapies, like Mindfulness Based Stress Reduction (MBSR), Acceptance and Commitment Therapy (ACT), and Dialectical Behavior Therapy (DBT). Apps such as Calm and Headspace lead a growing mindfulness industry which is valued at over 1.2 billion dollars.

The current mindfulness trend in the Western world has its roots in Eastern religions. The concept was popularized in the fields of psychology and medicine by Jon Kabat-Zinn, who was trained by Zen Buddhist teachers. To widen its appeal, Kabat-Zinn stripped mindfulness from its religious roots, focusing instead on the underlying psychological mechanisms. As defined by Kabat-Zinn (2003), mindfulness is "the awareness that arises from paying attention, on purpose, in the present moment and non-judgmentally" (*Mindfulness-Based Interventions in Context*, p. 145). The question for the Jewish consumer becomes: How do these now-secularized concepts fit within a Torah worldview?

For those steeped in the works of the Chasidic and Mussar masters, the concept of mindfulness is not new. This becomes clear in Rabbi Dr. Benjamin Epstein's book *Living in the Presence: A Jewish Mindfulness Guide for Everyday Life*, where he elucidates deeply insightful Torah teachings which revolve around important mindfulness techniques. Yet, despite many of the overlaps, it is important to highlight the potential points of distinction between a Jewish mindfulness practice and secular or Eastern mindfulness practices. One such distinction is apparent in the beginning of *Parshat Vayeishev*.

After years of exile, filled with painstaking labor, emotional distress, and physical pain, Yaakov finally returned home: "Now Yaakov was settled in the land where his father had sojourned" (Bereishit 37:1). The first Hebrew word of the *parsha* is *"Vayeishev,"* meaning that Yaakov "settled" in the land. Rashi, elaborating on a Midrash, sees within this word not just a physical description of location, but a longing for serenity (*shalva*). According to the Midrash, God does not respond to this mindset with affinity. The next world is for reward and relaxing, not this world. The moment Yaakov thought he could finally experience tranquility, the incredibly painful challenge of the loss of Yosef began to unfold.

The commentaries elaborate on the Midrash, framing what could be understood as a fundamental distinction between a Jewish mindfulness approach and one rooted in secular or Eastern concepts. Rabbi Yerucham Levovitz contends that the purpose of this world is not serenity, but spiritual growth borne out by challenges. *Sefat Emet* similarly suggests that the goal of life is to constantly toil for the sake of God, continually striving for perfection. The mentality of one who wants to dwell in peace, writes the Izhbitzer, usually leads to avoiding challenging situations, resulting in inaction that stems from fear.

The upshot of these responses is that Judaism does not view tranquility as the ultimate goal. As Rabbi Dr. Tzvi Hersh Weinreb so eloquently puts it: "The Torah's ideal is a life of action and involvement in worldly affairs. The Torah rejects the attitude of detachment and passivity, which is implicit in the teachings of Eastern religions. The Torah cannot envision the good life if that life is without challenge. Achievement of inner peace is not the ultimate value, especially not if it results in withdrawal from responsible action within society" (*The Person in the Parsha*, p. 97).

One of the closest religious terminologies that relates to mindfulness is *yishuv ha-daat*, often misunderstood as "peace of mind." Rabbi Dr. Epstein suggests that *yishuv ha-daat* does not mean peace of mind, but the act of "settling into (unifying with) present moment awareness" (*Living in the Presence*, p. 20). "In cultivating *yishuv ha-daat*," he writes, "we do not aim like some Eastern religions . . . to remove ourselves from whatever predicament, situation, or condition in which we find ourselves. Rather our goal is to enter fully into whatever is occurring in our lives and meet it with full presence" (p. 20).

If we take the Midrash to its logical conclusion, then Yaakov's mistake was seeking tranquility by avoiding his this-worldly responsibility, even for a moment. This world is for resilience and growth, not peace of mind, serenity, or tranquility. Jewish mindfulness isn't about detaching ourselves from the problems of this world, but about actively meeting those difficulties by being cognitively and emotionally engaged in the moment. By so doing, we will be better prepared to confront and grow from challenges, to improve ourselves, and to actively work towards the betterment of society.

Parshat Mikeitz

Need for Approval

How much do you care about what other people think of you?

On one level, it is natural and healthy to want the approval of others. If someone doesn't care what others think of him, he may do things that are harmful or immoral and end up being isolated from social groups, which in itself is not healthy. Yet the desire to be liked by others can easily become unhealthy if taken to an extreme. People who strongly need to gain approval or admiration from others determinedly seek ways to do so, sometimes at a high cost to their own goals. They tend to be more anxious and depressed, and to have lower self-esteem, which is contingent on what they think other people think of them.

The Talmud (*Berachot* 20a) relates that Yosef and his descendants are immune to the destructive power of the "evil eye." Before we understand why they are immune, we first need to understand this mysterious and controversial concept. Broadly speaking, as it is presented in the Talmud, when one person looks upon another with envy or jealousy, the act of looking alone can cause actual damage. There have been several explanations of this concept throughout the ages, including (subsequently disproven) scientific explanations of the eye's ability to emit a dangerous vapor or fire. An alternative explanation is the theological proposal that the first person's negative emotions toward the other provoke God to be extra meticulous towards the second person, an explanation which has its own set of controversial ramifications. Those who view the evil eye as a supernatural phenomenon either try to not draw too much attention to themselves, or else they use various mystical procedures to try and counteract it.

Others, however, provide a more rational, psychological explanation of the concept. Rabbi Avraham Yitzchak HaKohen Kook understands the evil eye to refer to general social influence. We can be easily swayed by other people's beliefs, opinions, and practices; *ayin hara* is the term used to indicate being negatively impacted by others (see *Ein Ayah* on *Berachot*, p. 102). Someone who has self-confidence and is sure that they are doing what is right in God's eyes won't be swayed by the negative influence of others, and would therefore be immune to the evil eye.

Similarly, Rabbi Joseph B. Soloveitchik (*Shiurei Harav, HaDarom* 61) assumes that *ayin hara* represents the negative social dynamics between two people. When one person disagrees, criticizes, or opposes another, he is putting an *ayin hara* on them. If a person's sense of self is too intertwined with what other people think of him, then when he receives any indication that others do not approve of him, he will be devastated. However, someone who has a developed and independent sense of self, and does not desperately require the approval of others, is immune to the *ayin hara*.

Taking a similar rational approach, Rabbi Immanuel Bernstein (*Aggadah: Sages, Stories & Secrets*) argues that Yosef was immune to the *ayin hara* because he was self-confident and not swayed by the opinions or negative influences of others. For instance, he told his brothers about his dreams even though they might not like him as a result (Bereishit 37:5–11). He resisted the solicitation from Potiphar's wife, even though he knew he might be punished, because it was morally and spiritually wrong (Bereishit 39:7–16). Additionally, when Pharaoh tells Yosef that he has heard that he can interpret dreams, Yosef brazenly corrects Pharaoh's mistake in public, saying that it is God who interprets the dreams (Bereishit 41:16). Yosef says and does what he believes God wants him to do, despite social pressure to do otherwise. This is what it means to be above the *ayin hara*.

From this perspective, we can all be immune to the *ayin hara*. We can stay firm in our sense of self, not needing the approval of others for our self-worth. When confronted by peer pressure to gossip or to cause undue pain to a third party, we can confidently refuse. When others try to influence us to sway us from following the Torah or performing certain *mitzvot*, we can stay firm and resist the strong pull to seek their approval. By doing so, we can be like Yosef, and rise above the *ayin hara*.

Freezing Emotions

Managing intense emotions can be difficult. In moments of distress, the body's sympathetic nervous system (SNS) is activated, which increases heart rate, blood pressure, and body temperature. In such a state, feelings may seem overwhelming and difficult to change. In order to calm down and take control, the parasympathetic nervous system (PNS) – which decreases heart rate, blood pressure, and body temperature – needs to be activated. The good news is that there are strategies which can help shift the physiological system from distress to calm, or from the SNS to the PNS. One such strategy, utilized in Dialectical Behavior Therapy (DBT), is to use cold water to alter body temperature. While there are several permutations of the exercise, the crux of the concept is to temporarily immerse your head in cold water while holding your breath. By doing so, your heart rate, blood pressure, and body temperature will decrease, "freezing" the emotion so that you can better handle the challenge.

Yosef, upon seeing his brother Binyamin for the first time in over 20 years, becomes overwhelmed with emotion (Bereishit 45:14). While we probably have a sense of how Yosef felt in the moment, the *pesukim* do not relate the exact thoughts and emotions he experienced. There are several suggestions in the commentaries. Sforno and Alshich suggest that he was feeling empathy, thinking of all the anguish that his father and brothers had endured throughout the years. Alternatively, Netziv suggests that he was distressed by the fact that he could not yet tell them who he was, and that he knew that his upcoming plan would cause them anguish (see Rashi for an alternative explanation).

Regardless of the precise reason, the verses make it clear that Yosef's feelings were intense. He turns away from his brothers, unable to fight back tears, and weeps in a different room. However, being overwhelmed with emotion threatened to ruin his overall plan. He needed to continue to act as the viceroy at the feast, and set the stage to frame Binyamin for stealing the silver goblet. How could Yosef shift from being overwhelmed with emotion to being calm, cool, and collected?

Although incredibly difficult, Yosef made a strong effort (*va-yitapak*), exerting control over his emotions, and stopping himself from crying. As part of that process, we are told *"va-yirchatz panav"* – that he washed his face. Rabbi Yosef Bechor Shor explains that the reason he washed his face was to remove the traces of the tears, ensuring his brothers wouldn't know he was crying. However, Shmuel ben Chofni Gaon, as understood by *Otzar Mefarshi HaTorah*, suggests that washing his face also served to remove the pain and change his emotional experience, allowing him to now have a meal with his brothers.

While we cannot know the temperature of the water Yosef used to wash his face, we nonetheless see traces of the DBT technique at work. Yosef was able to quickly control his strong emotional experience by washing his face, which then allowed him to proceed. When we are overwhelmed with an emotion that is getting in the way of our goals, we can utilize the cold water technique. This will lead to lower heart rate, blood pressure, and body temperature, helping us to focus on what we need to do to cope effectively.

Parshat Vayigash

Perspectives of the Past

How do we evaluate the past? How do we spend our time in the present? How often do we think about the future? In his book *The Time Paradox: The New Psychology of Time That Will Change Your Life*, Dr. Philip Zimbardo outlines six subjective time perspectives that people experience as they relate to the past, present, and future. Dr. Zimbardo argues that it is better to evaluate the past positively. While there are objective "facts" regarding what happened to us in the past, we can choose whether we provide the past narrative with a positive or negative spin. Past-negative perspectives are associated with depression and getting stuck ruminating in past experiences, while past-positive perspectives help ground us in the present and allow us to focus on the future.

Yaakov's life can be summed up as one traumatic event after another. First Esav threatened to kill him, then he suffered Lavan's continual trickery, Dinah's abduction, constant family strife, the death of his beloved Rachel, and finally the "death" of his cherished son, Yosef. When Pharaoh asked him his age, Yaakov responded with the past-negative perspective that his life had been short and bad (Bereishit 47:9).

We can empathize with Yaakov's response given all the hardship he had experienced. However, the Midrash (quoted by the *Daat Zekeinim*) critiques Yaakov's perspective. Instead of looking back and giving a subjective stamp of disapproval on his life, he should have shifted perspectives. Instead of focusing on the trauma, he should have realized that God *saved* him from Esav and Lavan, and *returned* Dinah and Yosef. The Midrash suggests that for each word mentioned in that interaction (33 in total), a year was taken off Yaakov's life. While Yitzchak lived for one hundred and eighty years, Yaakov only lived for one hundred and forty-seven.

Rabbi Dr. Abraham J. Twerski contrasts this Midrash with another one that critiques Yaakov. The Midrash states that while Yaakov was mourning Yosef, he exclaimed that God had turned away from him. It then criticizes Yaakov's complaint by projecting God's response: "I am busy setting things into motion to make his son the viceroy, and he is complaining that I have turned away?" Yet this Midrash does not identify any punishment. Why is Yaakov punished for saying his life was short and bad, but not for stating that God had turned away? Rabbi Dr. Twerski suggests that there is a fundamental difference between a response given during an ordeal and one given afterward. While ideally Yaakov should not have questioned God even amidst suffering, he was not punished because the pain was so great that he was not held accountable in the moment. After the suffering was over, when he had already been saved from his enemies and his children had been returned, Yaakov is held accountable for not shifting his perspective. He was expected to look back at the past and not complain.

In contrast to Yaakov, Yosef's success seems to stem from his ability to have a past-positive time perspective, which perhaps led to his ability to be future-oriented. He named his first son Menashe precisely because God allowed him to forget the traumas of his childhood. Yosef's ability to totally forgive his brothers required a firm belief in God's providence over past events, and a strong desire to move forward and not get stuck in what had already transpired. His success as Pharaoh's viceroy stemmed from the ability to predict Egypt's future economic climate, and more importantly, to devise and execute a plan to successfully avert national disaster.

We cannot criticize Yaakov because we should not judge how people react to traumatic events, and because we cannot fully grasp the greatness of our forefathers. But the Midrash teaches us a valuable lesson. If we shift our own perspectives toward the past from being past-negative to past-positive, we will be able to better appreciate the present and plan for a more successful future.

Contradictory Emotions

After Yehudah passionately pleads to take Binyamin's place to stay in Egypt, Yosef could no longer maintain his ruse. In what is perhaps the most emotion-laden scene in all of *Chumash*, Yosef bursts out crying, and reveals his identity: "I am Yosef! Is my father still alive?" (Bereishit 45:3). His brothers are shocked, although it is unclear what emotions they are experiencing. Some commentators assume that they are ashamed and embarrassed. Others argue that they fear retaliation. Yosef attempts to comfort them, although since they are speechless, he is forced to speculate as to the cause of their negative reaction. He tells them "Do not be pained [*al te-atzvu*] and do not be angry in your eyes [*al yichar be-eineichem*] that you sold me here," because it was all orchestrated by God for the purpose of being able to provide sustenance (Bereishit 45:5).

Yosef assumes that they are pained and angry, but it is not clear what the "pain" is, nor what they would be angry about. Several commentators assume that the pain refers to the constellation of self-referential negative emotions they may be feeling as it relates to the wrongdoing of the sale, such as regret, shame, anxiety, or sadness. The nature of the anger, however, is less clear. Why would Yosef assume that they would be angry? Additionally, Rabbi Chaim ibn Attar asks: Anger is rooted in the ego, while regret and sadness are rooted in the opposite place – not the ego, but in a broken spirit. If so, how could Yosef think the brothers would be angry?

Perhaps Yosef thought they would be angry at themselves because their plan backfired. Anger generally surfaces when our goals are obstructed, and there is little that is more anger-inducing than having our goals thwarted by the very actions we took to achieve them. The brothers sold Yosef as a slave so that he wouldn't rise to greatness, yet that act precipitated his greatness.

If this is correct, then how could they also feel regret and pain? They should either feel regret for what they had done to him, or angry that their plan failed. Malbim maintains that Yosef was not sure what his brothers were feeling, so he addressed both possibilities. Similarly, Netziv writes that Yosef was targeting his statement to two subsets of his brothers. While some brothers probably regretted their actions, others may have felt no remorse but instead were angry that their plan didn't work. Addressing both these concerns, whether they felt remorse or anger, Yosef argued that they should realize that this was all done by God for the sake of their survival.

However, there is another possibility. One of the core principles of Dialectical Behavior Therapy (DBT) is that, while it may be difficult, people could hold two seemingly opposite perspectives at the same time. We often run into emotional difficulties when we engage in all-or-nothing thinking. Once we accept that our emotions are complex and often contradictory, we can learn to accept these competing perspectives, and work on changing to improve our situation.

Based on this, perhaps our original assumption was wrong. Maybe the brothers could feel *both* remorse *and* anger, and not *either* remorse *or* anger. They could simultaneously regret what they did to Yosef *and* be frustrated that their plan didn't work out. By acknowledging both the moral sentiments of regret and the darker parts of their anger, they would be better able to move forward with repentance and reconciliation.

While sometimes our emotions are clear and straightforward, at other points they are confusing and contradictory. If we allow ourselves to identify and accept competing emotions, we will be better able to both understand and manage our emotional experiences.

Parshat Vayechi

Elements of Resilience

There is no one "right" way to respond to a traumatic event, and most people deal with trauma differently. However, research indicates that certain environments, perspectives, and behaviors lead to more adaptive responses that create the opportunity for healing. Yosef, a survivor of several traumatic events, serves as a paradigm of resilience. By analyzing Yosef's mindset and behavior as presented in the *pesukim* and Midrashim at the end of *Sefer Bereishit,* we can identify several strategies that serve as protective factors for dealing with traumatic events in a healthy way.

We naturally respond to trauma by avoiding the pain of the experience. Yet, research indicates that the more one tries to avoid the pain by either trying to not think about the traumatic event or by distancing oneself from anything that reminds one of the event, the greater the likelihood of developing post-traumatic stress disorder (PTSD). Consequently, besides talking about the painful experience, one of the strategies in trauma-focused cognitive behavioral therapy (TF-CBT) is revisiting the site where the trauma occurred, under the guidance of a therapist. Revisiting the site of trauma can create "time distancing," meaning the person begins to experience the trauma as belonging to the past, rather than continuing to experience the trauma in the present.

There is a fascinating group of Midrashim that suggest that on the way back from burying Yaakov, Yosef took a detour to revisit the scene of his original trauma – the infamous pit where his brothers left him to die. Standing over the pit, gazing into the abyss, he confronted the site of the trauma. At that moment, he recited a *bracha*: "Blessed is God (*HaMakom*) Who performed a miracle for me in this place (*bamakom hazeh*). This *bracha* reflects and reveals two important mindsets. First, as is indicated by the past grammatical tense, the *bracha* presupposes a break from the

47

past. By being able to acknowledge being saved *in the past*, Yosef solidifies a "then-versus-now" perspective.

The *bracha* also demonstrates a second important protective factor for Yosef – the ability to find positive meaning in the trauma. Broadly speaking, the *bracha* serves to spiritualize and sanctify the experience. More specifically, the wording of the *bracha* reveals a powerful message. The word used to connote God in the blessing is "*HaMakom*," which literally means, "the Place," but is a common euphemism for God. Yosef declared, "Blessed is the Place [God], who performed a miracle for me at this *place*." By choosing the same word to mean two different things, Yosef acknowledges that the whole narrative, starting with the trauma that happened at *this place*, reflects the will of *HaMakom* – of God Himself. This is the positive meaning within the trauma: God orchestrated each element of the story for the survival of the descendants of Yaakov in Egypt.

Finally, the story closes with Yosef demonstrating one more protective factor, namely, helping others in their healing process. The brothers feared that Yosef, now in a position of power, would seek retribution after Yaakov died. Yosef not only reassured them that he would not harm them, and that he would provide sustenance for them, but he also "comforted them and spoke to their hearts" (Bereishit 50:21). Rabbi Samson Raphael Hirsch suggests that Yosef was helping them with their healing process by trying to assuage their feelings of guilt by emphasizing the Divinely-ordained elements of what transpired, and the positive outcomes of everyone now having enough food to survive.

We hope to never experience traumatic events. However, if we are confronted with a trauma, we can learn several powerful strategies from Yosef. These include: revisiting the scene in a safe context to foster a "then-versus-now" perspective, finding meaning and positive benefit within the event, and helping others heal through their own healing process.

The Birth Order Effect

In a fascinating analysis of 700 brothers who played Major League Baseball, psychologist Frank Sulloway found that younger brothers were 10.6 times more likely to try and steal a base, and 3.2 times more likely to be successful at stealing one than their older counterparts. This study aligns with previous research which indicates that sibling birth order influences personality development. The oldest sibling is generally more intellectual, responsible, and conforming. To carve out a space for themselves, younger siblings take more risks, are more creative, and tend to be non-conforming. Despite the supporting evidence, these findings are hotly debated. Subsequent studies showed that utilizing more robust research methods yielded no significant personality differences among siblings based on their birth order.

Without taking a stand on which side of this debate is more convincing, the topic of birth order is clearly central to the entire *Sefer Bereishit*, reaching its full development in *Parshat Vayechi*. This theme begins with the deathly rivalry between Kayin and Hevel, and continues with the contentious relationships of Yishmael and Yitzchak, Esav and Yaakov, Leah and Rachel, and Yosef and his brothers. While each relationship had its own dynamic that added to the drama, having a younger sibling take the spotlight away from an older one is a theme that cuts through each episode. This is particularly accentuated in the story of Esav and Yaakov, where Esav sells his firstborn rights and the brothers contend for their father's blessing of the firstborn.

To the chagrin of his older children, Yaakov, the youngest child, favored his two youngest children, Yosef and Binyamin. This contributed to the eventual sale of Yosef and set the stage for the reunification of the family in Egypt. While in retrospect the culmination of the plot was fortuitous, the tragedy and trauma of the years of separation took a toll on all the parties involved, especially Yaakov. It is therefore surprising that when blessing Yosef's two sons, Menashe and Ephraim, Yaakov switches his hands and gives the better blessing to the younger son, Ephraim. Yosef, having experienced the dangers inherent in favoring one child over the other, especially a younger child over an older one, tries to intervene, and tells his father that he has the order wrong. Yaakov, however, responds that his preference for Ephraim is intentional. He, after all, will become greater than Menashe, and is thus deserving of the greater blessing.

Does Yaakov not realize the dangers of his decision? Why does he insist on favoring one over the other at the end of his life?

Perhaps Yaakov is communicating to his children, grandchildren, and to all subsequent generations, that success in life should have nothing to do with birth order. While being born first may have advantages, it does not determine one's future accomplishments. Being born second, third, or twelfth, may have some disadvantages, but birth order does not dictate one's place in the world. The youngest child can succeed more than the oldest child, and for that matter, the oldest child can succeed more than the younger ones. Starting with Kayin and Hevel and culminating with Ephraim and Menashe, *Sefer Bereishit* subverts the accepted norm in which the oldest is automatically endowed with greatness and privilege. This sets the stage for *Sefer Shemot*, where a younger brother, Moshe, surpasses his older siblings, and everyone graciously accepts that their roles are based on merit alone.

As the scientific community continues to debate whether birth order statistically impacts personality, perhaps the message of *Sefer Bereishit* is that, either way, we should not let it impact our accomplishments. Success should be based on merit, not birth order.

Parshat Shemot

Bystander Effect

In 1964, Kitty Genovese was stabbed and killed in Kew Gardens, Queens. *The New York Times* reported that 38 witnesses saw or heard the attack, and nobody did anything to help. This article (which was later shown to be exaggerated) motivated social psychologists John M. Darley and Bibb Latané to attempt to better understand why no one offered to help. In a series of experiments, Darley and Latané demonstrated what they termed the "Bystander Effect." They found that people are less likely to help someone in distress when there are other people present. Over the years, several different explanations were presented for this phenomenon. These include the assumption that someone else will act, termed the "diffusion of responsibility," uncertainty about if and how to act, and fear of physical or social repercussions, amongst others.

In the second chapter of *Sefer Shemot* we are presented with Moshe's brief yet powerful origin story. After being saved and raised by Pharaoh's daughter, Moshe matures (*va-yigdal*) and observes the reality of Egyptian slavery (Shemot 2:11). He first notices the pain and plight of the *Ivri* slaves (*va-yar be-sivlotam*). Rashi explains that Moshe notices and empathizes with their distress. Rabbi Yochanan Luria, in his commentary on Rashi, *Meshivat Nefesh*, indicates that this wasn't just a cognitive or emotional exercise. Rather, he was actively seeking to help others and protect the oppressed from the hands of the oppressor. Three successive stories follow which demonstrate this core character trait.

First, when Moshe witnesses an Egyptian beating a Jew, "he turns this way and that way, sees that there is no man" and kills the Egyptian (Shemot 2:12). One way to understand Moshe's behavior is that he turned in each direction to make sure that nobody would see him so he wouldn't get caught. Conversely, Rabbi Yaakov Tzvi Mecklenburg offers a completely different explanation which changes the way we understand the whole scene. He suggests that the Egyptian was hitting the slave in the presence of other *Jewish* slaves. Moshe turns in each direction not to see if there is anybody else present, but to see if any of the other Jews present would stand up and defend their brother against the Egyptian. Moshe sees that there is no "*ish*," no person of substance or stature willing to act in this situation. While there were plenty of bystanders, Moshe alone takes action to defend the Jewish slave.

In the second story, Moshe intervenes to stop two Jews from fighting against each other. The details of the fight are unclear within the *pesukim*, and commentators offer differing suggestions to fill in the gaps. Rabbi Yitzchak Arama assumes that both parties bear responsibility for the fight, and argues that Moshe demonstrates an essential leadership quality, namely, the ability and willingness to step in and adjudicate the conflict. In contrast, Rabbi Chaim ibn Attar suggests that this scene involves a perpetrator and a victim, paralleling the earlier story with the Egyptian and the Jew. Moshe intervenes, once again acting on behalf of the oppressed.

In the final story, Moshe approaches a well in Midian and sees shepherds harassing a group of young girls. Moshe perceives the injustice and saves the oppressed from the hands of the oppressor. What makes this third story even more compelling is that it comes right after Moshe was forced to pay a price for intervening in the first two stories. Moshe was not rewarded for his courageous behavior but had to run for his life because he intervened. Yet, confronted with a third injustice, he did not let the negative consequence of his previous actions prevent him from doing what was right.

Rabbi Yitzchak Karo, in his commentary *Toldot Yitzchak*, points out that there is a powerful progression in each of these stories. While each intervention is impressive, the first is perhaps the most understandable as Moshe is protecting one of his own from an outsider. The second story offers more justification for inaction as the perpetrator is a peer, yet he acts anyway. Finally, even in the third encounter, where both parties are strangers and Moshe could have easily ignored the injustice, Moshe stepped in and saved the shepherdesses.

With these three stories the Torah provides us a paradigm of what it means to be an upstander instead of a bystander. We may know people who are being bullied, harassed, or maligned by others. There are many psychological factors that can lead to inaction in such scenarios, including assuming someone else will stand up for them, or fear of retribution from the perpetrators. Yet, despite these factors, when those around us are in need, we would do well to emulate Moshe and intercede on their behalf.

Compassionate Empathy

Empathy is essential for our personal, social, and religious development. We generally associate empathy with the ability to feel sorry when someone else is struggling, but this is only one side of empathy, referred to as emotional or affective empathy. A second type of empathy, called "cognitive empathy," refers to the ability to intellectually understand the perspective of other people, identifying what they may be feeling, why they may be feeling that way, and how their behavior reflects what they are feeling. Someone who has cognitive empathy for another person may not feel emotional about the other's plight but will intellectually understand it better.

Experiencing either of these types of empathy is not inherently beneficial to other people. Some people who feel intense emotional empathy may be so overwhelmed by their own negative feelings that they are unable to help. Intellectually understanding what someone else is going through also does not necessarily lead to helping behaviors. In fact, sociopaths often score high on scales of cognitive empathy; they understand what people are feeling, and often use that knowledge to hurt and manipulate others. Empathy that leads to helping behaviors is called "compassionate empathy." It is morally and socially important to develop cognitive and emotional empathy, but only when that leads to the benefit of others.

In describing Moshe's path to becoming the leader, prophet, and teacher of *Bnei Yisrael*, the Torah and the commentators emphasize his ability to empathize. According to the Midrash (*Shemot Rabbah* 1:27), brought by Rashi, when first witnessing his brethren's suffering, Moshe "gave his eyes and heart, and felt troubled for them." The Midrash adds that Moshe cried after seeing their suffering. Moshe, in other words, felt emotional empathy for the plight of his people.

In his commentary (on Shemot 2:11), the Netziv adds a cognitive component to Moshe's "seeing." He writes that Moshe carefully analyzed how Pharaoh was making them work, and concluded that the work did not serve any functional purpose. Rather, the goal was to make the Jews suffer. The Netziv's interpretation may be based on the same Midrash that Rashi quotes, which also inserts a cognitive element to Moshe's empathy. Moshe paid attention to the fact that people were forced to do jobs that did not match their physical abilities. The weak, small, and young were forced to do jobs that were for stronger, bigger, and older people. Men were forced to do jobs generally designated for women, and women were forced to do jobs generally appropriate for men. Thinking through the nuances of this situation and identifying how his brethren must have been feeling is an integral part of cognitive empathy.

Yet, Moshe's empathy was not just limited to the affective or cognitive realms. He took action to help alleviate their pain. The same Midrash writes that Moshe "extended his shoulders to help carry the burden of each person." Moshe exerted himself to make the work easier for *Bnei Yisrael*. Moshe's cognitive and emotional empathy led to compassionate empathy, setting the stage for his consequent growth and development.

Moshe is someone who thought, felt, and acted to save and help those in pain. It is this blend of cognitive, emotional, and compassionate empathy that makes Moshe the great leader, prophet, and teacher of the Jewish people.

Parshat Va'era

Deep Breaths

Deep breathing is one of the first and most central interventions to help manage difficult emotions. When we feel intense emotions, such as anxiety, depression, or anger, our bodies tend to react physiologically by taking shorter and shallower breaths. By counteracting those quick and narrow breaths with a deeper breath, we increase the supply of oxygen to our brains, stimulating the parasympathetic nervous system, and signaling to our bodies that we can calm down. As strange as it might sound, deep breathing often requires training and practice. Many people take deep breaths with their upper chest, which can actually increase breathing rate and cause hyperventilation. An effective deep breath is known as diaphragmatic or belly breathing because it is done by focusing the breath below the rib cage, moving the stomach, rather than the chest.

Toward the end of *Parshat Shemot*, we are informed that after *Bnei Yisrael* saw the signs that Moshe performed and were told that God took note of their hardships, they were convinced and believed in the upcoming redemption (Shemot 4:30–31). Yet, in the beginning of *Parshat Va'era* when Moshe elaborates on the message of redemption, *Bnei Yisrael* do not listen *mi-kotzer ruach u-mei-avodah kasha*, "from shortness of breath and from hard work" (Shemot 6:9). Many commentators understand these to be two distinct reasons for not listening (see *Or HaChaim*): It was difficult to process the information because of the hard physical labor (*avodah kashah*), but there was an additional psychological component of being short of breath (*kotzer ruach*) that contributed to their inability to listen. What was this psychological impediment?

If we survey the commentators, we can identify three distinct emotions that may have impaired their ability to listen. The Midrash (*Pesikta Zutarta*) suggests that *Bnei Yisrael* were angry, and that led them to subvert

57

their original belief in the redemption. While the Midrash does not state explicitly what they were angry about, perhaps it was because following the promise of redemption, nothing changed. Rabbi Elimelech of Lizhensk suggests that they could not process the message of hope because they were depressed. Rabbi Eliyahu Mizrachi alludes to this as well, suggesting that *Bnei Yisrael* were not psychologically prepared or receptive to messages of comfort because they were devoid of any hope. Rabbeinu Bachya goes so far as to suggest that they had lost the will to live. A third group of commentators focus on fear and anxiety as hindering the message of hope. For instance, Maharal suggests that in addition to the actual physical difficulty of the labor, they were emotionally stressed and worried about the sheer magnitude of what they were expected to accomplish. Ramban adds that *Bnei Yisrael* were afraid that Pharaoh or the officers would kill them.

Whether only one of the approaches is correct or if there is truth to all three, it is fascinating that they are all rooted in the term *kotzer ruach*. The metaphor used to encapsulate emotional distress – whether anger, depression, or anxiety – is shortness of breath. Without critiquing our ancestors' reaction in Egypt, perhaps we can learn a message for our own lower-level *avodah kashah* experiences. When we are confronted with difficulties and react with the shortness of breath of an unhealthy emotion, that emotion may impede our ability to maintain a positive outlook and seek a solution. Instead, we should take a step back and take some deep breaths. If we can manage our anger, depression, or anxiety, perhaps we will have enough emotional fortitude to listen to the messages of hope and redemption.

Confirmation Bias

The only thing harder than changing someone else's opinion is changing our own opinion.

Pharaoh's behavior throughout the plagues is perplexing. Despite their miraculous nature and the devastation they wrought upon Egypt, Pharaoh refused to acknowledge God or to let *Bnei Yisrael* leave Egypt. One explanation which would obviate the need to understand Pharaoh's behavior on a psychological level would be to posit that God took control of his decisions and made him inhumanely stubborn. Even if we were to resolve the philosophical challenges of God removing a human's free will, we would be left with the textual challenge regarding the first five plagues, where the Torah explicitly states that Pharaoh hardened his own heart. It is only after the sixth plague that the Torah indicates that God hardened Pharaoh's heart (see Rashi on Shemot 7:3). How can we understand such extreme and self-destructive rigidity?

Researchers at Stanford recruited participants for an experiment based on their attitudes towards capital punishment, where half the recruited students were in favor of capital punishment and half against. The students were given two studies to read: one which provided data in support of capital punishment's ability to deter crime, and another that provided data against its efficacy to deter crime. Students who had previously favored capital punishment rated the data in support of their view highly compelling and the data that challenged their view as unconvincing, and the reverse was true for those holding the opposite view.

In truth, the data were fabricated in order to provide what were objectively similar claims in both studies. Although there was no logical reason to support their own side over the other, each side believed the evidence that proved their point and disregarded the conflicting evidence. This phenomenon, known as the "confirmation bias," helps us understand why it is so hard to change both our own and other people's opinions. Once we hold a certain belief, our minds search for evidence to support it and we tend to disregard evidence that calls our beliefs into question.

Pharaoh's refusal to believe in God's miraculous power is evident even before the plagues begin. When Aharon's staff swallows up the necromancers' staffs (Shemot 7:12), Pharaoh is not impressed. To make the evidence conform to his own way of viewing the world, he hardens his heart, assuming it is just stronger magic (see Ibn Ezra). The same is true for the first two plagues. Pharaoh assumes that Moshe and Aharon are just beating his own necromancers at their own game. The stronger challenge to his worldview comes when the necromancers proclaim that the third plague is beyond their abilities – "It is the finger of God" (Shemot 8:15). Despite the evidence, Pharaoh still hardens his heart. In fact, Ramban points out that this is the last we see of these necromancers. He dismisses and silences the opinions that do not conform to his own. Even by the fifth plague, which clearly only impacts the Egyptian animals and not those of Bnei Yisrael, Pharaoh still refuses to look at the counterevidence and hardens his own heart (see Sforno).

From this perspective, Pharaoh's irrational and self-destructive behavior is just an extreme version of a common human condition, which is present within us all. If we find ourselves constantly confirming our own opinions and easily rejecting any opposing evidence, it may be time to take a step back and try to evaluate things on a deeper level. Perhaps our opinions are correct, but to account for the confirmation bias, it may be wise to analyze and weigh all evidence in an objective and balanced manner.

Parshat Bo

Fake It Till You Become It

Sometimes a task seems so difficult, daunting, or incongruent with our personality that we choose to avoid it. We may garner some motivation for action from phrases such as "fake it till you make it," but still resist because we feel inauthentic or disingenuous to make it by faking it. In one of the most popular Ted Talks, and in her bestselling book *Presence: Bringing your Boldest Self to your Biggest Challenges*, social psychologist Amy Cuddy encourages us to adapt the phrase from "fake it till you make it" to "fake it till you become it." She makes her case for this subtle, yet significant, difference, based on her research on body posture. When people change and "fake" their body posture from one reflecting distance and timidity to an open, power posture (such as Superman's pose), they feel more confident and are more willing to act courageously. Even their body chemistry changes: their cortisol (the stress hormone) decreases and their testosterone (the assertiveness hormone) increases. "Faking" their body posture doesn't just help them succeed, it actually changes their personality until they "become" it.

As *Bnei Yisrael* prepare to leave Egypt, they are given many laws related to the *korban Pesach*. One of these laws is the prohibition against breaking any of the bones of the sacrificed animal (Shemot 12:46). Commentators struggle to understand the meaning and depth behind this commandment. In one of his suggestions, Ralbag proposes that this is another example of something we do differently on Pesach night so that children will ask why this night is different from others. Rabbi David Zvi Hoffmann bases his interpretation on both the historical context and the thematic context of the verse. The verse begins by commanding that the sacrifice must be eaten within one house, from which it cannot be removed, and concludes by prohibiting the breaking of any bones. Rabbi Hoffmann argues that the custom during regular, non-Pesach meals was to break off part of the portion of the animal and send it to a friend's house so they could partake as well. Since sending the food out of the house is prohibited in the case of the *korban Pesach*, the Torah explicitly prohibits even the breaking of the bones in order to prevent someone from removing it from their house.

Other commentators argue that there is a deeper significance to not breaking the bones. Some suggest that it serves to reflect the rushed mindset that was essential for leaving Egypt. People in a rush don't have time to break bones and suck out the marrow. They quickly eat the meat and throw away the bone (see Rashbam, Bechor Shor, and Chizkuni). Others see the act of breaking the bones as the expression of a character flaw. Breaking a bone to suck out the marrow can seem gluttonous and excessive, which reflects poorly on the eater and demeans the respect befitting to the sacrifice (Ralbag). It also calls into question the sacrifice's validity, as it needs to be eaten when one is full (Chizkuni).

It is within the context of this mitzvah that *Sefer HaChinuch* presents his famous thesis that our personality is influenced by our actions (*"acharei ha-peulot nimshachim ha-levavot"*). Preempting his son's question as to why the Torah would provide so many laws related to the Exodus, *Sefer HaChinuch* explains that the purpose of this mitzvah, and *mitzvot* in general, is to provide us with actions that inculcate character. By not breaking the bones, we demonstrate our break from slavery and our new existence of freedom. It is not proper, he argues, for people of stature to break bones while eating. Therefore, when exiting servitude, *Bnei Yisrael* are called upon to act like royalty, even if they do not feel like royalty. They – and by extension, we – are encouraged to not just fake it till we make it, but to fake it till we become it.

Learning by Teaching

If you want to learn better, become a teacher.

Learning by teaching, or what is sometimes termed "The Protégé Effect," is an effective strategy to enhance learning. When learners take on the role of teacher, experience and research shows that the learner becomes more motivated and understands the material better. In a foundational paper on the topic in the *Journal of Educational Psychology*, John Bargh and Yaacov Schul outline the mechanisms that can account for these cognitive benefits. One important factor is that when someone learns something in order to teach it, the way they experience the material is deepened. Their thinking becomes more organized, they look for relationships between ideas, and actively think about the best way to communicate it to others.

The time had finally come for *Bnei Yisrael* to be freed from slavery. In this pivotal moment, Moshe gathers the people to deliver important instructions related to the rituals they are to perform before they are redeemed, as well as the rituals for commemorating this momentous occasion in the future. In framing his teaching, Moshe could have spoken about several topics directly relevant to that particular moment. He could have decried the evil of slavery or underscored the responsibilities of freedom. He could have created continuity by connecting the present to the tradition of *Bnei Yisrael*'s ancestors or prepared them for future challenges and tribulations. Instead, Moshe spoke about children and education. At that moment, in Rabbi Jonathan Sacks' words, "the Israelites were told that they had to become a nation of educators."

In a passage that set the stage for the Rabbinic conceptualization of the "Four Sons" in the Haggadah, Moshe prepared *Bnei Yisrael* for the questions their children would ask in the future. "And when your children say to you, 'What does this ceremony mean to you?'" (Shemot 12:26), or "When your son asks you, 'What does this mean?'" (Shemot 13:14), he instructs, "On that day tell your son..." (Shemot 13:8). Moshe's broad message is critical and explains the "why" of education. Education is an essential pillar of Jewish life. Teaching our children is foundational to freedom. Again, in Rabbi Sacks' profound words, Moshe "realized that a people achieves immortality not by building temples or mausoleums, but by engraving their values on the hearts of their children, and they on theirs, and so on until the end of time" (*Radical Then, Radical Now*, pp. 32–33).

Embedded in the narrative is not just the essential "why" of education, but also a strategy for "how" to be an effective educator. Moshe tells *Bnei Yisrael* to think about how they will communicate and explain the experience to future generations, and even more striking is his timing. He did not deliver his message as a reflective debriefing after the performance of the *mitzvot*. Rather, it was conveyed before they even performed the original rituals themselves.

Moshe was intimating that the initial experience of each person should be infused with the knowledge that they will eventually communicate this experience to their children. Everything should be learned with an eye for how it will be taught in the future. While at the moment they were merely learners, Moshe helped transform *Bnei Yisrael*'s own learning experience by charging them from the outset with being teachers.

Even if you are not a formal educator, try to become a teacher. The next time you learn something, think about how you could communicate the idea effectively to someone else. Not only because we are a nation of educators, but because by teaching, you yourself will learn more effectively.

Parshat Beshalach

Feed Your Brain

We are generally aware that what we eat impacts our overall health, and that eating unhealthily can put us at risk for the development of numerous physical diseases. In addition, there is mounting research that what we eat also greatly influences our intellectual abilities and our emotional health. Our diets affect the neurotransmitters in our brains which regulate our cognitive functioning and our moods. Diets high in refined sugar impair our thinking abilities and tend to focus us on pursuing even more food with high sugar content. Cognitive decline has also been associated with diets high in cholesterol and saturated fats. In contrast, diets high in fruits, vegetables, whole grains, nuts, and unsaturated fats, like omega-3 fatty acids, are linked with increased cognitive and emotional health.

God initially frames the concept of the manna as a test, to determine whether *Bnei Yisrael* will follow in His laws (*le-maan anasenu ha-yeileich be-torati im lo*, Shemot 16:4). The commentators differ in their understanding of the nature of this test. Rashi suggests that the test is whether they will follow the rules specific to the manna, which includes a restriction against leaving any leftovers or going out to collect it on Shabbat. Ramban disagrees, writing that the test is not whether they will follow the laws, but whether they will trust God enough to follow Him through the wilderness, despite the lack of natural food sources. Chizkuni offers a third interpretation: since God is providing free food from Heaven – which requires little preparation time – the test is whether *Bnei Yisrael* will use their free time to study Torah.

Elaborating on this last theme, Rabbi Shlomo Ephraim Luntschitz suggests that the manna served to counteract each of three broad categories of impediments to learning Torah. The first is our tendency to spend a lot of time in the pursuit of securing food. Since *Bnei Yisrael* were in the desert, they would have to spend an inordinate amount of time and energy just to find food, something they did not have to do once they had the manna. A second impediment is that those who have lots of food (or money) tend to spend a lot of time busying themselves with protecting and increasing their savings, which can detract from the amount of time learning. Therefore, there were strict limitations on the amount of manna one could gather, preventing anyone from amassing a distracting amount of food. A third impediment to proper Torah learning is the food itself. Writing in the seventeenth century, Rabbi Luntschitz observed that certain coarse and heavy foods diminished the clarity and effectiveness of people's thinking so that they could not focus properly on intellectual pursuits. The manna did not have any of these detrimental cognitive effects, ensuring *Bnei Yisrael*'s ability to focus on learning Torah. The test, therefore, was whether *Bnei Yisrael* would use their free time for the pursuit of Torah when all these impediments were removed.

We are not blessed with the miracle of manna now, but we would do well to try and incorporate some of the lessons it brought into our own lives. This includes a broad reminder about following God's laws and trusting in Him to provide for us. But it also encourages us to reflect on our eating habits and how they affect our general spiritual productivity. Do we spend more time than necessary buying, preparing, and eating various foods that are not essential to our well-being? Could we use some of that time for learning Torah and doing acts of kindness instead? Can we prioritize eating foods that help boost our cognitive abilities and stay away from ones that give us brain fog and make us feel sluggish? Perhaps even without the manna we can do our best to replicate the benefits our ancestors were afforded with this powerful, yet challenging, miracle.

Active Hope

If you want to have better physical and mental health, work on boosting hope. Research shows that high levels of hope are correlated with a host of positive outcomes, such as healthier habits (better sleep, healthier eating, increased exercise), greater success in school and at work, more fulfilling relationships, and greater overall satisfaction with life. But there is one caveat. The benefits of hope only apply when the hope is directly tied to actively pursuing a goal. Hope associated with passivity is not hope. Hope is not just the belief that the future will be better than the present, but most importantly, it is the belief that you can actively do something to make the future better.

At first glance, hope, so defined, has very little to do with *Parshat Beshalach*. The themes of the *parsha* seem to be faith and trust that it is God, and not people, who can make the future better. There is little human agency in the narrative, as God dominates the story; it is He who destroys the Egyptians in Yam Suf. The same could be said of the previous two *parshiyot* as well. God performs the ten plagues and is alone responsible for *Bnei Yisrael*'s exodus from Egypt.

However, it would be incorrect to describe *Bnei Yisrael* as entirely passive. After God destroyed the Egyptian army, *Bnei Yisrael* were attacked by Amalek. According to the *pesukim* (Shemot 17:8–16), the war was fought through natural means. Yehoshua, sword in hand, led the army against Amalek. The Torah relates that when Moshe's hands were lifted, *Bnei Yisrael* would gain momentum and when his hands were lowered they would start losing, but this was less Divine intervention and more Divine inspiration. The Mishnah (*Rosh Hashanah* 3:8) explains that Moshe's raised hands motivated *Bnei Yisrael* to think about God, which gave them the courage to prevail.

The episode of God defeating Egypt followed by *Bnei Yisrael* defeating Amalek is the first of three cases of what Rabbi Jonathan Sacks refers to as a "double narrative" (*Covenant and Conversation: Exodus*, p. 120). Each of these cases consists of an act performed entirely by God, with *Bnei Yisrael* being passive, followed by a narrative in which *Bnei Yisrael* partner with God by taking a fully active role. The second double narrative where this occurs is the Revelation at Sinai, where God is dominant, followed by the building of the Tabernacle, which is primarily constructed by *Bnei Yisrael*. The third double narrative is the formation of the *luchot*: the first set was entirely God's doing, while the second set involved Moshe's active participation. God teaches *Bnei Yisrael* to take an active role in their own development. In Rabbi Sacks' words: "God is transformed from doer to teacher. In the process, human beings are transformed from dependency to interdependency" (p. 121).

Rabbi Sacks uses the destruction of the Egyptians as an example of *Bnei Yisrael*'s passivity, but, upon closer inspection, this is not entirely true. While it is God who was primarily responsible for the redemption of *Bnei Yisrael* from Egypt, He also required active participation from *Bnei Yisrael*, even in the process of the redemption. Most prominently, when they are trapped between the quickly-approaching Egyptian army and Yam Suf, God tells Moshe to stop crying out in prayer and just start traveling (Shemot 14:15). The Talmud adds the celebrated courage of Nachshon ben Aminadav to the narrative, the man who was the first to enter the water (*Sotah* 37a). It was necessary for human action to precipitate the miracles at Yam Suf. Rabbi Dr. Yehudah Brandes (*Torat Imecha*) suggests that the same theme is evident when God commands *Bnei Yisrael* to bring the *korban Pesach*. It was essential that they become active partners in the redemption, and not just passive recipients.

If we want a better future, we can't just sit back and hope or pray to be saved. Hope tied to passivity is not really hope. We must be willing to actively try to bring about the change we want to see. By linking our hope to action, we partner with God to improve our future.

Parshat Yitro

Emotional Responsibility

How can the Torah command us to feel or not feel certain emotions?

Many of us are under the impression that our emotions just happen to us without our input and against our will. Something or someone pushes our emotional buttons, which triggers a neural circuit in our brain and causes a physiological reaction; and there is nothing we can do to stop it from happening. My coworker makes me angry, my spouse makes me happy, traffic makes me anxious, and my neighbor causes me to be envious. Dr. Lisa Feldman Barrett, a neuroscientist and psychologist, labels this perspective as the "classical" view of emotions. It has roots in ancient philosophy and advocates in modern psychology. Yet, she argues, based on decades of research, this perspective is utterly incorrect.

In her bestselling book *How Emotions Are Made: The Secret Life of the Brain*, Dr. Barrett describes her theory of constructed emotion, contending that our emotions are constructed and created by us. We are the architects of our own emotions through our own interpretations of events, which can be based on our past experiences and our social and cultural environments. This theory can be both empowering and anxiety-provoking, as it confers upon each of us to take responsibility for our own emotions.

Writing in the 12th century, Rabbi Avraham ibn Ezra addresses the subject of emotional responsibility as it relates to the 10th commandment, namely, the prohibition against coveting. Many people, Ibn Ezra writes, believe that we are not in control of our emotions, and therefore assume that the Torah cannot command us to feel a certain way. They could understand the legislation of behavior, but not laws which aim to regulate our internal emotional state. As opposed to these opinions, Ibn Ezra argues that the Torah can and does command us to regulate our emotions, and that it is within our control to do so.

Ibn Ezra provides a parable whose relatability may have diminished in the modern era, but its message still resonates. He argues that a pauper living in the 12th century would not be desirous of a princess because he would believe the prospect of courting her to be preposterous. He likens such a desire to wanting to have wings and to be able to fly. Since it is impossible, such thoughts will not lead to an emotion. Similarly, there are certain religious perspectives, beliefs, and interpretations that we are expected to construct that will help prevent us from being envious of our friends. If we were to firmly believe that God provides us with all that we need, and we were to work on being content with our own lot, then we would not feel envious. These may not be easy beliefs to inculcate, but since we are able to work on doing so, we are held responsible for the emotions we experience.

Building upon Ibn Ezra's idea that we can construct and control our emotions, later commentaries provide alternative strategies for how to limit our feelings of envy. Rabbi Yosef Dov Halevi Soloveitchik in his commentary *Beit Halevi* suggests that if one has a strong desire or temptation and is then startled, the temptation will be drowned out due to the fear. So too, if one has awe of God, that awe would preempt the temptation. Alternatively, Rabbi Yaakov Tzvi Mecklenburg suggests that if one's heart is filled with love and passion for God, there would be no room for feeling envious.

While these strategies may seem lofty, they position our emotions within our own ability to control them. It may not be easy, and may take time and effort, but we can work on constructing our worldview such that we take responsibility for our own emotions. By doing so, we can live more empowered, spiritual, and emotionally healthy lives.

Effective Feedback

Most people don't like to be criticized. Even delivering helpful and useful feedback to others can backfire. If not done correctly, the recipient can easily get defensive and become even more entrenched in his or her errant ways. Organizational psychologists study the optimal way for managers to deliver feedback in the workplace. Educational psychologists research the most effective way for teachers or administrators to provide feedback to students or colleagues. Therapists often work with individuals, couples, and families to learn how to provide useful feedback to friends or family members. While there are several components to effective feedback delivery, we will focus on three of the themes found in the psychological literature that we can glean from an analysis of *Parshat Yitro*.

On the heels of victory against the Egyptians and of a newfound freedom, Moshe finds himself spending his days adjudicating disputes between people according to God's laws. Moshe's father-in-law, Yitro, hears about the miracles and wonders that God performed for *Bnei Yisrael* when saving them from the Egyptians, and comes to visit Moshe. He observes Moshe spending all day answering the people's questions, and criticizes him for it. Moshe accepts the feedback, and subsequently adjusts his practice. While this demonstrates Moshe's great humility, the commentators point out several nuances within Yitro's method of criticizing which increased the likelihood of Moshe accepting his words.

First, one of the most important factors in the delivering and receiving of feedback is the relationship between the giver and the recipient. The better the relationship, and the more the recipient believes that the criticizer speaks with the benefit of the recipient in mind, the more likely the feedback will work. Yitro's critique of Moshe's system comes only after the verses highlight the warm and positive relationship they enjoy. The critique works because Moshe knows how much Yitro respects and appreciates him.

Second, regarding content, feedback is more effective when it is specific and not communicated as criticism of the entire individual. When the person providing the feedback exaggerates and generalizes, saying the equivalent of "you always do this," the person receiving the feedback will likely get defensive. The verse that communicates the imperative to provide feedback for religious offenses states that "You shall surely rebuke your fellow and do not bear [*lo tisa*] a sin because of him" (Vayikra 19:17).

This is generally understood as a directive to not embarrass the person during the process of rebuke. However, Rabbi Gedaliah Schorr provides an additional layer of meaning to the text, suggesting that *lo tisa*, originally translated as "do not bear," can also be interpreted as "do not lift," meaning, when you criticize someone, do not lift the sin above the person you're rebuking. The Torah is teaching us that we should not generalize it to all circumstances. Rather, we should focus specifically on the single issue at hand and criticize the action or the problem – not the person. This is exactly what Yitro does when he critiques Moshe. Yitro specifically isolates one problem, saying, "this thing that you are doing is not effective" (Shemot 18:18). He emphasizes the problematic action, not the person.

Finally, feedback is more effective when it is followed by practical advice for improvement. Rashi, based on the Midrash, writes that Yitro had seven names, one of which is Yeter, meaning "addition," because a section was added to the Torah in his merit. While Yitro's critique starts in verse 14, the part that is considered added in his merit is where he begins to offer advice on how to fix the problem in verse 21 (*ve-attah techeze*). Rabbi Avraham Pam (*Atarah La'Melech*) explains that anyone can complain and criticize. In fact, even without Yitro's advice, *Bnei Yisrael* would have eventually complained about the flaws in the judicial system, so the critique would have been in the Torah either way. The legacy of Yitro is that he balanced his critique with constructive advice as to how to correct the issue.

Whether in personal or professional settings, it is a difficult – but essential – skill to learn how to provide feedback in an effective manner. Analyzing Yitro's critique of Moshe, we can learn the importance of fostering a good relationship, being targeted and specific in the feedback, and offering advice on how to fix the problem.

Parshat Mishpatim

The Dangers of Groupthink

Psychologists have linked Pearl Harbor, the Bay of Pigs Invasion, the Vietnam War, the Watergate Scandal, NASA's Challenger and Columbia shuttle disasters, and the invasion of Iraq in 2003 to the concept of groupthink. Dr. Irving Janis, in his pioneering 1972 book *Victims of Groupthink*, describes that groupthink occurs when like-minded people gather to make a decision, and due to social conformity, they all gravitate towards the same conclusion, without fully analyzing all sides of the issue. Several factors make groupthink more likely, including high group cohesiveness, high stress situations, and a closed leadership style in which the leader states his or her decision first and suppresses dissenting views.

In a fascinating paper entitled "Groupthink and the Sanhedrin: An Analysis of the Ancient Court of Israel Through the Lens of Modern Social Psychology," Rabbi Dr. Eliezer Schnall and Dr. Michael Greenberg argue through various examples from the Talmud that the laws regulating the Sanhedrin serve to counteract groupthink. The Sanhedrin tended to be a group of like-minded individuals who were charged with making very important decisions in high stress situations, such as adjudicating capital cases. Without proper safeguards in place, they were in danger of groupthink.

Drs. Schnall and Greenberg cite a plethora of Talmudic proofs to bolster their argument – all conceptually rooted in *Parshat Mishpatim*. In a sharp formulation, the *pasuk* states, "You should not follow a multitude to do evil" (Shemot 23:2). Rabbeinu Bachya understands this verse as a general exhortation to not associate with people who are behaving inappropriately. However, most commentators, including Rashi, argue that the *pasuk* is speaking directly to judges. In a situation where all the other judges decide that someone is either guilty or innocent, if one judge, based on his own reasoning, is convinced that the others are incorrect, he is obligated to state his dissenting opinion. Even if this distinguished group exerts social pressure to suppress his opinion and keep the decision unanimous, the dissenting judge must state his argument.

The *pasuk* concludes *ve-lo taaneh al riv lintot acharei rabim lehatot,* which also lends itself to a number of possible interpretations, but seems to reiterate the importance of upholding justice and not just conforming to the majority (see *Haamek Davar*). Rashi points out that the word *riv* (disagreement), which is usually spelled *reish, yud, vet,* is spelled in this *pasuk* just *reish, vet,* without the middle *yud.* This allows for a non-literal reading of the word as *rav,* which means "teacher." According to this interpretation, the message is that one should not disagree with one's teacher when deciding a legal ruling. Yet, since this principle would suppress a junior judge's honest opinion, the less experienced judges in the Sanhedrin presented their opinions first, before listening to their teachers or the experts' decisions. This open leadership style is essential for avoiding groupthink.

None of us sit on the Sanhedrin, but the lessons gleaned are generalizable to other situations. Broadly speaking, it is important to stand firm for what is right and just even when others disagree. Additionally, to whatever extent we make decisions as a group, we should do our best to counteract the threat of groupthink. We can do this by modeling open leadership styles, allowing others to speak before the higher authorities, and by encouraging dissenting opinions.

Verbal Sensitivity

Sticks and stones can break my bones, but words can crush my self-esteem, and lead to depression, anxiety, life-long mental illness, and declining health. Physical, sexual, emotional, and verbal abuse are all interpersonally damaging and morally reprehensible. Verbal abuse is no less damaging than other forms of abuse. Yet, as the original "sticks and stones" adage hints at, many people underestimate the damage that can be inflicted with "just" words.

In *Parshat Mishpatim,* the Torah delineates dozens of interpersonal commandments, reflecting the vigilance we must demonstrate regarding other people's property, and the care we must take to avoid physical damage. While both categories of laws are extremely important, the third category, being sensitive to the ways in which our words impact another's emotional space, often gets overlooked. In a striking passage, God commands us to "not cause pain to any widow or orphan," where the consequence of violating this law is that "if you cause him pain and he calls out to me, I will hear his outcry. My wrath will blaze and I shall kill you by the sword, and your wives will be widows and your children orphans" (Shemot 22:21–23).

According to Ralbag, the pain being described in these verses includes physical and financial pain, as well as emotional distress caused by verbal abuse. The harsh punishment described reflects the seriousness and egregiousness of the crime being committed. In the Torah, the orphan and the widow represent people who are vulnerable and do not have family to protect them. Through the commandment and the punishment, God acts as their protectors.

The ramifications of this concept are broader than we may think. While the verses specify the widow and the orphan, Rashi, quoting the *Mechilta,* argues that it is forbidden to oppress anybody. The Torah provides common examples of people who may be vulnerable and sensitive, but it is forbidden to oppress anyone. Additionally, based on the double language of *im anei te'aneh* ("if you cause him pain"), the *Mechilta* further suggests that the prohibition is not only violated by a large affliction, since even a small affliction is forbidden.

Rabbi Dr. Abraham J. Twerski (*Twerski on Chumash,* p. 151) points to a different part of *Parshat Mishpatim* to underscore the same message. One who either strikes or curses his parent is punished with death (Shemot 21:15 & 17). Yet, as Rashi points out, the form of the death sentence for the one who curses his parent is more severe than the punishment for the person who strikes his parent. Different explanations are given for this idiosyncrasy, but at its basic level, Rabbi Dr. Twerski argues that verbal abuse can sometimes be more damaging than physical abuse. Perhaps, as Rabbi Yaakov Yitzchok Ruderman (*Sichot Avodat Levi*, 40) argues, the Torah makes the consequences more severe for cursing because verbal abuse is both more prevalent and generally not considered problematic.

Parshat Mishpatim exhorts us to stay away from any form of interpersonal damage. Because verbal damage is particularly harmful and often overlooked, an added emphasis should be placed on being sensitive to the damage we can do with our words. Not only does this mean avoiding mean-spirited attacks, but it also requires us to be mindful that we don't unintentionally cause pain through our words. Words really can cause serious psychological pain and we would do best to instead use our words to heal, not harm.

Parshat Terumah

Knowing Nothing

"The only thing I know, is that I know nothing." This idea, known as the Socratic Paradox, lays the groundwork for the perspective that knowledge is not something to be attained. In modern psychology and educational literature, this idea is expressed in the distinction between achievement and mastery orientations. People who have an achievement orientation want to demonstrate that they have accomplished and learned, while those with a mastery orientation want to develop their abilities, irrespective of actual attainment of a goal or an understanding of a particular piece of knowledge. Those that display a mastery orientation tend to do better academically, put in more effort, persist through challenges, and tend to love learning more than those with an achievement orientation.

In a striking passage, Rabbi Simcha Zissel Ziv (*Chochmah U'Mussar,* p. 344) quotes this view from the Sages, which he suggests is identical to that of Socrates. Featured most prominently in his argument is the fact that the term used to describe a person engaged in Torah study is "*talmid chacham.*" Even the greatest sage, who has amassed encyclopedic knowledge and can plumb the depths of Talmudic analysis, is still called a student.

To bolster his idea, Rabbi Simcha Zissel Ziv quotes the *Baal HaTurim* (Shemot 25:18) who suggests, based on the Gemara (*Sukkah* 5b), that the *keruvim* (cherubim) that sat above the ark were fashioned in the image of children. This understanding is based on the fact that the word *keruv* is usually spelled *kaf, reish, vav, vet,* but in this instance, it is spelled just *kaf, reish, vet* (without the *vav*). Rabbi Abbahu connects this to the Aramaic word *ravya,* which means "child." A *keruv* is *ke-ravya* – like a child. The image of the child represents a never-ending curiosity, thirst, and quest to learn and discover.

Rabbi Shlomo Ephraim Luntschitz (*Kli Yakar*) finds the same idea embedded within the dimensions of the ark. He first observes that the dimensions of the Altar were five *amot* by five by three (5x5x3); the dimensions of the Table (*shulchan*) were two by one by one and a half (2x1x1.5); and the dimensions of the Ark were two and a half by one and a half by one and half (2.5x1.5x1.5). The Altar was comprised of whole numbers, the Table of a mixture of whole and half numbers, and the Ark exclusively of half numbers. He explains the symbolism of this pattern for the Altar and the Table, but for our purposes, his explanation of the Ark's half numbers is pertinent. The Ark's dimensions were based on half numbers, he argues, because the Ark represents Torah, and half measurements represent incompleteness. Every learner should take the perspective that they are not a finished product. There is always more to learn, and there is always room to grow.

This message is countercultural. We are a society obsessed with certificates, grades, accolades, and accomplishments. Our systems, institutions, and classrooms tend to foster achievement orientations. Yet, we can never become complete and whole in our learning, for there is no graduation. To the extent that we can cultivate a mastery orientation for ourselves, for our children, and for our students, we will become better learners. We are all students, we are all *keruvim*, we are all children, we are all incomplete. The only thing we really know, is that we know nothing.

The Limits of Authenticity

Be yourself. That is, unless your self is meanspirited, obnoxious, and insufferable. Then be someone else.

Being authentic is generally viewed as a valuable trait. Knowing your thoughts, emotions, beliefs, and values, and then acting and interacting with the world based on those internal characteristics, is a core principle behind several psychotherapeutic frameworks. Recent research has demonstrated that higher levels of authenticity are associated with increased general well-being and can improve personal relationships and overall job satisfaction.

On the surface, *Parshat Terumah* outlines the measurements for the different components of the Tabernacle. However, the commentators were sensitive to unpacking various hidden symbolisms relating to personal growth from amongst the construction instructions. The Ark was to be covered with pure gold: "From within and from without you shall cover it" (Shemot 25:11). The Talmud (*Yoma* 72b) relates in the name of Rava that this verse teaches the importance of authenticity: "Any Torah scholar whose inside is not like his outside [*tocho ke-varo*] is not to be considered a Torah scholar."

Yet, as Rabbi Norman Lamm (*Derashot Ledorot: Exodus*, pp. 147–153) contends, this maxim does not present the full picture of Jewish law and ethics. There are differences embedded between how we behave inwardly and outwardly. Concepts such as *mar'it ayin* require us to be "inauthentic" and to put on a show for the outside, even when we know that there is nothing inherently wrong with our actions. Additionally, violating the Shabbat or profaning God's Name are markedly more serious when done in public than in private. So how precisely are we to understand the value of having our insides like our outsides?

A close reading of Rava's statement helps uncover the boundaries of his message. Rava does not suggest that our outsides should be like our insides, but rather that our insides should be like our outsides. There are parameters of how we are to behave on the outside. There is proper etiquette and there are commandments that we are instructed to follow, even if our insides are not properly refined. If our insides are "cruel and filthy and corrupt," in Rabbi Lamm's language, then we are still better off projecting an image of being "clean and compassionate" to the outside world. Rava is not saying that if our insides are deficient, then we should be deficient for the sake of authenticity. Rather, we should feign being "clean and compassionate" on the outside while working to transform our insides into also being "clean and compassionate."

Another limitation to consider when aspiring to be authentic, is whether there actually is a stable and unified self that one can express in all situations. While philosophers and psychologists have hotly debated this question, there is one particular application of this discussion related to the vessels of the Tabernacle worth reflecting on. Rabbi Yitzchak Zilberstein (*Aleinu L'Shabei'ach* 2:442) quotes his father-in-law, Rabbi Yosef Shalom Elyashiv, who highlights that there is a second vessel besides the Ark that a Torah scholar is compared to, namely, the Menorah. He suggests that each of these vessels represents a different part of the scholar's personality and responsibility. The Ark is hidden, representing the private and introverted aspect of his nature, yearning for study, meditation, and introspection. The Menorah symbolizes the opposite – the need to shine for others, and the importance of influencing the public for good. While there are several important lessons to glean from this idea, the one relevant to the discussion of authenticity is that it is normal, healthy, and warranted to have different, even seemingly contradictory, parts of our personalities, which manifest differently depending on the situation.

In sum, authenticity is a worthwhile trait, but it has its limitations. It does not mean that there is only one solitary way to think, feel, and behave in all situations. Different parts of our personalities can express themselves in varied circumstances. It is also not an excuse to behave inappropriately. It is better to be inauthentically compassionate than to be authentically cruel. Ideally, we strive to have our insides and our outsides be authentically good. If we are not yet up to that level, we should strive to behave properly and work on having our internal states follow. With all this nuance, perhaps instead of advising people to "be yourself," we should change the advice to "be clean and compassionate."

Parshat Tetzaveh

Appreciating Beauty

How often do you feel awe, admiration, and elevation while witnessing beauty and excellence? Appreciation is one of the twenty-four character strengths outlined by psychologists Christopher Peterson and Martin Seligman (2004) that enhance well-being. They define appreciation as the "ability to find, recognize, and take pleasure in the existence of goodness in the physical and social worlds" (p. 537). Peterson and Seligman make an important distinction between three different types of goodness for which one can feel and show appreciation: 1) physical beauty, 2) skill or talent, and 3) virtue or moral goodness. In a recent study, Dr. María Luisa Martínez-Martí and her colleagues reported that individuals who score high on an Appreciation of Beauty and Excellence scale (which includes all three types of appreciation) generally report higher senses of well-being, life-satisfaction, purpose, and hope. They also report more impactful spiritual experiences, and are more empathetic, sympathetic, and concerned for the well-being of others.

It is clear from the sheer number of verses related to the construction of the *Mishkan*, its vessels, and the clothing of the *kohanim*, that the Torah is deeply interested in transmitting a theology of beauty. In the beginning of *Parshat Tetzaveh*, Moshe is commanded to make holy garments for his brother Aharon *le-kavod u-le-tifaret*, "for honor and for beauty" (Shemot 28:2). The commentators differ on the exact meaning of this phrase. Elements of the dispute rest on a textual ambiguity, which perhaps also reflects a deeper spiritual message.

Textually, it is unclear which noun "for honor and beauty" is modifying. Ralbag understands that the clothing itself must be honorable and beautiful, so that if it is ripped or worn out, it becomes invalid. Ramban argues that it is the *Kohen Gadol* who is being honored and beautified by the clothing, as the garments described were also worn by royalty. Rambam suggests that it is not the clothing, nor is it the *Kohen Gadol*, who is being honored, but that the special clothing glorifies the *Mishkan*, while Sforno says that the special clothing glorifies God Himself. Regardless of which approach we take, it is evident that since physical beauty relates deeply to sacred rituals, there is an inherent value in glorifying and elevating it.

Yet, our sense of awe and appreciation is not limited to the realm of mere physical beauty. Inherent in witnessing and experiencing the presence of the *Kohen Gadol* was also an appreciation of his skill and talent. As is evident from the verses describing the performance of the sacrificial rituals, especially in the context of Yom Kippur, the work of the *Kohen Gadol* was complicated and required practice, precision, and determination. Spectators witnessing the *Kohen Gadol* (and even modern readers imagining the ancient scene) no doubt felt a sense of awe and appreciation of the skill and talent required to successfully execute the rituals.

In his commentary *Aderet Eliyahu*, Rabbi Yosef Chaim of Baghdad, better known as the *Ben Ish Chai*, adds another dimension of appreciation, namely, virtue and moral goodness. He argues that clothing cannot be an inherent symbol of character. If someone who is known to demonstrate base moral character wears royal or regal attire, the contrast between internal flaws and external pretense makes the wearer even lower in the eyes of others. It is only if the onlookers are certain of the pristine character of the wearer of the garments that the clothing can enhance his or her stature. There is a Talmudic tradition that the *Kohen Gadol* could only emerge from the Holy of Holies on Yom Kippur if he was of high moral character. Therefore, when the *Kohen Gadol* exited the Holy of Holies on Yom Kippur, his emergence affirmed his virtue. The beauty of his priestly garments was integrally intertwined with the beauty of his virtue, character, and moral goodness.

The *Mishkan*, and particularly the role of the *Kohen Gadol* within it, provides a paradigm for how to nurture our own sense of appreciation. We should be mindful of all the excellence that we encounter. We can learn to cultivate this trait, combining an appreciation of beauty, talent, and virtue, all within a spiritual paradigm. In so doing, we can enhance and deepen our relationship with ourselves, with others, and with God.

Multiple Intelligences

Howard Gardner transformed how we conceptualize intelligence. Until the 1980s, the predominant view was that there is one type of general intelligence that can be accurately captured in an intelligence test, and that IQ scores are typically predictive of overall "success." In contrast, Gardner proposed a theory of multiple intelligences incorporating eight different types of intelligences, instead of just one. The eight intelligences span a large range of areas, including linguistic (effectively using spoken and written language), logical-mathematical (analyzing), spatial (recognizing and manipulating patterns), kinesthetic (strategically directing one's body to accomplish goals), musical, interpersonal (understanding and working well with others), intrapersonal (self-awareness and self-management), and naturalistic (understanding nature) intelligences. He later proposed a ninth type, existential intelligence, related to ideas of transcendence and concepts overlapping with spirituality.

This broader view of how to understand intelligence is evident when analyzing the design and creation of the priestly clothing in *Parshat Tetzaveh*. God tells Moshe to instruct those who are *chochmei leiv* to make the clothing for Aharon and his sons (Shemot 28:3). The words *chochmei leiv* can be translated literally as "wise of heart," but what exactly does this prerequisite characteristic entail?

Ibn Ezra maintains that in the Torah, the *leiv* (heart) is the seat of wisdom. Consequently, calling someone "wise of heart" is just another way of calling that person intelligent. However, as Gardner observed, there is more than one kind of intelligence, and using his terminologies, it would – at a minimum – require logical-mathematical intelligence to compute the measurements, spatial intelligence to visualize the patterns, and kinesthetic intelligence to sew and weave.

Assuming a more popular distinction between heart and mind, Rabbi Naftali Tzvi Yehudah Berlin (the Netziv) contends that "wise of heart" cannot mean classical wisdom (*chochmah*) because that is located in the brain, while the heart is the seat of emotion. Therefore, he suggests, "wise of heart" means possessing fear or awe of God (*yir'at Hashem*). This emotional experience is felt in the heart and is the beginning of wisdom. Yet, it is clear that, since the Torah still denotes this emotional experience with the word *chochmah* there is a component of intelligence within this emotional experience. The ability to harness and utilize our emotions to

shape our behaviors is an integral part of Gardner's concepts of intrapersonal intelligence and interpersonal intelligence (when it impacts others).
The fact that *chochmah* is contextualized within a spiritual framework relates
it to existential intelligence as well.

Others assume a third explanation of *chochmei leiv* as meaning the
ability to be mindful. Ramban presumes that the priestly clothing was
required to be made *"lishmah"* – with the proper intention. Sforno adds
that the makers of the clothing needed to have in mind that the clothes
will endow sanctity. Rabbi Yaakov Tzvi Mecklenburg extends this idea
of *lishmah*. It wasn't enough to make the clothing knowing they would
bestow sanctity; rather they had to be made with specific people in mind
(*le-shem baaleihem*) who would wear the clothing. According to these
commentators, the craftspeople needed to be intrapersonally intelligent,
with the ability to have the presence of mind, intentionality, and mindful
awareness while performing various tasks.

The craftspeople were required to possess diverse types of intelligences.
Beyond the intelligences related to the general skills of craftsmanship,
they needed to have well-developed interpersonal, intrapersonal, and
existential intelligences. Taking their lead, we should work to identify and
utilize our own multiple intelligences and apply them to Divine service.
Consider reflecting on which non-traditional aspects of intelligence you
are blessed with and search out ways to cultivate them further and utilize
them effectively in your daily life.

Parshat Ki Tisa

The Dangers of Rigidity

At the risk of sounding too rigid: Inflexibility is at the core of many mental health struggles. Cognitive rigidity, or the inability to adapt thinking to new demands or situations, is connected to anxiety, depression, phobias, and obsessive-compulsive disorder. Even in the absence of a diagnosable disorder, being rigid, stubborn, and inflexible can lead to various negative personal and social outcomes. Learning how to appropriately adapt to new situations without getting stuck in old and unhelpful paradigms of thinking and acting lies at the core of several therapeutic approaches. In a popular TED talk, the founder of Acceptance and Commitment Therapy (ACT), Dr. Steven C. Hayes, vividly describes his own personal journey struggling with panic attacks that set the stage for the development of his therapeutic system. His experience, combined with over a thousand research studies, point to the underlying cure for such psychological distress, and that is psychological flexibility.

It is rather remarkable, Rabbi Simcha Zissel Ziv (*Chochmah U'Mussar*, p. 133, see also Rabbi Norman Lamm's *Derashot Ledorot: Exodus*, pp. 185–189) points out, that after the grave sin of creating and worshipping a graven image, God's main criticism of *Bnei Yisrael* is that they are a stiff-necked people – an *am keshei oref* (Shemot 32:9), and are therefore worthy of destruction. The depravity and blasphemousness of the idol worship takes a back seat to flawed character. Rashi, explaining the language of being "stiff-necked," writes that they stick the back of their necks out to those rebuking them, refusing to offer a receptive ear. This trait impedes any ability to admit mistakes, to listen to criticism, or to repent. God can forgive an egregious sin, but only after acknowledgement and contrition; both of which are unfeasible for those who are stiff-necked.

Rashi's conceptualization of being stiff-necked incorporates an element of self-assuredness within the stubbornness. In a slightly different interpretation, Rabbi Avraham ben HaRambam understands being stiff-necked as a metaphor for being set in one's ways. It is not about being arrogant, but about being stuck in habit. *Bnei Yisrael* were steeped in a culture of idol worship, and could not adapt to a new paradigm of thinking and being. This point is particularly compelling when considered in its psychological context. They thought Moshe was taking too long, and in that moment of nervousness they reverted back to old habits. Stiff-necked people are creatures of habit, and those habits become especially rigid during times of stress.

Abarbanel offers a third understanding of the symbolism of being stiff-necked. He writes that God purposefully created us with the ability to flexibly turn our necks from side to side, allowing us to see any danger that may come from behind us. Stiff-necked people cannot turn back to see what is heading towards them. This, Abarbanel argues, is a metaphor for not being able to anticipate the consequences of one's actions. *Bnei Yisrael* were acting without thinking about the ramifications of what they were doing. Being flexible means being able to foresee what may happen in the future and modify one's behavior accordingly.

Each of these approaches provides us with important lessons for our own lives. Being stiff-necked, whether that means being closed off to criticism, getting stuck in habit, or not foreseeing the consequences of our actions, is detrimental to our well-being. Being functionally flexible and adaptable are essential characteristics that will help us thrive socially, emotionally, and spiritually. If you are interested in practically working on becoming more flexible, ACT identifies six different therapeutic processes to help people attain this prized trait, including acceptance, cognitive defusion, being present, self as context, values, and committed action. To learn more, see the sources in the Further Reading section.

Dignity Culture

Cultural psychologists Angela Leung and Dov Cohen distinguish between three paradigms of culture: dignity, honor, and face. In dignity cultures, honor and dignity are intrinsically possessed by all. Everyone has inherent worth, which cannot be taken away and does not depend on others' conferral. In honor cultures, one must claim honor to possess it and it must then be reciprocated and given by others. Otherwise, one does not have honor. In face cultures, people are placed into general social hierarchies and have a "face," or social standing, within that hierarchy. They cannot claim more face than allowed in their position, and they could lose face depending on their actions. Since these are just paradigms, sometimes a given population or group may espouse different components of the varying concepts.

In his book *Created Equal*, Professor Joshua Berman argues that in contrast to the other ancient Near Eastern cultures of the time, the Torah argues for what we can loosely call a "dignity culture." From his analysis of political hierarchies, economics, education, and narrative accounts, he concludes that the Torah is generally egalitarian in how it treats individuals and promotes equality amongst all. His research was inspired by the writings of Rabbi Jonathan Sacks, who argues in several of his works that one of the central tenets of the Torah is that "every human being, regardless of color, culture, class or creed, was in the image and likeness of God" (*Not in God's Name*, p. 4). There is an intrinsic honor and respect, referred to by the Sages as *kavod haberiyot*, that is inherently granted to all.

The beginning of *Parshat Ki Tisa* relates the obligation to give the half-shekel, which functioned both as a way to count the people and as a monetary donation to the *Mishkan*. Everyone was obligated to give the same exact amount – "The wealthy shall not exceed nor shall the poor fall short of a half-shekel, to give the offering of God" (Shemot 30:15). Rabbi Moshe Feinstein notes that the language used by God in telling Moshe to take a census of *Bnei Yisrael* is strange. The word used to denote the counting of the half-shekel is *tisa*, meaning "raise" or "carry," which is a rather inexact way of saying to collect. A more precise word choice, Rabbi Feinstein suggests, would have been "*timneh*" or "*tifkod*." The use of the word "*tisa*" must have a hidden message embedded within.

Rabbi Feinstein suggests that one might have thought that the righteous, the rich, or the privileged classes should be more involved and give more money. The symbolism behind everyone giving the same half-shekel is that everyone is equal, and everyone has the potential to contribute substantively. This is why the verse uses the word "*tisa*," which also means "to lift up," alluding to the fact that the contribution elevates the people by leading them to realize their equality and worth. The message is one of dignity for all.

This idea has important ramifications for both the interpersonal and intrapersonal realms. When it comes to how we treat others, it is important to remember that all humans are created in the image of God and that everyone has a basic right to dignity and worth. Keeping this in mind will help us interact more civilly and respectfully with those with whom we may disagree.

In terms of how we relate to ourselves, many people struggle with rejection, feelings of worthlessness, and shame. These sentiments can stem from traumatic experiences and can be very hard to shake. Rehearsing the core belief that we have inherent dignity (in the technical sense) and worth, gifted by God as being created in His image, which is immutable and irrevocable, despite what others or our inner critic may say, could be a helpful strategy to help cope with such difficulties.

Parshiyot Vayakhel-Pekudei

Moments Ripe for Anger

This essay was originally published on March 18, 2020, at the beginning of the COVID-19 epidemic. While the message was particularly pertinent at the time, it's relevance can be generalized to other contexts, as well.

Before Moshe provides his long delineation of the details of the *Mishkan*, he begins with a brief message related to Shabbat, highlighting one specific prohibition: "you shall kindle no fire throughout your dwellings on the day of Shabbat" (Shemot 35:3). Commentators wonder about the connection between Shabbat and the *Mishkan* and why the location of "your dwellings" is singled out for the prohibition; surely the prohibition applies no matter where one is located. Rabbi Shmuel Goldin, in his book *Unlocking the Torah Text*, suggests that the reason "your dwellings" is singled out is to emphasize "the primacy of that fundamental unit – the centrality of which is underscored, over and over again, at critical points in Jewish history – the Jewish home" (p. 304). Shabbat and the *Mishkan* are connected to teach us that "as central as the Sanctuary and Temple will be in your experience, their role will pale in comparison to that of your homes and families.... The Sanctuary is meant to inspire and to teach, but the lessons it teaches will reach their fulfillment only within your homes" (pp. 304–305).

The *Zohar* famously sees the fire referenced in this *pasuk* as a metaphor for anger. One should not get angry on Shabbat. But then we can ask a simple question: Why is the prohibition of anger emphasized only on Shabbat? Shouldn't it be a problem on other days as well? Perhaps the problem of getting angry is highlighted on Shabbat, since Shabbat is a symbol of peace, and getting angry is antithetical to the spirit of the day.

Alternatively, while Shabbat is in theory emblematic of tranquility, this often does not translate well into practice. The Mishnah (*Shabbat*

2:7) requires us to ask before Shabbat starts, "Have you tithed? Have you prepared the *eruv*? Light the candles!" But we are implored to say it with calmness because the sense of urgency caused by the rush of Erev Shabbat makes it an apt time for anger, especially if those close to us are not receptive to our demands and timelines. Shabbat is also a time when people are home from work and families are united together for a long period of time without the distractions of a regular routine. The environment is ripe for anger, frustrations, and disagreements, so it is important to remain tranquil when we talk – even when reminding someone to do *mitzvot* like lighting Shabbat candles.

A related therapeutic strategy, also found in the Mussar literature, is to predict times we are prone to get angry and to imagine beforehand what will likely happen. After we become aware of how we would usually react in such a scenario, we should rehearse, in our minds, ways to react effectively when that moment inevitably does surface. That way, when we are confronted with the rush of Erev Shabbat, or with the building frustrations that may surface on a long Shabbat afternoon, we are already equipped with an adaptive response.

Due to the requirements of social distancing, and *shul* and school closures, we are now in a time where the same environments that are apt for angry responses are not limited to Shabbat, but are present throughout the week as well. Our synagogues are closed, but, as Rabbi Goldin argued, their roles "pale in comparison to that of our homes and families." It is incumbent upon us, both on Shabbat and during the week, to be aware of situations where we tend to get angry. By identifying these patterns, we can work on being better prepared with a healthier response. This will go a long way to maintaining and sustaining the beauty and sanctity of our homes and of Shabbat as we confront and respond to new challenges.

The Benefits and Detriments of Humor

Humor is one of the most lauded traits in the positive psychology literature. People who have a sense of humor have more positive moods, fewer negative moods, a more engaged and pleasurable life, and an increased satisfaction with life in general. Laughter, the physiological manifestation of humor, is beneficial for mental health, and can be a valuable means for coping with stress and enriching relationships. Laughter has physical health benefits as well, as it can relax muscles, improve blood circulation, reduce blood pressure, and enhance respiration.

Yet, there is an important caveat. Dr. Rod Martin, who meticulously studied the psychology of humor for over three decades, distinguished between different categories of humor. Some types of humor can be beneficial to the self or others, while others can be damaging. Affiliative humor, which is used in a non-hostile manner to lighten the mood and to make the self or others feel better, is psychologically beneficial. But aggressive humor, used to put down the self or others, whether through sarcasm, teasing, derision, or ridicule, can be psychologically damaging.

As a powerful example of affiliative humor, the Talmud (*Taanit* 22a) relates a story about Rabbi Berokah Hozaah who was walking through the marketplace when he met Elijah the Prophet. Rabbi Berokah asked Elijah if there was anyone in the marketplace who merited a share in the World to Come. Elijah identified two average-looking individuals.

Investigating what their secret was, Rabbi Berokah asked them their occupation. They replied that they were jesters and when they see people who are sad, they cheer them up with a good joke. This documented case of affiliative humor shows the Sages appreciated the healing power of humor and the extreme reward one receives for using this power to heal others.

In stark contrast, a paradigm of aggressive humor is the scoffer (*leitz*). Proverbs, the Sages of the Talmud, and later works of religious-ethical growth in our tradition, all caution against becoming a scoffer. Rabbi Yitzchak Hutner (*Pachad Yitzchak: Purim*, pp. 25–31) elaborates on the spiritual sickness that a scoffer represents, being unable to revere, appreciate, or experience awe. The impulse of the scoffer is to be cynical and sarcastic, denigrating anything of significance. This is the trait embodied by Amalek, the archrival of the Jewish people.

Parshat Pekudei provides a detailed – and what at first glance seems unnecessary – accounting of all of the material used to construct the

Tabernacle in the desert. The Midrash (*Shemot Rabbah* 51:6) inserts a bothersome backstory, which suggests the context for this detailed account. Moshe overheard a conversation between two scoffers. One pointed to the robust size of Moshe's neck and thighs, accusing Moshe of eating and drinking in excess, as he had more means and wealth than the rest of the nation. "He is responsible for all of the money collected for the Tabernacle and there is no oversight," his friend responded. "What do you expect? That he wouldn't get rich?"

It is rather remarkable that someone can accuse Moshe, who led *Bnei Yisrael* out of Egypt and spoke directly to God, of stealing from his people in the place where God dwells. Yet, this is the degenerative power of cynicism and scoffing. This aggressive type of humor against others may get a short-lived good laugh, but it damages relationships, and is corrosive to living a meaningful life.

Humor has the power to heal and the power to destroy. Let us try to not fall into the tempting trap of aggressive and cynical humor, which is antithetical to a religious personality. Instead, we can harness the power of affiliative humor. By doing so, we can enhance our own and others' psychological and spiritual well-being.

Parshat Vayikra

Mistakes Were Made

In their book *Mistakes Were Made (But Not by Me)*, Drs. Carol Tavris and Elliot Aronson explain the psychology behind why many of us have difficulty admitting mistakes. They describe the various tricks our brains use to defend our egos from noticing our shortcomings, including cognitive dissonance, confirmation bias, naïve realism, and memory distortions. The basic gist behind all these tricks is that our mind "yearns for consonance and rejects information that questions our beliefs, decisions, or preferences" (p. 299). Yet, the thrust of Tavris and Aronson's argument is that we could neutralize these cognitive errors by just being aware that they exist and place us in danger of deluding reality.

The Torah describes four different inadvertent sins that require different sacrificial atonements, depending on who sinned: the High Priest, the court, the leader (*nasi*), or a regular individual (Vayikra, chapter 4). The Torah frames the sacrifices for the High Priest, the court, and the individual as conditional, "if" they sin (*im*); but when it comes to the leader, the *pasuk* uses the word *asher*, "*when* the leader sins*." Commentators are troubled by the assumption that the leader will inevitably sin.

Ibn Ezra circumvents the problem by arguing that the word *asher* is synonymous with the word *im* and also means "if," not "when." However, other commentators place greater significance upon the change in wording, and suggest that there is a fundamental difference between a leader and the other three groups. Rabbi Jonathan Sacks quotes three different explanations for this linguistic shift. First, a leader is more prone to arrogance (Sforno), second, he is more involved in secular pursuits (Rabbi Eliyahu Munk), and third, he can be easily swayed by popular opinion (Rabbi Meir Simcha of Dvinsk). Rabbi Sacks suggests a fourth answer which stresses the inherent difficulty and uncertainty in making political decisions.

93

Rashi, quoting the Midrash, takes the discussion in another direction by focusing on a different function of the word *asher*. Rashi notes that this word also doubles as an allusion to the word *ashrei*, meaning "happy, praiseworthy, or fortunate." "Fortunate is the generation," he writes, "whose leader sets his heart to bring an atonement sacrifice even for an inadvertent sin; how much more certain is it that he will repent for his willful sins." It is not easy for any of us to admit our mistakes, since we have many cognitive distortions that conceal our flaws from our awareness. It is even more common for leaders to not see their mistakes because the stakes are higher. We should pause and celebrate leaders who are willing to admit their mistakes and are able to model proper behavior for others.

How do we overcome the obstacles that prevent us from seeing our mistakes? I believe the answer lies within a careful reading of Rashi's commentary, since he formulates the idea slightly differently than the sources he quotes. The Tosefta, the Talmud Bavli, the *Sifra*, and the *Yalkut Shimoni* all write, "fortunate is the generation whose leader offers a sacrifice for his unintentional sins." Rashi adds the words *notein leiv*, "sets his heart."

"Fortunate is the generation whose leader is *notein leiv* to offer a sacrifice for his unintentional sins." The path to be able to admit mistakes is to pay attention – to be *notein leiv*. As Drs. Tavris and Aronson argue, the way to overcome our biases is to be aware that we have them in the first place. If we become aware of the tricks our minds play to protect our egos, and we become mindful and pay attention, we will more likely be able to recognize and admit when we make mistakes.

Fearless Sacrifices

Harvard Professor Amy Edmondson argues that the best organizations are "fearless." By fearless, she does not mean that they make bold and daring decisions, but that they create a culture of psychological safety, where employees are not afraid to make suggestions, ask questions, or admit mistakes. By removing fear from the equation, the business can innovate, grow, and thrive. Part of the process of becoming fearless is to promote the detection and reporting of intentional or unintentional failures, both big and small, as early on as possible. After detection, it is essential to thoroughly analyze failures to understand their root causes and then try to mend them and learn for the future.

Parshat Vayikra details the intricacies of several different types of sacrifices. The first three are optional (*olah, mincha,* and *shelamim*) and the last two are mandatory (*chatat* and *asham*). The latter two are obligatory because they usually come as a result of a sin. Failure requires atonement. The *chatat,* though, requires explanation. It is brought for sins committed unintentionally (*shogeig*). Why should an unintentional sin require atonement?

Perhaps one of the goals of requiring these sacrifices is to create psychological safety within the context of sin and failure. The institution of sacrifices balances the normalization of sin with responsibility and accountability. We need to try to detect all levels of failure – intentional and unintentional. When we become aware of shortcomings, we should own up to them. There is a system in place for everyone, even the anointed priest (*Kohen Mashiach*) and the leader (*Nasi*), to atone for their unintentional sins. We should not be afraid to admit our failures.

After detection and acknowledgment, it is important to analyze the root cause of the failure. Professor Edmondson argues that most businesses only conduct a superficial review and do not sufficiently detect the underlying factors. For the purposes of the *chatat* sacrifice, this may be a little tricky. If the sin was committed by accident, what deeper reason could be ascribed to the shortcoming?

While the particulars of each case should be analyzed individually, there are several broad approaches in our tradition that may serve as a starting point for a personalized investigation. One possibility is to assume that while the act was inadvertent, there may be a subconscious desire lurking beneath conscious awareness. Such a perspective, which overlaps with a Freudian understanding of the subconscious, is suggested by both the *Shem MiShmuel* (Vayikra 5671) and the Lubavitcher Rebbe (*Likutei Sichot*, 3:944–946). Taking a slightly different approach, Rabbi Eliyahu Dessler (*Michtav me-Eliyahu* 3:138–139) suggests that a person does not make mindless errors in an area that is integral to their identity. The mistake reveals that the value in question was not adequately prioritized or internalized. Finally, Rabbi Samson Raphael Hirsch contends that even though it was not done on purpose, the failure is indicative of a lack of attention and carelessness. This lack itself requires atonement.

The key point common to all the above perspectives is that there is a lot one can learn from failures, even inadvertent ones. The *chatat* offering provided both the context and safety to recognize failures and the space and framework for self-reflective analysis. Even in the absence of these sacrifices in the present day, we would do well to learn from the eternal message by creating spaces where we can all healthily admit and analyze mistakes for the sake of personal and communal growth.

Parshat Tzav

The Fresh Start Effect

New Year's is a time for a new you. Changing the calendar from one year to the next serves as a marker and motivator for personal change. Wharton professor Katherine Milkman termed this psychological phenomenon the "fresh start effect." In explaining the mindset behind this theory on Freakonomics Radio, Milkman argued that we dissociate ourselves from last year's failures: "Those are not me. That's old me. That's not new me. New me isn't going to make these mistakes." Her formulation is reminiscent of Maimonides' language in his Laws of Repentance (*Hilchot Teshuvah* 2:4), where he writes that part of the change process requires a symbolic name change, as if to say, "I am a different person and not the same one who sinned."

Milkman and her colleagues hypothesized that this dissociation with our past selves is not just confined to New Year's, but there are other temporal landmarks throughout the calendar that spark improved behavior. To test their theory, they downloaded eight years' worth of Google searches for the word "diet" and found that people search "diet" more at the outset of a new week, month, year, and semester; or after a birthday or a holiday. They found similar results when investigating when people go to the gym – there is a boost in attendance after these "new" opportunities for a fresh start.

From a Jewish calendrical perspective, Rosh Hashanah, the Ten Days of Repentance, and Yom Kippur embody a fresh start perspective, where change is embedded within the framework of the new year. However, it can be severely limiting to constrain change and fresh starts to just that time of the year. Each new month also presents an opportunity for transformation. This is highlighted with Rosh Chodesh celebrations, and is especially pertinent for those who have the custom of fasting and repenting the day before each new month (known as *Yom Kippur Katan*).

Yet, new years or new months are not exclusive opportunities for change. *Parshat Tzav* begins with laws relating to the burnt offering (*olah*). An essential part of the sacrificial process is that the priest ceremoniously separated the ashes of the previous day's sacrifice and removed them from the camp (Vayikra 6:4). Rabbi Samson Raphael Hirsch explains that this act signifies that every day is a fresh start, calling us "to go to our mission with full new devotion and sacrifice." One application of this symbolism, Rabbi Hirsch asserts, is the importance of not being complacent with yesterday's accomplishment, starting fresh with the same energy despite the somewhat repetitive nature of existence.

Perhaps we can suggest another message. Despite the "burnt" parts of yesterday, we are called on each day to remove yesterday's shortcomings, and to start fresh from scratch today. While new years, months, and weeks provide an opportunity for reflection, the truth is that every day does so as well. The imperative of repentance and improvement is one that is operative all year long, not just during the High Holidays.

It is important to look for temporal landmarks on the calendar to boost our motivation to change. But we don't have to wait for the first of the year, the first of the month, or next Monday until we start improving. Every day is a fresh start.

Pay It Forward

In a series of fascinating studies, Dr. David DeSteno and colleagues demonstrate that when people feel grateful for receiving a benefit, they are more likely to pay that goodwill forward, with either time or money. As he delineates in his book *Emotional Success: The Power of Gratitude, Compassion, and Pride*, this applies not only to reciprocating back to the benefactor of the initial good; in fact, people are even more likely to pay the good forward to others. Additionally, gratitude is contagious. It can spread virally through social spheres, creating an upward, virtuous cycle. Even seeing someone else express gratitude can create a positive emotional momentum, leading to more gratitude, compassion, and kindness.

Parshat Tzav details various peace offerings, known as *shelamim*. As a rule, one who offered this type of sacrifice could eat it on the day that it was brought, on that night, and on the following day. An exception is the thanksgiving offering, known as the *todah*. The thanksgiving offering was brought when one wanted to extend gratitude and praise to God, generally, although not necessarily, after being saved from a dangerous situation. Unlike the other peace offerings, the thanksgiving offering was only allowed to be eaten the day it was brought and that night; on the following day, the leftovers were forbidden. Another difference between the thanksgiving offering and the other peace offerings is the requirement that it be accompanied by forty loaves of bread. Why the differences?

Sforno suggests that the increased amount of food and decreased amount of time to eat incentivized people to invite guests. Unlike other sacrifices which may be more private in nature, the ideal thanksgiving offering is a public affair. The social setting allowed the benefactor of God's graces to recall the details of His wonderous deeds to a larger audience, glorifying God's name among the attendees.

Perhaps, based on Dr. DeSteno's research, we can suggest that beyond the benefit of proclaiming God's beneficence, the public meal provided two other essential functions. First, since inviting guests to a festive meal is itself an act of kindness, the thanksgiving offering is an opportunity to pay the gratitude forward. Bringing the sacrifice is not only an act of gratitude and acknowledgment of the benefactor (God), but is also a means of doing good for others. In a sense, there is no better way to show gratitude for all that God does for us than by using His gifts as opportunities to do for others.

Second, while a private moment of deep gratitude may be even more powerful and humbling than a public gesture, the public demonstration has an essential social function, serving as a signaling device to others. When we see others perform acts of gratitude, we ourselves get caught up in the positive energy, and are more likely to act virtuously. The thanksgiving offering needed to be done in public, not just to praise God, which is a worthwhile pursuit on its own, but also to increase moral virtue amongst those present.

In contemporary times we lack the actual sacrifice, but we can create other opportunities to demonstrate gratitude in public. By making gratitude a social experience, we can create an increasing spiral of positive energy that can help propel us forward to continued virtue in service of God and other people.

Parshat Shemini

Mistaken Anger

The Eighth Day of the inauguration of the *Mishkan* calls for a celebration, as God's Glory appears and a fire descends, symbolizing the successful acceptance of the sacrifices (Vayikra, chapter 9). Yet the elation turns quickly to tragedy when another fire descends, this time to consume Aharon's sons Nadav and Avihu for offering a "foreign" fire on the altar (Vayikra, chapter 10). Aharon is silent. The usual regulations of mourning are suspended, for the ceremony must proceed as planned. Moshe informs Aharon and his remaining children to eat from the *mincha* and *shelamim* offerings as intended, but does not mention anything specifically about the *chatat* offering. When he discovers that they burned the whole animal and did not eat it, Moshe expresses anger.

Aharon defends the decision, arguing that after all he has experienced on that day, God would not want them to eat the sacrifice. Moshe hears Aharon's argument and is pleased. The Sages explain that Moshe had previously known that according to the law they shouldn't have eaten the *chatat* offering, but Moshe forgot. The Midrash (*Vayikra Rabbah* 13) identifies this as one of the three times that Moshe became angry and consequently forgot a law.

Another Midrash (*Sifra, Shemini* 2:12) reports a fascinating dispute between two Sages as to the sequencing of the events. Did Moshe's anger cause him to make a mistake, or did his mistake cause him to get angry? Chananiah ben Yehudah argues that Moshe's anger led to his mistake. However, Rabbi Yehudah questions this analysis because if it were not for the mistake, he never would have become angry in the first place. The mistake led to the anger, not the other way around.

Regarding Moshe, it is unclear which Sage is correct. Yet, to appreciate the psychological message, we don't have to pick a winner. They are both true. Anger both causes mistakes and is rooted in mistakes. The fact that anger causes mistakes is obvious. When we are angry, we tend to speak or act in ways that we later regret. Mistakes caused by anger destroy careers, damage relationships, and devastate families.

Less apparent, yet perhaps more important, anger is also rooted in mistakes. Some argue that we cannot control the way we feel. Emotions, they claim, just happen to us without any conscious control. Yet mounting evidence indicates otherwise. Our thoughts, beliefs, expectations, perceptions, and attitudes impact the way we feel. A core principle of Cognitive Behavioral Therapy (CBT) is that by working on identifying, challenging, and changing our thought processes, we can make our emotional experiences healthier.

The thoughts that lead to unhealthy anger are almost always mistaken. They are what psychologists refer to as cognitive distortions or irrational beliefs. We should always be hesitant of critiquing Moshe Rabbeinu, but following the lead of the two above Midrashim, at the very least we can try to glean a lesson for our own self-improvement. In Moshe's case it seems his mistake was not remembering all the applicable laws of the case, and consequently jumping to the conclusion that the others were mistaken. Are we prone to arriving too quickly at conclusions, making judgments before we have all the facts? Do we yell at our kids, siblings, parents, friends, coworkers, or employees, before clarifying the whole story? If so, we should perhaps train our brains to slow down, examine the situation from all sides, and ask clarifying questions of others. By changing our mistaken thinking, we can avoid becoming angry, helping us avoid the negative consequences that anger can have on our relationships.

Aharon's Silence

Dr. Bessel van der Kolk is a world-renowned trauma expert, and a colleague of Dr. David Pelcovitz. Dr. Pelcovitz relates a story where Dr. van der Kolk showed him a picture of a man's brain that was taken using an fMRI, a machine which measures brain activity by detecting changes in blood flow in different regions of the brain. This particular image was taken while the man was experiencing a flashback to the traumatic experience of being caught in the stairwell of the World Trade Center on 9/11. At that moment there was absolutely no brain activity in the part of the brain dedicated to language, known as Broca's area. The memory of the trauma rendered him speechless. Only after therapy, where Dr. van der Kolk helped the man give words to the pain, did later images show brain activity in the language centers.

Perhaps, Dr. Pelcovitz suggests, this vignette can help us understand Aharon's silence in *Parshat Shemini*. After they brought a "strange" fire to the altar, a fire burst forth and consumed Aharon's sons Nadav and Avihu. Moshe then told Aharon, "This is what God meant when He said: Through those near to Me I shall be sanctified, and gain glory before all the people." The verse then ends, *va-yidom Aharon*, "and Aaron was silent" (Vayikra 10:3).

How are we to understand Aharon's silence? Does silence mean a lack of crying, a lack of speech, or both? Does it mean that he could not say anything, had no urge to say anything, or that he desperately wanted to cry out but controlled himself? What exactly would he have said, and why didn't he speak at all? What was his facial expression? Did he just control his speech but "leaked" out his emotion in some other way, or was he stoic in his expression as well?

Ramban assumes that upon witnessing their deaths, Aharon started weeping. It is only after Moshe quoted God as saying, "Through those near to Me I shall be sanctified" that Aharon was silent. This assumes that Aharon experienced a natural emotional reaction and was subsequently consoled. Rabbi Yaakov Tzvi Mecklenburg disagrees and says that if he was crying and then went silent, the word used should have been *va-yishtok*. *Va-yidom* connotes an absence of any noise. According to Rabbi Mecklenburg, this word reflects that Aharon accepted God's decree without hesitation or doubt.

The Chofetz Chaim suggests that it was not only that Aharon did not voice any protest, but that the absence of reaction was reflected in his facial expression as well. The word *va-yidom*, he argues, is related to the word *domem*, an inanimate object. His face was like a rock, lacking even a hint of negative expression.

The latter two commentaries align well with Rashi, who quotes the Talmud (*Zevachim* 115b), which states that Aharon was rewarded for his silence. The question is: why is silence rewarded here? Why couldn't Aharon cry out in mourning? Some look to Aharon as a paradigm for how all should react to tragedy: Accept God's judgement and don't question "why." Alternatively, Rashbam suggests that Aharon's silence does not indicate that one should not demonstrate emotion upon the loss of loved ones. Rather, this was an exception, requiring a higher level – and perhaps super-human level – of self-control. Aharon was commanded to (at least temporarily) suppress his emotions, as his presence was needed for the public sanctification of the Tabernacle.

As a rather bold alternative, Rabbi Shmuel Goldin (*Unlocking the Torah Text: Vayikra*) suggests that Aharon chose silence as his way of dealing with loss. Moshe attempted to console Aharon by telling him that God is sanctified by those who are close to Him, meaning that Nadav and Avihu were precious to God. Yet, Rabbi Goldin suggests that in Aharon's silence he is responding: "Moshe, there are times when words do not suffice, when they are, in fact, hurtful. I reject your attempt to explain the inexplicable. No words or comfort will assuage my heart's deep pain. I am willing to accept God's justice, but I know that I will never fully understand. For me, in the face of overwhelming loss there is only one meaningful response: Silence" (p. 68).

Despite their variations, the aforementioned opinions all assume that Aharon chose to stay silent. Dr. Pelcovitz, based on his interchange with Dr. van der Kolk, suggests that maybe Aharon's silence was not a conscious choice. Rather, his silence was a natural reaction to the trauma of witnessing his two sons dying. Broca's area in his brain was inactive; he literally could not speak. There were no words.

Perhaps the range of explanations indicates another important lesson that Dr. Pelcovitz emphasizes. It is normal for different people to react differently to distress. There is no one right way to cope. While we may never know Aharon's inner thoughts and emotions, the diverse possibilities model and validate various ways one can respond to tragedy.

Parshiyot Tazria-Metzora

Biases of the Self

Precise and accurate knowledge of the self is elusive. Psychologists have identified a number of self-serving biases which serve to protect our egos. The fact that most of us attribute successes to our abilities and mistakes to matters beyond our control, and that many of us think we are above average, reflects this self-serving bias. In fact, some cleverly designed studies demonstrate that we even have a bias to deny the fact that we have biases. We are quick to identify the self-serving bias in others but think that we ourselves are immune to it.

This idea is alluded to in a law that is sourced in *Parshat Tazria*. Kohanim were responsible for diagnosing and overseeing the purification process of *tzaraat*. Even if a person presented with all of the symptoms, if a Kohen did not officially declare the affliction as *tzaraat*, it lacked the status of the disease. However, a Kohen did not have the ability to self-diagnose. Even if he "knew" he had the illness, a different Kohen needed to assess it because of the rule stated in the Mishnah (*Negaim* 2:5), "A person may inspect anyone's afflictions, other than his own." Rabbi Menachem Meiri interprets this legal ruling homiletically. The word *negaim* is literally a reference to physical afflictions like *tzaraat*, but could also be interpreted as shortcomings, inadequacies, and failings of personality. We can see the flaws of others, but we fail to detect those same defects in ourselves. To remedy this blind spot we all have, we are encouraged to "acquire a friend" (*Avot* 1:6), someone who can help identify our weaknesses, so we can be inspired to self-improvement.

Being aware of and trying to change our self-serving biases is essential for religious growth. It helps stave off arrogance, which is perhaps the most strongly condemned character trait throughout Jewish literature. Coming to the realization that we may not be as great and faultless as we think is important for the inculcation of humility and an accurate, not inflated, sense of self. However, there is a whole category of biases that are the opposite of self-serving. Instead of a biased self-perception which leads to arrogance, many people reach inaccurate conclusions about the self which lead to depression. Instead of attributing success to ability and failure to circumstance, they think failures result from their lack of ability while successes are attributed to chance. Instead of thinking they are above-average, they think they are worthless and hopeless.

While it is difficult to identify our own self-serving biases, the same is true regarding self-denigrating biases. People tend to be inaccurate judges of themselves, either in the positive or the negative direction. Having another person, whether a teacher, friend, family member, or therapist who can help identify our self-related biases, is essential for spiritual, emotional, and personal growth.

Confronting our biases and striving for accurate self-awareness is an emotionally daunting task. If we feel that our core sense of self is threatened, we can experience deep anxiety, making precise self-analysis more difficult. Perhaps another lesson from this week's *parsha* can help define the emotional context which is most conducive to self-reflection. Describing someone who sees symptoms of what might be *tzaraat*, the verse states (Vayikra 13:2): "When a person shall have in the skin of his flesh a rising, or a scab, or a bright spot, and it became in the skin of his flesh the plague of *tzaraat*..." *Or HaChaim* writes that the verse uses the words "in the skin of his flesh" to teach us that *tzaraat* is only skin deep, so to speak. It does not permeate the essence of a person's being. This message is essential if we want to work on our own biases or help others with theirs. A person's flaws never become the entirety of his or her identity. This realization could help us loosen our defenses and be more receptive to scrutinizing our self-related biases, with the ultimate goal of an accurate sense of self conducive to a more authentic persona.

Hedging for Humility

Embedded in the complex and esoteric laws of *tzaraat* is a simple, yet powerful, message related to the power of speech. Although the verses themselves do not explicitly state what causes *tzaraat*, the Talmud associates it with seven sins, most famously with *lashon hara*. The detrimental effects evil speech has on others is obvious. While we may have difficulty being mindful of or controlling what we say, few people would deny the damage that hurtful speech can inflict. Yet *lashon hara* is not just problematic for its interpersonal effects; it also stems from a deficiency of character. One of the other seven sins responsible for *tzaraat* is arrogance. These two sins may be linked: Speaking ill of others may reflect an arrogant personality.

Dr. James W. Pennebaker is a leading psychologist in the field of language and personality. Using complex computer programs, he analyzes people's word usage to mine an individual's thoughts, feelings, motivations, and relationships with other people. Pennebaker demonstrates in several studies that the words we use not only affect others, but reflect our selves as well.

One example of this is our use of "hedges." When asked "What's the weather like outside?," we could respond "It's cold" or we could respond "I think it's cold." In his book *The Secret Life of Pronouns: What Our Words Say About Us*, Pennebaker argues that when we say, "I think it's cold" instead of "It's cold," we are implicitly acknowledging that "Although there are different views on this – and you may indeed come to a different conclusion – my own personal belief is that it might be cold outside. I could be wrong, of course, and if you have a different sense of the weather, I won't be offended" (p. 44). "I think" implies nuance. It leaves room for multiple perspectives and different opinions. In short, it reflects humility.

Describing the laws of *tzaraat* as it relates to houses, the verse tells us that when a person sees something that looks like *tzaraat* on his house, he approaches the Kohen and says "Something like a plague has appeared upon my house" (Vayikra 14:35). The Midrash (quoted by Rashi) is sensitive to the fact that the verse could have just stated "a plague has appeared upon my house." The fact that the qualifier "something like" (*ke-nega*) a plague is used must be teaching something of significance. Even if the person approaching the Kohen is a scholar who knows conclusively that it is a plague, says the Midrash, he should still hedge his statement. He should not say I saw a plague. Rather, he should say, I saw something like a plague.

Rabbi Eliyahu Mizrachi, in his supercommentary on Rashi, finds a moral message within the Midrash. The Torah is teaching us proper behavior (*derech eretz*): we should speak using hesitant language. He connects it to another comment of the Sages, namely, that we should train ourselves to say, "I don't know" (*Berachot* 4a). Rabbi Samson Raphael Hirsch explains that hedging our statements and admitting when we are not sure of something reflects a humble character.

In what is becoming an increasingly toxic social and political climate, the Sages' suggestion, rooted in the biblical text, provides us a framework for proper character development and effective communication. While there may be a place for indisputable facts and speaking with conviction, if we consider everything we think and say as definitive truth, it may be time to take a step back and reflect. Is it a plague, or something like a plague? Am I so sure of everything, or can I perhaps admit that I don't really know? If we can hedge our communication with a hint of humility, we will be well on our way to cultivating our own character and improving our relationships with others.

Searching for Meaning

Viktor Frankl was a famous Jewish psychiatrist and a Holocaust survivor. In his 1946 book *Man's Search for Meaning*, he chronicles his experiences in Auschwitz and the tenets of his psychotherapeutic method, logotherapy. This method, he argues, helped him cope with the traumatic and horrific experiences during the Holocaust. Three of the essential and related messages of logotherapy are that (1) we all have free will to choose our mental responses, even amidst suffering; (2) our mission in life should be to seek meaning, not to merely gain pleasure or to avoid pain; and (3) we obtain meaning by living a life that focuses on values and ideals.

In describing the wisdom, internal structure, and depth of the Hebrew alphabet, the mystical work *Sefer Yetzirah* highlights the connection between the word *nega* (affliction; spelled *nun, gimmel, ayin*) and the word *oneg* (pleasure; spelled *ayin, nun, gimmel*): "There is no good higher than *oneg* and no evil lower than *nega*." The word *nega* is used often in *Parshiyot Tazria* and *Metzora* to describe the disease of *tzaraat*. Building off of *Sefer Yetzirah*, several commentators reflect on the relationship between the *nega* of *tzaraat* and the inverse concept of *oneg*.

For example, Rabbi Yissocher Frand quotes and elaborates on the *Chidushei HaRim*, pointing out that the only difference between *oneg* and *nega* is the place of the *ayin* within the word. In *oneg* the *ayin* is in the front of the word and in *nega* it is at the end. When explaining the laws pertaining to *tzaraat* of clothing, the Torah states that if after washing, "the affliction has not changed its appearance [*ha-nega lo hafach et eino*]... it is contaminated..." (Vayikra 12:55). The *Chidushei HaRim* suggests a homiletic reading. The term *et eino*, translated as "its appearance" can be read as "its *ayin*," referencing the letter *ayin*, with an additional layer of meaning, namely, its eye, or vision. The difference between a *nega* and *oneg* is a matter of *ayin*, or perspective.

To be clear, *oneg* in this context does not mean physical pleasure, nor does it necessarily mean a surreal, detached, obliviousness to pain. *Oneg* is a spiritual pleasure, which does not completely negate pain, but can alleviate it by infusing meaning. It is the pleasure that comes when, despite pain, we can change our perspective and still commit to living a life steeped in values and ideals.

Perhaps this is why, as *Sefat Emet* explains, the impurity of the *metzora* lasts seven days, ensuring that he or she experiences Shabbat as part of the process. The pleasure and meaning one derives from Shabbat are reparative. *Sefat Emet* also points out that the word *tzaraat* (*tzadi, reish, ayin, tav*) has the same letters as the word *atzeret* (*ayin, tzadi, reish, tav*), which is a reference to the holiday of Shavuot. Shavuot, representing the acceptance and study of Torah, provides the antidote for the pain and suffering of *tzaraat*.

We generally hope to avoid pain and suffering, but there are cases where the only thing we can control is our response. While it is incredibly challenging, we can work on shifting our perspective and investing our lives with value and meaning, despite the pain. By suffusing our lives with the meaning that permeates a Torah lifestyle, we can hopefully change any *nega* we may experience to one of *oneg*.

Parshat Acharei-Mot

The Power of Confession

The conversation of Jewish self-improvement revolving around Yom Kippur tends to focus on *teshuvah*, or repentance. Whether increasing positive spiritual habits or decreasing negative ones, the focus of *teshuvah* tends to be action-oriented. If a person steeped in sin successfully ceases his wayward behavior, we tend to think of him as completing the process of *teshuvah*. However, the absence of *viddui*, or confession, calls into question the efficacy of this process. The concept of confession is sourced in the Yom Kippur rituals of the *Kohen Gadol*, found in this week's reading of *Acharei Mot*. According to Rambam, confession is an absolutely necessary part of repentance. But why is this so? If my behavior has improved, why is the verbalization of my past indiscretion compulsory?

In their review of spiritual confessions (*Understanding Spiritual Confession: A Review and Theoretical Synthesis*), psychologist Aaron Murray-Swank and his colleagues from Bowling Green State University identify four mental health benefits attainable through confessing. Two of these are impression management, meaning that (1) people tend to judge those who confess more positively, and (2) there is an increased social connection between the confessor and the person or people hearing the confession. These two benefits are irrelevant to Jewish ritual confession, as they involve confession to another person. Within Judaism, confession is between man and God – there is no middleman. The third benefit is the emotional catharsis that confession provides. Suppressing emotions can be unhealthy, while verbally expressing them can help reduce feelings of guilt and shame. The last benefit is that confession allows the confessor to better understand what had happened: "The act of translating thoughts and feelings into language," they write, "provides coherence and structure to human experience" (p. 284). This is the reason why confession is essential to the process of *teshuvah*.

The Gemara in *Yoma* (36b), based on the verse in this week's *parsha* (Vayikra 16:6), states that the confession of the *Kohen Gadol* suffices to effect atonement (*kapparah*) on its own, even in the absence of a sacrifice. According to Rabbi Samson Raphael Hirsch, the root of the word for atonement, *kapparah*, means to "bury" or to "cover up." When we confess, God buries our past sins. Yet, Rabbi Hirsch contends, the sin is benevolently covered up only from God's perspective. From our perspective, the sin should not be buried, but remain vivid and clear in our minds. This is because the function of confession in Judaism is not disclosure to another human being, but an admission to oneself (as is evident from the reflexive form of *hitvadah*).

As long as our thoughts are bottled up in our minds, Rabbi Joseph B. Soloveitchik elaborates in *Al Ha-Teshuvah*, they are definitionally unclear. We cannot fully grasp what we are thinking or feeling unless we verbally express it. The act of constructing logical and grammatical sentences allows the fleeting and unintelligible chatter in the recesses of our brains to become coherent. Consequently, confession requires the courage to confront shortcomings that we may have otherwise buried. Therefore, Rabbi Soloveitchik argues, the confession of the *Kohen Gadol* suffices for atonement even without the official sacrifice. The confession itself is the sacrifice: "A confession which is not just simple lip-service, but which emanates from an anguished soul and an aching heart is accounted as an offering on the altar...Just as we burn an offering on the altar, we burn our resolute serenity, cultivated pride and artificial life with the act of confession" (translation from *New Studies in Vayikra* by Nehama Leibowitz, pp. 224–225).

Without confession, self-improvement is incomplete. To obtain the requisite self-awareness required, we must concretize our thoughts through speech. By verbalizing our misdeeds, this will assist us in fully engaging in the *teshuva* process, moving us toward *teshuvah sheleimah*, a complete return to God.

The Limits of Responsibility

A core principle of many types of psychotherapy is personal responsibility. If we want to improve, we need to take responsibility for the things that we can change. Yet, such an approach can be dangerous. Sometimes we take responsibility for things that we cannot change, or that aren't our fault. This could lead to unhealthy shame and self-blaming, which could make matters worse. It is difficult, yet essential, that we find the balance between taking responsibility for things we can change and realizing what is beyond our control.

As part of the sacrificial service on Yom Kippur, the *Kohen* would take two goats and draw lots. The Mishnah (*Yoma*, chapter 6), building on Vayikra 16, explains that the two goats needed to be exactly alike in appearance, size, and value, and they needed to be purchased at the same time. Based on the lots drawn, one goat was designated "for God" and the other "for Azazel." The goat "for God" had the privilege of becoming a sin offering in the *Mishkan*. The goat "for Azazel" had no such luck. It was sent through the wilderness and, as an act of atonement, was thrown off a cliff. Although they were virtually identical, their destinies, as determined by the chance of a lottery, were not.

How are we to understand this cryptic and seemingly capricious ceremony? When considering repentance and atonement, the same tension exists between taking personal responsibility and acknowledging external circumstances beyond our control. On the one hand, repentance requires us to own up to our shortcomings; on the other hand, not everything that goes wrong is completely our fault. In a powerful analysis of the deeper symbolism of this ritual, Rabbi Joseph B. Soloveitchik explains, "The secret of atonement is thus indicated in the ceremonious casting of the lots. It reflects the basis for the penitent's claim to forgiveness, that his moral directions were similarly influenced by forces beyond his control, that his sinning was not entirely a free and voluntary choice" (*Reflections of the Rav*, p. 46). Just like the destiny of the goats was determined by lots, so too, we ask God to view our actions as being beyond our control.

While we have free will, man "does not choose the family into which he is born and reared, nor the society whose values will have such an impact on him. He makes choices, yet major aspects of his life seem to be governed by capricious, chance events and circumstances beyond his control. He is a vulnerable creature whose serenity may suddenly be jarred by overpowering temptations, peculiar turns of events, unexpected political coups, an economic collapse, a terminal illness, or traumatic shocks" (*Reflections of the Rav*, p. 41). According to Rabbi Soloveitchik, the ceremony of the goats acts as a plea to God to keep in mind all of the circumstances that are beyond our control which may have influenced our decisions.

Accordingly, this ceremony provides a healthy counterpoint to the generally appropriate and worthwhile pursuit of self-accountability required for change. It is important for us to take responsibility and strive to improve, but it is equally as important to not overdo it to the point of unrealistic and unhealthy self-blame. The ceremony of the goats reminds us to put things in perspective and realize that not everything is under our control, and not everything is our fault.

Parshat Kedoshim

Assertiveness Training

Imagine for a moment that someone you loved or cared about harmed you in some way. Hopefully it wasn't too easy to conjure up a scenario, but we are all, at some point, let down by those closest to us. How do you generally react in such a situation? While context obviously matters, is there a recommended way to respond when we are hurt by others? There is one verse in this week's *parsha*, as elucidated by Rambam, that encapsulates an entire therapeutic approach to handling such circumstances.

Albert Ellis, the founder of Rational Emotive Behavior Therapy (REBT), distinguishes between three types of responses to being hurt by others: unassertive, assertive, and aggressive. Being "unassertive" when someone does something we don't like, means to react passively, keeping our feelings inside without expressing them at all. While this may seem like a good way to avoid conflict, one of the problems associated with being unassertive is that it often leads to internal resentment and hostility. On the other extreme is an "aggressive" response. Instead of keeping it inside, we express our emotions in a harmful, often retaliative fashion. This could take the form of insulting, offending, denigrating, or yelling at the other person. It may feel good in the moment, but hardly leads to positive long-term consequences. According to Ellis, the preferable behavior is "assertive." We are assertive when we express what we are thinking and feeling in a non-aggressive, yet straightforward, fashion.

In the beginning of *Parshat Kedoshim* the Torah lumps three concepts into the same *pasuk*, which don't intuitively seem to fit together: (1) don't hate your brother in your heart, (2) reprove your fellow, and (3) don't incur a sin on his behalf (Vayikra 19:17). Rambam in the sixth chapter of *Hilchot De'ot* connects each piece of the verse, providing a framework similar to the therapeutic one discussed above. If someone does something to hurt us, we should not allow the feelings to fester inside, as that will lead to resentment and hatred (unassertive behavior). Rather, we should approach the person and reprove him by initiating a conversation about his actions (assertive behavior). However, upon doing so, we must be careful to not incur our own sin by embarrassing the person (aggressive behavior).

Rambam adds two important criteria that helps ensure the effectiveness of the reproof and avoid aggressiveness. First, the conversation should be conducted in private. This minimizes the degree to which we embarrass the other person. Second, it should be done in a gentle and soft manner. Tone of voice and word choice are essential to keeping the conversation productive and non-hostile. Rabbi Yaakov Tzvi Mecklenburg in his commentary, *Haketav Vehakabbalah*, adds that we should try to speak in a way that is not blatantly accusatory. Instead of jumping to conclusions, we should ask questions to clarify what happened, so that the person does not become defensive.

If we generally react to being hurt with either an unassertive or an aggressive behavior, it may be time to revisit our approach. Not only are these approaches not helpful in resolving conflicts with those we care about, they may also be violations of two Torah principles. Taking an assertive approach may require training and practice, but it is a worthy investment that pays dividends in psychological, social, and spiritual growth.

Expansion of the Self

What is love? We usually relegate its exploration to the arts, but there are psychologists who conduct scientific research to try and better understand this elusive concept. One theory of love which has some empirical backing was presented by a married couple, Arthur and Elain Aron, in the 1980s. Their theory, the "self-expansion" model of love, has two primary components. One component is that we are generally motivated to expand our sense of self by entering into relationships with others, which helps increase our own potential. The other component is that the drive to expand ourselves through relationships causes other people to become, to some extent, included in our own sense of self. We expand our own identities to include others.

In his introduction to his Talmudic work, *Shaarei Yosher*, Rabbi Shimon Shkop presents a fascinating analysis of two fundamental directives in *Parshat Kedoshim* that relates to love as being an expansion of the self. The two concepts are to be holy (*kedoshim tihiyu*) and to love your fellow like yourself (*ve-ahavta le-reiacha kamocha*). Both are broad in scope, coloring numerous interactions and influencing many decisions. Yet, both holiness and love are abstract and complex concepts that defy easy definition. What does it really mean to be holy? What does love entail? Is it realistic to expect us to love another person as much as we love ourselves?

The Torah states that we should be holy because God is holy (Vayikra 19:2). This is difficult to understand. What does it mean to be holy? Any definition of holiness we suggest must be applicable to God as well. The Midrash adds a curious insertion into the text. After commanding us to be holy, the Midrash has God ask rhetorically: "Perhaps you may think that you could be as holy as I am? That is impossible, for My holiness is greater than your holiness." If we follow the midrashic reading, our definition of holiness must also contain a hierarchical component of God's holiness being greater than our own.

Rabbi Shkop argues for a definition of holiness which encompasses no less than "the entire foundation and root for our life's purpose." Holiness, according to Rabbi Shkop, can be defined as existing and acting with complete dedication to helping others. As such, God, who created and directs this world for the sake of others, with no "personal" benefit, serves as the ultimate paradigm of holiness.

Yet, as the Midrash makes clear, we can never reach such a level nor should we even aspire to such an intense degree of holiness. God created us with an ego; we are all self-interested. The commandment of "loving your fellow like yourself" is formulated by Hillel in the negative: "That which is hateful to you, do not do to someone else." This is because, Rabbi Shkop argues, when it comes to bestowing positive benefits, it is fitting for us to prioritize ourselves. In addition, Rabbi Akiva teaches us that our lives take precedence over our friends' lives, so that we should prioritize saving ourselves before others. We need to avoid harming others, but we otherwise come first.

The challenge becomes balancing these two concepts that seem to be pushing in different directions. On the one hand, we are egoistic and focus on ourselves, and on the other hand, we are to be holy and serve others. The key to reconciling these concepts, Rabbi Shkop suggests, lies within our definition of self (our "*ani*"). Our starting point is a self-absorbed "*ani*," which only cares about the physical self. We can then expand the definition of self to include our spiritual elements. A step further would be to include our family members within our senses of self, and continue to expand until we include the Jewish people, and perhaps even the entirety of creation, within our definition of self.

To be holy is to do for others. To ignore self-interest is delusional. We must start with a healthy and developed self, whose psychological and physical needs are prioritized, but we strive to not stop there. We work to expand our definition of self, to care and help as many others as we can, aspiring to be as holy as humanly possible.

Parshat Emor

Sefirat HaOmer: Process and Outcome

When you set a goal, do you concentrate your mental energy on the means to achieve it, or on the aspired end of attaining it? In the psychological literature on goal-pursuits, these two different perspectives are called "process focus" and "outcomes focus." A process focus is more concrete; it emphasizes the how and accentuates the journey. An outcomes focus is more abstract; it emphasizes the why and accentuates the destination. Researchers are trying to determine which approach is more effective in goal-fulfillment. To date, studies present conflicting evidence. Some studies indicate that focusing on the process is more rewarding and less anxiety-provoking. Others demonstrate that focusing on the outcome helps promote grit and perseverance. The secret may lie in striking a balance, and learning to alternate between a process focus and an outcomes focus.

Within the Torah itself, the exact purpose of the counting of the *Omer* is ambiguous. The Torah, in *Parshat Emor* (Vayikra 23:15–16), instructs us to count seven weeks, culminating in the various sacrifices brought on the fiftieth day. The commentators offer various suggestions for the commandment to count the days, many of which relate to the chronological placement of the *Omer* in between the holidays of Pesach and Shavuot. The entire goal of leaving Egypt, writes Rambam (*Moreh Nevuchim* 3:43), was to receive the Torah. Therefore, we enhance our appreciation for the end-goal of Shavuot by counting, from Pesach, toward it. *Or HaChaim*, on the other hand, focuses less on the end-goal. He connects the reason for counting to the process of purification that was necessary after leaving the impurities of Egypt.

Within the same outcome-focused approach as Rambam, *Sefer HaChinuch* (Mitzvah 306) asks, if *sefirah* is about anticipation, why do we count up (Day 1, Day 2…) and not down (Day 49, Day 48…), as we often do to build excitement? He answers that if we were to start counting down from 49, we would get discouraged from the long wait until we reach the goal, so we start with 1 in order to not be dissuaded. Approaching it from a process focus, Rabbi Shimshon Pinkus provides a different answer to *Sefer HaChinuch*'s question. *Sefirah* is an exercise of self-growth. As a consequence, counting upwards represents the fact that we should be developing and building from one day to another.

Rabbi Soloveitchik, quoted by Rabbi Shmuel Goldin (*Unlocking the Torah Text: Vayikra*, p. 202), argues that these two ideas are inherent within the word *sefirah*. In contrast to the word *minyan* (counting), in which counting is only essential to the attainment of an ultimate goal, *sefirah* means counting towards a goal (outcome) in which every individual unit becomes a goal unto itself (process). Counting highlights both the process and the outcome. Both are important to effective goal-pursuit and knowing how to keep one aspect in mind enhances the other.

The process of self-growth, inherent in the counting-up method, will be more efficacious if the goal of Shavuot is underscored; and the goal of Shavuot will be more meaningful if the process of self-growth is more successful. As we count during *sefirah*, we would do well to combine both approaches, thereby enhancing the meaning of our experience.

Happiness & Wholeness

Toward the end of *Parshat Emor*, the Torah presents a description of the various holidays spanning the Jewish calendar. The seventh month – what we now call *Tishrei* – is jam-packed with holidays, starting with Rosh Hashanah, continuing with Yom Kippur, and culminating in Sukkot and Shemini Atzeret. After describing the holidays of Rosh Hashanah and Yom Kippur in great detail, Rabbi Samson Raphael Hirsch summarizes their essence as a buildup and counterpoint to the holiday of Sukkot. Both Rosh Hashanah and Yom Kippur are serious and somber days, permeated with negative emotions. Rosh Hashanah is "a day of *Teruah*, a day of shatteringly shaking us up out of ways of life displeasing to God" and Yom Kippur makes us "appear before God, 'poor' in every justification for further living and working" (Judaica Press translation). In stark contrast, on Sukkot we celebrate by "taking of the produce of the earth to gain the joy of living and working in happiness before God."

Rabbi Hirsch then adds one simple, yet powerful, observation. Both Rosh Hashanah and Yom Kippur are one day each, yet Sukkot is comprised of seven days. The lesson he gleans from this straightforward calculation is that the Torah is prescribing what our baseline mood should be throughout the year. It should not be the "bowed down broken feeling" associated with Rosh Hashanah and Yom Kippur, but the "happy joy of life" experienced while living "a life faithfully devoted to duty," symbolized by the seven days of Sukkot.

If our primary mood should be one of happiness, the challenge becomes how to attain such a state. There is an entire field, called "positive psychology," dedicated to the study of happiness and well-being. One important observation that several psychologists have made is that relentlessly pursuing happiness usually does not lead to happiness. Moreover, unless we are able to understand and accept our negative emotions, we are not likely to find lasting happiness. When experienced in a healthy manner, negative emotions such as sadness, frustration, concern, guilt, and embarrassment have a functional value. If we try and suppress these negative emotions because they make us feel uncomfortable and we want to be happy, the less likely it is that we will actually be happy.

Rabbi Hirsch may be subtly hinting to this idea as well. While we should generally strive to serve God in a state of happiness, we must also make time and psychological space for those more negative emotions. There is an important place for the "bowed down broken feeling" symbolized by Rosh Hashanah and Yom Kippur, and that must be experienced if we want to build toward the happiness of Sukkot. Our pursuit of serving God with joy needs to incorporate a healthy experience of negative emotions, as well.

This may also be reflected in another aspect of the Jewish calendar mentioned in *Parshat Emor*, namely, the counting of the *Omer*. We are commanded to count seven *temimiyot* weeks, meaning "whole" or "complete." While "wholeness" in this context has a serial connotation to it, in the sense that we should not miss a day, "wholeness" here can also hint at the development of our personality. On the one hand, counting the *Omer* represents an exciting build-up and progression, whether agriculturally or as preparation for receiving the Torah. On the other hand, it is a time (on a Rabbinic level) of mourning and solemnness. Perhaps the "wholeness" of this time requires us to validate and experience both the positive and negative emotions simultaneously. With this, we serve God with our whole selves, and it is within this wholeness that we can truly experience psychological and spiritual flourishing.

Parshiyot Behar-Bechukotai

Portion Control

Most of us are under the impression that we know when we are satiated. We can accurately determine, based on internal cues, that we are full and do not need to eat any more. Most of us, however, are wrong. In a series of studies, Dr. Barbara J. Rolls from Penn State University has demonstrated that people's overall consumption of food and internal feelings of satiety are easily manipulated with portion sizes. If my level of being satisfied was based only on internal feelings, the size of my sandwich shouldn't influence how much of it I eat before I feel sated. However, studies show that whether eating subs, potato chips, macaroni and cheese or salads, people tend to eat more and need more food to feel satisfied when there is more food present.

In *Parshat Behar* we read about the mitzvah of *Shemittah*, where we are informed that every seventh year the land must rest. Although we are not permitted to work the land, the Torah promises that God will provide nourishment and that we will eat to the point of satiation (*ve-achaltem la-sova*, Vayikra 25:19). However, the *pesukim* continue with what seems to be a redundancy. "And should you ask, what are we going to eat if we can't sow the field and gather our crops?" The Torah answers (Vayikra 25:20–21) that God will bless the produce of the sixth year, so that it will yield enough produce for three years: the sixth, the seventh (*Shemittah* year), and the eighth (which would otherwise not have any produce, as none would be planted during the seventh year). But the previous *pasuk* had already promised that we will eat to the point of satiety! Why, then, does it tell us not to worry, for God will assure us enough food for three years?

Rabbi Ovadia Sforno explains that this perceived repetition reflects two different potential blessings which God offers. The first, and what seems to be the ideal situation, is that God will bless our food's potential to satiate. Its nutritional value will increase, and a smaller dose of food will keep us satisfied longer. This is similar to what the Sages tell us about the manna, which, despite its small size, was able to provide adequate nutritional and satiation value. This is the ideal blessing – smaller portion sizes, longer-lasting satiation. The Torah then adds a contingency blessing. If our belief is lacking and we fear that the smaller portions will not suffice, then God will increase the quantity of the food as well. Our eyes will perceive the vast quantities of food and we will feel calmer and more satisfied.

Sforno is highlighting the subjectivity of satiation. The first blessing would have been enough if not for their anxiety of the portions being too small. To avoid any such anxiety related to observing the mitzvah of *Shemittah*, God is willing to give in to this human frailty and give us bigger portions just so we would feel more secure. Yet, the ideal would be for us to be satisfied with the smaller portion.

If we can expand from *Shemittah* to our normal eating habits, the message is clear. Our ability to feel satiated is not entirely biological. There are psychological processes involved as well. Our portion sizes and the environmental cues, such as the size of our plates and cups, influence how much we eat before we feel full. If we can train ourselves to eat in a healthy way, perhaps with the guidance of a nutritionist or a psychologist, we may be able to eat less while still obtaining important nutrients and feeling just as satisfied.

Individualism vs. Collectivism

Given the choice, would you sacrifice your own goals, dreams, and desires for the sake of your family or the welfare of your group? Dutch social psychologist Geert Hofstede conducts pioneering work in the field of cross-cultural psychology, analyzing the differences between cultures. Two essential elements of his work include the characterization of "individualist" versus "collectivist" cultures. Individualist cultures – such as the United States and Western Europe – tend to value independence, autonomy, and uniqueness. In contrast, collectivist cultures, typified by East Asian countries, value group membership and harmony over the expression of one's personal values or opinions.

Does the Jewish tradition fit into an individualist or into a collectivist framework?

The passage of rebuke found in *Parshat Bechukotai* represents a collectivist trend within Jewish thought. In a haunting description of destruction, the Torah states that even with no one pursuing them, *Am Yisrael* will run away in such a panic that they will stumble over one another (Vayikra 26:37). In this imagery, the Sages find an allusion to the idea that all of Israel is responsible for one another: *kol Yisrael areivim zeh bazeh*. This principle has ramifications for several laws, but also serves as a deeper ethical, spiritual, and metaphysical message of collective responsibility. Through the challenges and the celebrations, we are in this together. That notion generates moral and religious responsibilities towards one another.

Yet, despite this indication of the Torah being a collectivist system, we find several individualistic notions within Torah as well. As an example, every individual is obligated to say, "the world was created for me" (Mishnah, *Sanhedrin* 4:5) In addition, we may not sacrifice an individual in order to save the community, and one is obligated to save oneself before saving somebody else (*Bava Metzia* 62a).

Jewish thought does not fit well into either paradigm, as it clearly contains both collectivist and individualist impulses. Rabbi Joseph B. Soloveitchik explains in his essay, *The Community*: "The greatness of man manifests itself in his inner contradiction, in his dialectical nature, in his being single and unrelated to anyone, as well as in his being thou-related and belonging to a community structure" (p. 25). The different sources that push and pull in opposite directions reflect this tension, and require us to balance the individual and collective components of our natures.

This blend of individualism and collectivism is further reflected in the concept of counting, as related to counting the 50 years until the *Yovel* (Jubilee) and the counting of the weeks and days of the *Omer*. While discussing the laws of *Yovel* in *Parshat Behar*, the verse states in the singular *ve-safarta lecha*, "you should count" (Vayikra 25:8). The Sages understand this as a directive towards the court. There should be one singular count for the entire population done by the *Beit Din*. When discussing the counting of the *Omer*, there are two different verses, with two distinct addressees. One verse uses the singular when mandating the count, *tispor lach* (Devarim 16:9), while the other verse states the same idea in the plural, *u-sefartem lachem* (Vayikra 23:15). The Sages learn from this that the obligation to count is placed on both the individual as well as on the courts, which represent the communal level.

The counting of the *Omer*, Rabbinically symbolic of our preparation for receiving the Torah, incorporates the dual elements of individual and communal responsibility. We are both an individualistic and collectivist culture, and it is our job to use the guidelines and framework of the Torah to strike a balance between prioritizing ourselves and serving our community.

Gritty Torah

Does it make sense to work hard? There is a certain appeal to relaxing, coasting, and procrastinating. There is a natural pull towards inertia, motivating us to remain in a restful state, not having to exert ourselves. This is particularly true when there is no immediate benefit to leaving our state of comfort. A biological argument can also be made in favor of conserving physical energy. Why put in effort when we could just take it easy?

In her landmark paper, *Grit: Perseverance and Passion for Long-Term Goals*, Dr. Angela Duckworth, a psychologist from the University of Pennsylvania, defines "grit" as perseverance and passion for long-term goals, which entails "working strenuously toward challenges, maintaining effort and interest over years despite failure, adversity, and plateaus in progress" (pp. 1087–1088). From a certain perspective, being gritty does not make sense. Why would someone work strenuously towards a goal and invest so much effort into doing something so difficult? If things are hard and a person does not see immediate success, it is natural and perhaps even smart to give up and move on to something else.

Parshat Bechukotai delineates the rewards and punishments related to the service of God. Rewards in the form of rain, sustenance, security, and the resting of the Divine Presence can be attained by following God's laws (*im bechukotai teileichu*), protecting his commandments (*mitzvotai tishmoru*), and performing them (*ve-asitem otam*). At first glance, the *pasuk* (Vayikra 26:4) seems redundant. The same broad message (follow God's commandments) is stated in three synonymous ways. However, with the assumption that the Torah does not repeat itself for the sake of poetic embellishments, the *Sifra*, quoted by Rashi, assumes that each of these three components alludes to different aspects of following *mitzvot*. Following God's laws (*bechukotai teileichu*) cannot just mean doing the *mitzvot*, because that is explicit in the last part of the *pasuk* – "and perform them" (*ve-asitem otam*). Rather, following God's laws (*bechukotai teileichu*) is an allusion to the concept of toiling in the learning of Torah (*teheyu ameilim ba-Torah*).

Later commentators present many questions and interpretations to try and understand the depth of this Midrash. In fact, *Or HaChaim* presents forty-two different explanations of these few words. For the present discussion, one question stands out. In many contexts the word *bechukotai* references the category of *mitzvot* that don't seem to make any sense. For example the mitzvah of *parah adumah* (Bamidbar 19) is the quintessential *chok*. We cannot grasp its meaning or significance, yet we do it anyway because God commanded it. If we understand *bechukotai* here as a mitzvah that does not have a rational basis and that refers to laboring in the study of Torah, the question becomes: does it not make sense to work hard while learning? Why is learning categorized here as a *chok* which stands above reason?

Viewed from a short-term perspective, toiling in Torah is a *chok*. It does not make sense to invest so much cognitive energy into something that is so difficult and whose positive results may not be immediately apparent. If I force myself to focus after a long day of exhausting work, I may not see the blessings which God promises right away. The rain may not fall as I open the book, I may not feel secure from my enemies as I start reading, and I may not even feel the Divine Presence as I turn page after page. Even more frustrating, I may not even see success in my learning! It makes sense to stop. It makes sense to give up. It makes sense to go to sleep. But we learn anyway, because it is a *chok*.

Though we may not see any immediate reward, our hard work will pay off over time. Dr. Duckworth's research demonstrates that people who are gritty tend to be more successful at attaining long-term academic and professional accomplishments. Therefore, she suggests that schools invest resources into teaching children how to be grittier. As is apparent from this Midrash, grittiness has been essential to Torah education for millennia. We push, we toil, and we labor even when it does not make sense, and we trust that when we follow this essential *chok*, that God will grant us the long-term reward.

Parshat Bamidbar

Unified Diversity

Muzafer Sherif was a Turkish-born psychologist who moved to the United States for graduate school, then moved back to Turkey in the 1930s to teach in Ankara University. He was imprisoned and placed in solitary confinement for criticizing the Nazi party and the Turkish government. He subsequently moved back to America, and became a pioneering social psychologist.

Sherif is known for one of the most famous experiments related to intergroup conflicts and resolutions. He gathered twenty-two boys in Robbers Cave State Park, Oklahoma, and divided them into two groups – the Eagles and the Rattlers. At first, the two groups did not interact with each other, and naturally built their own group identity. In the second stage of the experiment, the two groups were placed in situations where they had to compete for various rewards and resources. As a result, hostility between the groups increased, engendering hatred and creating conflicts. In the next stage, the groups interacted without competition; however, this did not decrease the feelings of conflict. Tensions decreased, and intergroup cohesion was created only after the two groups were made to work together towards a mutual goal that required cooperation (termed a "superordinate goal").

The beginning of *Parshat Bamidbar* delineates the details of a census that Moshe, at God's command, took of all Jewish males over the age of twenty. The Torah presents the numbers according to the different tribes, and also describes the specific tribal formations. The first *pasuk* relates that God spoke to Moshe on the first day of the second month of the second year after they left Egypt. Rabbi Yaakov Kamenetsky (*Emet LeYaakov*) asks why they waited until the second year to take this census and create the tribal formations. Would it not have made more sense to do this in the first year?

Rabbi Kamenetsky explains that *Bamidbar* presents an inherent danger of tribalism. Separating people by groups, and standing behind flags, creates an us-versus-them, or adversarial, mentality. When people stand in groups behind their own flags, they tend to favor their own group and be hostile to other groups. One way to overcome this natural human tendency is to create a unifying, superordinate goal. In our case, that is the function of the Torah. Only with the Torah in the center can we attempt to create a healthy, cooperative group dynamic. Only with the *Mishkan* in the center of the formation could the tribes march separately. That is why God waited until the second year, after the Torah was given and after the *Mishkan* became the epicenter, to take the census. The danger of having different tribes was mitigated only after they had come together in unity.

Rabbi Samson Raphael Hirsch also highlights the tension between the in-group and the out-group. Introducing the census (Bamidbar 1:1–2), God tells Moshe to count the heads of the entire congregation of Israel (*adat Bnei Yisrael*) according to their families (*le-mishpechotam*) and the house of their fathers (*le-veit avotam*). Rabbi Hirsch argues that *adat Bnei Yisrael* represents the unified whole of the people in the desert. However, there is a second aspect, focusing on the families and the households. This second part represents the individual differences between families and tribes. Once there is a unified whole, there is a value in acknowledging diversity and differences between families.

As we prepare for Shavuot, may we merit finding our own unique voices and contributions to the Jewish people, while not allowing these differences to create divisiveness. This can be accomplished if our focal point is serving God, not ourselves or our in-groups, which will enable us to stand unified in heart and mind as we accept the Torah.

Intellectual Humility

Parshat Bamidbar is generally read the week before Shavuot, motivating the commentaries to find a thematic link between the *parsha* and the holiday. *Bamidbar*, translated as "in the wilderness," gets its name from the opening verse which relates that "God spoke to Moshe in the wilderness of Sinai" (Bamidbar 1:1). The Midrash (*Bamidbar Rabbah* 1:7), highlights the juxtaposition of wilderness and Sinai, and explains the deeper significance of God giving the Torah in a desert. It suggests that "whoever does not make himself ownerless [*hefker*] like a wilderness, cannot acquire wisdom and Torah." What does it mean to make oneself ownerless? Chanoch Zundel ben Yosef, in his commentary on the Midrash, *Eitz Yosef*, explains that this teaches that a person needs to be humble enough to learn from all and to teach all, as Torah cannot be found in an arrogant person.

Pirkei Avot, which is also customarily read before Shavuot, begins with a tradition of the Torah's transmission from Sinai through the time of the early Sages – "Moshe received the Torah from Sinai and transmitted it to Yehoshua," and so on. One of the many oddities of this first Mishnah is its starting point. We would expect it to state that Moshe received the Torah from God, but instead we read that he received it "from Sinai" (*mi-Sinai*). Why is a mountain, and not God, viewed as the first link in the chain of tradition?

The commentaries provide close to a dozen explanations to this question, but the one with the most moving moral message is provided by Rabbi Israel Lipschitz in his commentary *Tiferet Yisrael*. Weaving together various statements of the Sages, Rabbi Lipschitz suggests that there is a common thread between Moshe, Torah, and Sinai, and that is the trait of humility. Moshe, we are told, is the humblest of all people (Bamidbar 12:3). The Torah, we are told, is compared to water. Water symbolizes humility, as it abandons its high position and streams downwards until it collects in lowly places. Sinai was chosen because it was the humblest of mountains.

The fact that Moshe, Sinai, and Torah share the same trait may be enough to warrant this allusion to humility in the beginning of *Pirkei Avot*, but the message is deeper than just an association of nouns. Other than the person, place, and object, the Mishnah also uses a verb – *kibel* – meaning, "to receive." Moshe was only able to receive the Torah because of his humility. This Mishnah omits the name of God and highlights Sinai instead, to reveal the necessity of humility in Torah learning and observance.

Why is humility such an essential trait for acquiring Torah? Humility not only positively impacts our relationship to God and to others, but also assists in improving our intellectual abilities. Dr. Liz Mancuso from Pepperdine University conducts psychological research on the concept of intellectual humility. Intellectual humility is a more specific construct than regular humility, as it pertains specifically to ideas, knowledge, beliefs and opinions, and not to global perceptions of self. People with intellectual humility accept that their cognitive faculties are not perfect, and that their perspective may not be accurate. They are not overconfident about their knowledge, they respect others' viewpoints, and are willing to revise their own viewpoints if necessary. The research suggests that people higher in intellectual humility tend to have wider general knowledge than those who are intellectually arrogant.

Her explanation for this finding can serve as commentary on another Mishnah in *Pirkei Avot* (4:1), "Who is wise? He who learns from everyone." Dr. Mancuso explains that intellectual humility is associated with a love of learning, an openness to ideas, and an ability to learn with and from others. This includes listening and reflecting on other people's opinions, and disagreeing assertively when appropriate, without being aggressive or prematurely dismissive. Conversely, people who are arrogant tend to be so preoccupied with their desire to be seen as intelligent that there remains little cognitive space for focusing on actual ideas. These people are so distracted by egotistical concerns that they cannot learn and understand effectively.

Humility is essential to learning because it allows us to focus on learning, instead of on our egos. It is essential for accepting and receiving the Torah. On the humblest mountain of Sinai, the humblest man, Moshe, received the Torah, a paradigmatic representation of humility. To emphasize the point, all this took place in the "ownerless" wilderness.

Intellectual humility is not only desirable; it also facilitates our ability to receive and learn Torah. May we all feel motivated to acquire this valuable trait.

Parshat Naso

Situational Control

The struggle for self-control is one of the most important, hardest-fought battles of all time. Unfortunately, there are many casualties, and our will-power often loses to temptation. To become a *nazir*, we are told in *Parshat Naso*, one must take a vow, and commit to abstain from grape products, from defiling oneself through contact with a human corpse, and from cutting one's hair. The Torah uses a strange word to describe the act of vowing: *yafli*. Ibn Ezra offers two possible meanings for this word. The first is that it connotes setting oneself apart (*yafrish*). The second is that it means wonder (*pele*): where most people tend to give in to temptation, the *nazir*'s commitment to self-control, Ibn Ezra argues, is so rare and powerful as to be called wondrous. On the one hand, the *nazir* inspires us to have more self-control, and on the other, he or she reminds us that most people fail to restrain themselves, or worse, do not even try.

The topic of *nazir* is immediately preceded by that of *sotah*. A woman whose husband warns her, in front of witnesses, to not seclude herself with another man, yet does so anyway, must undergo the *sotah* ceremony to determine whether she committed adultery. Intrigued by the juxtaposition of these two seemingly unrelated concepts, the Midrash proposes a connection. *Nazir* comes after *sotah* because anyone who witnesses the downfall of the *sotah* will be so dedicated to avoiding such a demise, that he or she will commit to not drinking any wine out of fear that intoxication may lead to adultery.

The connection the Midrash is making between *nazir* and *sotah* is not tangential or coincidental; it reveals the core message behind both concepts. The mitzvah of *sotah* and the mitzvah of *nazir* both teach us that the ideal way to deal with temptations is by avoiding the battle in the first place. To avoid becoming a *sotah*, we should not put ourselves in an environment that is conducive to sin. This includes not drinking wine as well as avoiding situations of seclusion that are primed for temptation. Along come the laws of the *nazir*, and the idea becomes intensified. Very often, the Sages institute additional restrictions as fences and barriers to help distance us from biblical prohibitions, but the case of the *nazir* is one of the few examples where the Torah itself provides added restrictions to protect the original law. The *nazir* avoids not only wine, but all grape products (Bamidbar 6:4). In addition, the Talmud adds that he should not even go close to a vineyard (*Avodah Zarah* 58b)!

In her article, *Situational Strategies for Self-Control*, Dr. Angela Duckworth argues that situational strategies are the most salient and effective ones for avoiding self-control failures, yet they are also the most underappreciated and underutilized. We often try to battle temptation directly, and eventually lose to that delicious-looking piece of chocolate cake. We think we will be able to study but are unable to avoid the allure of our phones. The smartest and most effective strategy is to not buy the chocolate cake in the first place, and to leave our phones off when we want to focus.

Yes, the struggle for self-control is a difficult one, but perhaps we are going about it the wrong way. Contending will-power against temptation should only be a last resort. Many have fallen in the heat of passion or the intenseness of an emotion: the better way, learning from the *sotah's* mistakes and taking the lead from the *nazir*, is to avoid the battle in the first place. If we avoid temptations and situations that could lead to sin, we can perhaps have better self-control, leading us to become happier, healthier, and more spiritually refined people.

Hierarchy of Needs

Abraham Maslow was a humanistic psychologist who taught at Brooklyn College and Brandeis University in the mid-twentieth century. He proposed a theory of motivation, known as Maslow's hierarchy of needs, which is taught in virtually all introductory psychology courses, and is also popular in the fields of business and education. While the theory is more nuanced than usually presented, the basic idea is that humans have five different levels of needs to be fulfilled. The hierarchy starts with physiological needs like food and water, and then moves to safety needs like shelter and protection from danger. The third need is to belong and connect socially, and the fourth is to feel respected and have a sense of self-esteem. The final need is self-actualization, which is the need to fulfill one's potential. In later works, he added a concept called self-transcendence, which is a need to become a part of something greater than the self.

Maslow's theory is often illustrated as a triangle, with the lower, physiological, needs placed at the bottom, progressing up to the pinnacle of self-actualization. However, researchers Todd Bridgman, Stephen Cummings, and John Ballard argue that Maslow himself never mentioned the concept of a triangle anywhere in his writings, and that the use of that icon to illustrate the theory was first done by a management textbook. While embedding the theory with the visual aid of a triangle has helped propel its widespread popularity, they argue that the way the triangle is used to symbolize the hierarchy leads to several misconceptions, a point to which we will return shortly.

Parshat Naso provides one of our most ancient and well-known prayers, namely, the Priestly Blessings or *Birkat Kohanim*. We recite this blessing several times a day, and it also has a special place on Friday night as part of the blessing that parents give their children. The verses state:

יְבָרֶכְךָ יְקֹוָק וְיִשְׁמְרֶךָ: יָאֵר יְקֹוָק ׀ פָּנָיו אֵלֶיךָ וִיחֻנֶּךָ: יִשָּׂא יְקֹוָק ׀ פָּנָיו אֵלֶיךָ
וְיָשֵׂם לְךָ שָׁלוֹם:

May God bless you and protect you. May God cause His countenance to shine upon you and favor you. May God lift His face to you, and grant you peace (Numbers 6:24–26).

Rashi explains that the first blessing is a material one – that our goods and property be blessed. Protection refers to physical safety, that "plunderers should not come and take your property." According to the Midrash

(*Bamidbar Rabbah* 11:6), the second blessing, which mentions light, is a reference to Torah, and represents a spiritual blessing. The third blessing, Professor Nehama Leibowitz (*Studies in Bamidbar*) argues, sums up the previous two and adds the concept of peace; because without peace, the previous blessings cannot prevail.

Professor Leibowitz writes: "Accordingly the three sections of the priestly benedictions illustrate an ascending order, starting with a blessing concerned with man's material needs and then dealing with his spiritual wants, and finally reaching a climax combining both these factors together, crowning them with the blessing of peace" (p. 67). If we juxtapose her analysis of the Priestly Blessings with Maslow's hierarchy of needs, we notice that the first verse deals with Maslow's two first levels – i.e., for material goods and for safety. The next verse refers to spiritual needs, which can be conceptualized to include social needs, self-actualization, and self-transcendence, as all of these values have corollaries in the spiritual realm through the performance of various *mitzvot*. The last verse, which she contends is a combination of the first two, highlights the need to integrate the physical and spiritual, an idea central to Jewish thought.

In conclusion, Professor Leibowitz writes, "This ascending order and increasing surge of blessing is reflected in the language and rhythm. The first phrase consists of three words, the second five, and the third of seven" (p. 67). In bolstering the argument of the literary precision, Rabbi Jonathan Sacks adds that not only are the number of words precise, but so are the number of letters! The first line has fifteen letters, the second has twenty, and the third, twenty-five. When centering the verses, the image that emerges should be familiar:

יְבָרֶכְךָ יְקֹוָק וְיִשְׁמְרֶךָ׃

יָאֵר יְקֹוָק ׀ פָּנָיו אֵלֶיךָ וִיחֻנֶּךָּ׃

יִשָּׂא יְקֹוָק ׀ פָּנָיו אֵלֶיךָ וְיָשֵׂם לְךָ שָׁלוֹם׃

If we compare the triangle depicted in the *Birkat Kohanim* with the triangle associated with Maslow, we can notice one glaring difference. Maslow's hierarchy is depicted as bottom up. The long part of the triangle on the bottom represents the physiological needs, while the uppermost point is self-actualization. One critique of this representation is that it can be interpreted as elitist – only a small number of people can ever reach self-actualization. A related critique is that this imagery could suggest that the most amount of time and energy exerted by most people is on the lower needs, for the most part ignoring the higher ones.

In the "hierarchy of needs" presented in the triangle of *Birkat Kohanim*, the starting point is not at the bottom but at the top. Perhaps this symbolism represents a counterpoint to the aforementioned critique of the triangle associated with Maslow. These blessings are for everyone, not just the elite. Everyone has the capability and the charge to reach their potential by blending the physical and spiritual. In addition, when prioritizing our time and our tasks, we should spend the least amount of time with purely material endeavors, and focus the bulk of our energies on serving God by combining the spiritual and the physical, with the hope and blessing that we can do so in a state of peace and tranquility.

Parshat Behaalotcha

Variety Effect

According to the "variety effect," people tend to eat more when there are more options (as we have likely experienced while partaking in a smorgasbord). When the color, flavor, or shape of a food is varied we ingest more than we would if there was just one choice. By satiating a range of sensory experiences, we can fulfill more desires with increased consumption. Perhaps unsurprisingly, variety-related eating habits are linked to obesity.

After over a year of consuming the manna, *Bnei Yisrael* had enough. Yes, it looked nice and tasted good, but food falling from the Heavens was not enough to prevent them from complaining. They wanted meat. They remembered with fondness the fish they ate in Egypt *chinam* (for free), as well as the cucumbers, melons, leeks, onions, and garlic. Yet upon further thought, we are left wondering: Are cucumbers, melons, leeks, onions, and garlic really superior to the manna? Was the food in Egypt really free and so easy to obtain that it surpassed the convenience of food falling from the sky?

The Midrash, cited by Rashi, is convinced that there is a deeper motivation behind the complaint. *Bnei Yisrael* could not have longed for the free food in Egypt, because, according to the Midrash, there was no free food in Egypt. The Egyptians made them work tirelessly to find their own straw in order to make their own bricks; they were certainly not handing out free food. Rather, behind *Bnei Yisrael*'s complaints, either consciously or subconsciously, was a more serious protest. They missed not the free food, but the freedom from restraints. In Egypt they were free from *mitzvot*, and now they were constrained with rules and regulations.

Unlike the Midrash, Ramban understands *chinam* ("free"), literally. In Egypt, he suggests, they had easy access to food. If they worked by the river, they were allowed to catch and eat fish. If they worked in the fields, there was such an abundance, that the field owners allowed *Bnei Yisrael* to eat what they liked as they gathered the crops. While the work was grueling and cruel, at least they could eat whenever they wanted, because food was so plentiful and available. Manna was also free financially, but it was not free from restrictions: they could only get a rationed portion within a specific schedule. The *Meshech Chochmah* points out that they even had meat available to eat, but they could only eat it by bringing it as an offering near the *Ohel Moed*. There was plenty of free food, but there were also restrictions.

Perhaps an additional part of the complaint is related to the monotony of the manna. It was the same food, every day. The nostalgia of cucumbers, melons, leeks, onions, and garlic is not about taste, but variety. On a similar level, the Netziv proposes that the foods they requested represent different courses. Instead of having just one course of manna, *Bnei Yisrael* wanted appetizers, dips, and dessert to go along with it.

God was trying to teach them controlled, scheduled, spiritually-motivated eating. *Bnei Yisrael* rebelled and complained because they desired the unbounded, unrestricted, smorgasbord variety of eating that they enjoyed in Egypt. In our own lives, whether in the context of food or otherwise, we may have a natural desire for variety and freedom from constraints. Yet, the message of the manna is that it is beneficial to curb this craving. If we are able to overcome this natural tendency for the variety effect, we will no doubt be able to live more psychologically, physically, and spiritually healthy lives.

The Limits of Conscientiousness

When researching and discussing different personality types, psychologists generally refer to what is known as "The Big Five" personality traits. These five traits, scored on a continuum, are conscientiousness (organized, controlled, goal-oriented), agreeableness (cooperative, kind, friendly), neuroticism (sad, moody, anxious), openness (imaginative, creative) and extraversion (sociable, excitable, expressive). Some psychologists assert that these five traits, sometimes referred to by the acronym CANOE (or OCEAN), subsume all other subcategories of personality.

Out of the five, the one that is consistently highlighted as important for success in various contexts such as school, work, and relationships, is conscientiousness. People high in conscientiousness tend to be organized and orderly. They create successful routines and thrive in structured environments. Sometimes, though, when they are deprived of consistent schedules and predictability, they struggle. In one study, people high in conscientiousness reported decreased mental health following unemployment. The lack of routine was hard on their psychological well-being.

Conscientious members of *Bnei Yisrael* would probably have struggled in the wilderness. In *Parshat Behaalotcha* we read that *Bnei Yisrael* would encamp and journey according to God's will, as reflected in the movement of the clouds. There was no advance warning or predictability to the pattern, as "[s]ometimes the cloud would be upon the Tabernacle for a number of days … and sometimes the cloud would remain from evening until morning … or for a day and a night … or for two days, or a month, or a year" (Bamidbar 9:20–22). Everything depended on God's command. Ramban (Bamidbar 9:19) elaborates on how physically and psychologically challenging this process must have been, as sometimes right after unpacking from a long journey, they would have to pack up and travel again. What purpose did this system serve?

Rabbi Samson Raphael Hirsch explains its importance, writing that "such was the training school of our wanderings through the wilderness in which we should have learned for all time to follow God's guidance with devotion and trust, no matter how incomprehensible it may seem to us." Following God's commands is easy when they are logical. The challenge is to serve God with a full heart when life does not make sense and is unpredictable.

Similarly, Rabbi Eliyahu Dessler (*Michtav me-Eliyahu* 4:230) writes that it is easy to live a life infused with Torah values when life is peaceful.

However, if we can only follow our routine of prayer, learning, and acts of kindness when there is structure and stability, we are setting ourselves up for failure. Life is rarely predictable, and our responsibilities vary. Without fail, our surroundings will vary and change. The erratic encampments in the wilderness served to train and model a life where we do God's will, despite the lack of external consistency.

While conscientiousness is generally worthwhile, the experience in the desert serves as a critical counterpoint. Striving for routine may be praiseworthy, but it is important to be adaptable and flexible when God's will demands us to be so.

Parshat Shelach

The Color of Tzitzit

There is a small, yet growing subfield within psychology called "color psychology." Researchers in this field are interested in how people perceive, relate to, and respond differently to various colors. Some reactions that we have to colors may be innate. For instance, since blood rushes to the face when one becomes aggressive, the color red, in both humans and animals, is a signal of dominance. Other reactions to colors may be based on a learned association between the color and another object. For instance, a Yankee fan may feel happy when seeing blue pinstripes because he or she associates that color scheme with the team.

Towards the end of *Parshat Shelach* the Torah discusses the mitzvah of *tzitzit*. We are commanded to place fringes on our garments, including a thread that is *techelet*. The purpose of this is explicitly stated within the *pesukim*: its function is to remind us of God's commandments and not to wander after our hearts and eyes. Later authorities debate the exact color of *techelet*. Some say it is blue, some say violet, and some green. Others debate how many of the strings must be *techelet* and how many are to be white.

How does wearing fringed garments remind us of the *mitzvot* and prevent us from wandering after our hearts and eyes? Our Sages offered numerous explanations, some focusing on number symbolism, others on the significance of garments, and still others on the importance of color. Focusing now on this last category, we can ask: How does wearing blue/violet/green strings interspersed through white strings remind us not to sin?

Rabbi Meir (*Menachot* 43b) tells us that looking at *techelet* sets off a series of associations that keeps us from sinning. *Techelet*, which he seems to understand as being blue, is a color similar to that of the ocean, which is similar to the sky, which is similar to the color of God's Throne of Glory.

Ramban adds that within the word *techelet* are the words *kol* (all) and *tachlit* (purpose). Meaning, *techelet* at its core reminds us of our mission in this world, which is to serve God by doing *mitzvot* and by avoiding sinning.

Rabbi Yitzchak Arama suggests that *techelet* imparts another important moral significance. This message is dependent on a medieval color theory which is not accepted in modern times. The assumption was that there were seven colors that flowed on a spectrum: white, yellow, red, green, blue, purple, and black. At the extremes of the spectrum were white and black, with green in the middle. Rabbi Arama, presumably understanding that *techelet* is green, argues that the symbolism behind *techelet* is that it is the middle ground between extremes. This serves as a model for our character traits, teaching us to follow the middle path.

Using Rabbi Arama's precedent to interpret the message of *techelet*, as based on the then-accepted science of color, perhaps there is another layer to understanding *techelet* that we can add by viewing it through the prism of modern color psychology. In a fascinating article researching how colors impact marketing strategy, Lauren Labrecque and George Milne summarize previous findings regarding the psychological significance of different colors. White, the total reflection of all the colors, is associated with sincerity, purity, and peace. Blue, which together with violet have the shortest wavelengths of all of visible colors, is associated with intelligence, trust, and duty. In contrast, colors on the longer end of the wavelength spectrum (like red, orange, and yellow) stimulate states of excitement and arousal, emotions which are oftentimes related to sin.

As the *pesukim* indicate, *tzitzit* function to counteract sin. If *techelet* is blue, perhaps the sense of duty and loyalty invoked by seeing blue and the purity associated with white are meant to balance and counter the excitement represented by the red of sin. In addition to the associations that lead us to think of God's throne, the psychological symbolism of the colors themselves may serve as an intervention to arrest the arousal of sin and remind us to be loyal to God.

The Self-Esteem of the Spies

Over his career, Rabbi Dr. Abraham J. Twerski published ninety books. After he had published sixty, someone asked him how he could possibly write so many different books. He responded that he hasn't written sixty different books, he has written the same book in sixty different ways. The unifying topic of his works is the significance of self-esteem. This includes delineating the destructive effects of low self-esteem, and strategies to strengthen it when it is low. The origin of his writings and emphasis on self-esteem, he writes, is sourced in *Parshat Shelach*.

The focus of *Parshat Shelach* is the story of the spies whom Moshe sent to survey the land. Ten of the spies return to report that the land has some benefits but they are not confident in Israel's ability to conquer the land. The nation responds by yearning to go back to Egypt. Consequently, that generation was forced to wander in the desert for forty years and not enter the land of Israel. It is not entirely clear within the narrative what the spies did wrong. They were asked to scout the land and report back, and that is what they did. The commentators offer several answers, but we will focus on the one that inspired the entirety of Rabbi Dr. Twerski's writings.

The spies report that they observed the *Nefilim*, the children of giants. In their report, they disclosed their own feelings of inadequacy, saying, "We were in our own eyes as grasshoppers" and then added "and so we were in their eyes" (Bamidbar 13:33). The verse does not tell us how they knew what the *Nefilim* thought of them. One approach, taken by the Midrash (*Bamidbar Rabbah* 16), is to assume that they had no way of knowing what the others thought of them. Speaking from God's perspective, the Midrash says, "That you think you look like grasshoppers, I can overlook that – but that they think you look like grasshoppers – how do you know what they think? Who says that they did not see you as angels?"

This, Rabbi Dr. Twerski argues, is exactly what low self-esteem does to our thinking: "The way you feel about yourself is how you think others perceive you" (*Twerski on Chumash*, p. 310) Because they thought so lowly of themselves ("like grasshoppers"), they assumed that that is how everyone else perceived them as well. God would have overlooked them calling themselves grasshoppers, though they were wrong to do so. But it was unforgivable to assume that the *Nefilim* also perceived them as grasshoppers – because at that point, they were projecting their own low self-image onto others, and that projection stunted their abilities and responsibilities. How did they know the *Nefilim* had such a low opinion of them, when maybe they viewed them favorably, as angels?

The Talmud concludes (*Sotah* 35a) that the spies actually *heard* the *Nefilim* call them grasshoppers. It was not a projection of low self-esteem; it was a reflection of reality. The others *did* think lowly of them! If this is the case, the message shifts from not having our low self-image distort how we think others perceive us, to not letting what others think of us distort our own self-perception. Even if the *Nefilim* thought of them as grasshoppers, this should not have stopped them from trusting God and having the internal courage to proceed.

Both messages are essential. When we do not know what people think of us, we should be careful to not project our own insecurities onto what we think others are thinking. But, even in cases where we do know that others do not think highly of us, if we are following the right path and proceeding towards the real or proverbial promised land, we should not let their low opinion of us derail us from our goals.

Parshat Korach

Unhealthy Conflict

Conflict is ubiquitous in many life situations, and there are numerous fields of research that study this fiery topic as it manifests in these different contexts. Industrial and organizational psychologists investigate conflict in the workplace, marriage and family therapists look at conflict between relatives, political psychologists work to understand conflict on a global scale, and social psychologists study conflict on a more general level. While there is naturally some disagreement amongst the research findings about conflict, there are generally accepted trends regarding the causes of conflicts and the best ways to resolve them.

Jewish tradition is also heavily concerned with conflict resolution and the pursuit of peace. Rabbi Dr. Howard Kaminsky, in his book, *Fundamentals of Jewish Conflict Resolution: Traditional Jewish Perspectives on Resolving Interpersonal Conflicts*, systematically gathers and summarizes ideas found in biblical and Rabbinic literature, comparing those sources with modern approaches to conflict resolution. What follows is a brief summary of his main points as they relate to *Parshat Korach*.

The Sages (*Sanhedrin* 110a) articulate a prohibition against perpetuating a quarrel, based on the *pasuk* that states "Do not be like 'Korach and his congregation'" (Bamidbar 17:5). In his commentary on the Talmud, the 12th-century French scholar, Rabbi Yehonatan mi-Lunil argues that even though Moshe was unjustly attacked, he would have violated this prohibition had he not tried to stop the dispute. Rabbi Natan Tzvi Finkel (*Or ha-Tsafun*, vol. 1, pp. 192–193) suggests further that we can learn from Moshe's continual attempts to resolve the conflict that the prohibition even applies after the other party rejects earlier attempts at reconciliation.

The Mishnah in *Avot* (5:17) distinguishes between the disputes of Hillel and Shammai, which are considered "for the sake of Heaven," and the dispute between Korach and his followers, which is not. We are given paradigms, without the delineation of any criteria for identifying a dispute for the sake of Heaven. The commentators try to fill in the gaps, and many use the nuances of the narrative reported in *Parshat Korach* to elucidate the parameters of worthy and unworthy disputes.

Summarizing and organizing the commentaries, Rabbi Dr. Kaminsky presents three criteria that indicate that a dispute is not for the sake of Heaven. One is that the party demonstrates a lack of intellectual integrity. They are uninterested in engaging in any clarifying or compromising dialogue. They consider themselves right, and nothing anyone can say will change their minds. A second criterion is the content and tone of the argument. If one side clearly condemns and insults the other party with a backdrop of animosity, then the dispute is not for the sake of Heaven. The final criterion relates to the motivation behind the dispute. If the provocation is rooted in anything but the pursuit of truth or peace, that is a strong clue that it is not for the sake of Heaven. Various Midrashim indicate that Korach's true motivation was rooted in arrogance, jealousy and hurt, and not a more noble internal impulse.

The difficulty, as Rabbi Yonatan Eybeschutz poignantly adds, is that most people are not always aware of these ulterior motives and subconscious motivations within themselves. Most people can rationalize away their participation in any dispute as being for the sake of Heaven, even if it is not. If we truly want to follow Moshe's paradigm and avoid Korach's example, we would be wise to reflect and engage in honest introspection before participating in any dispute. Are we listening to the other party and are we really concerned with intellectual integrity? Are we overcome with hostility and other unhealthy negative emotions towards the other party? Can we honestly say – knowing that it is so easy to delude ourselves – that we are not being driven by ulterior motives? If we are not confident that we pass these criteria, we would generally do well to avoid disputes as much as possible.

Would You Rather Be Right or Happy?

The strong desire of one or both parties to be right stands at the core of many high-conflict situations. Getting to the truth, the whole truth, and nothing but the truth, may be a value in court, but if used too often in relationships, it will lead to continual strife. When in a situation of conflict, we must first clarify the end goal. If the ultimate goal is justice, fairness, and truth, then we will have to suffer the consequences that generally come when others disagree. If the ultimate goal is peace, harmony, and sustained relationships, then we may have to swallow our desire to be right.

Commenting on the conflict that Korach instigates against Moshe, Maharal argues that people get into disputes because they act according to *din* – the strict letter of the law. They get sucked into a mindset of rigidity of purpose in their pursuit of justice and judgement. In the wake of their hunt, destruction and calamity tend to befall these justice seekers and those around them. Dr. Avivah Gottlieb Zornberg writes that this type of person "suffers from a kind of manic rationality" (*Bewilderments: Reflections on the Book of Numbers*, p. 182). In contrast, those who are willing to go *lifnim mi-shurat ha-din* – beyond the letter of the law – avoid unnecessary disputes. They either realize that there are two sides to the story, or they are willing to let things go, even if they "know" they are correct. They would rather have peace than be right.

In order to prove to all that Aharon was chosen to be the *Kohen Gadol*, God told Moshe to take a staff from the leader of each tribe and place all of the staffs in the Tent of Meeting. By the next day, Aharon's staff had blossomed and sprouted forth almonds. Rabbi Menachem Sacks, in his commentary *Menachem Zion*, finds deep symbolism in the fact that the staff produced almonds, and not a different fruit. Within the context of the laws of tithing, the Mishnah informs us that there are two types of almonds: those that are bitter when they are small and sweet when they develop, and those that are sweet when they are small and bitter when they grow bigger. Fights and disagreements often feel sweet and right in the moment but lead to bitterness and regret in the long run. Peace, on the other hand, is often difficult to maintain in the moment. It is difficult to bite our tongues and not respond when we think we are justified. But in the long run this will lead to ultimate sweetness.

This does not mean that we should never communicate our deeply-held beliefs just because someone might disagree. The Mishnah in *Avot* (5:17) identifies the conflict of Korach and his followers as a "dispute not for the sake of Heaven" and pits this against the disputes between Hillel and Shammai, which were "for the sake of Heaven." Obviously, there is a place for disputes, if they are "for the sake of Heaven." The difficulty is how to define what is considered "for the sake of Heaven." This is especially difficult since it is easy to justify and rationalize that one is pursuing truth and justice "for the sake of Heaven," even when that might not be accurate.

While a more comprehensive and individualized answer to this query is warranted, let it suffice for now to suggest that most of the arguments that we have on a regular basis with our spouses, children, family, friends, coworkers, neighbors, community members, and social media acquaintances, are probably not what the Mishnah would consider "for the sake of Heaven."

What is our goal? Do we want to be right or happy? If we want happiness, let us consider focusing less on truth, and more on peace.

Parshat Chukat

Self-Monitoring

One of the key techniques used in Cognitive Behavioral Therapy is self-monitoring. Keeping track of thoughts, emotions, or behaviors is a powerful intervention that affects change. For example, research by Dr. Aaron Beck demonstrates that when people who are depressed are asked to record thoughts that are self-critical, the number of such thoughts tends to decrease over time. The act of tracking itself causes the change. In addition, tracking also provides valuable information that can be analyzed to reveal a deeper understanding of what contributes to a person's thoughts, emotions, or behaviors.

As *Bnei Yisrael* approached the land of Canaan, they asked Sichon, the King of the Amorites, for permission to pass through his land. Sichon not only declined the request, but he waged war against *Bnei Yisrael*. This turned costly for Sichon, as he was defeated and *Bnei Yisrael* took over his land. In what seems like an odd tangent, the Torah dedicates several *pesukim* to explaining the history of Cheshbon, one of the cities taken over by *Bnei Yisrael*. Cheshbon, we are told, had belonged to Moav, but was conquered by Sichon from Moav, and only then conquered by *Bnei Yisrael*. "About this" conquest of Sichon over Moav, the Torah relates, "the poets would say: 'Come to Cheshbon; let it be built and established – the town of Sichon'" (Bamidbar 21:27). Who are these poets, and why do we care about what they used to say about the war between Sichon and Moav?

Rashi explains that the poets here are Bilaam and his father Beor, and the Torah is hinting at a backstory to set the stage for the next chapter in the *Chumash*. Originally, Sichon was unable to defeat Moav; he succeeded only after hiring Bilaam to curse Moav. When Balak the King of Moav later tells Bilaam that he knows that whomever he blesses will be blessed and whomever he curses shall be cursed, he is speaking from personal experience. Balak knows that he lost to Sichon because Bilaam cursed Moav, so he tries to hire Bilaam to curse *Bnei Yisrael*.

While Rashi attempts to expound the *pesukim* within context, Rabbi Yochanan, quoted in the Gemara (*Bava Batra* 78b), views the message of the *pasuk* as a religious and moral one. According to the Gemara, the *pasuk* should be read homiletically. The word for poets is "*ha-moshlim*," which can also be understood as meaning a ruler or master. Cheshbon, the name of the city, literally means an accounting. Rabbi Yochanan reads the *pasuk* as telling us that those who are rulers over themselves, meaning those that exhibit self-control, are skilled at monitoring and analyzing their religious decisions. They calculate the loss incurred by fulfilling a mitzvah against the reward of accomplishing it, and the pleasure derived from committing an *aveirah* against the loss suffered in the end. Rabbi Moshe Chaim Luzzatto in his classic work, *Mesillat Yesharim*, uses Rabbi Yochanan's explanation here as a springboard to a discussion of how essential self-monitoring is to religious self-improvement.

Rabbi Yochanan's reading seems to be completely removed from the context of the *pesukim*. However, Rabbi Yonatan Eybeschutz argues that this message of self-monitoring is enhanced when understood within the context of Sichon and Moav. He suggests that Cheshbon was a border town with a small population which the king of Moav largely ignored because of its seeming insignificance. Sichon took over Cheshbon with ease, and it then served as a strategic location for him to conquer other cities in Moav. The message for self-monitoring, Rabbi Eybeschutz writes, is that we too often ignore the "Cheshbons" of our behavior: those crumbs that don't count as calories or the one small sin that nobody really cares about anyway. These "unimportant" oversights often lead to unwanted outcomes over time.

To gain a better mastery of ourselves, we need to improve our self-monitoring skills. We can improve our mental and physical health by tracking our thoughts, emotions, and behaviors in a Cognitive Behavioral Therapy framework, and enhance our religious commitment through tracking *mitzvot* and *aveirot*. We can become *moshlim*, masters over our own lives, if we make a proper *cheshbon*, an honest accounting of ourselves.

Blocked Goals

If something hinders us from achieving our objective, we are prone to respond with anger. This can be particularly challenging for parents or educators who try to inculcate certain values, traits, or behaviors into children, while the children may not always be receptive. In those moments when their teaching goals are blocked, whether due to lack of understanding or due to defiance, the parent or educator is susceptible to feelings of frustration and anger.

Still stuck in the desert after almost 40 years, *Bnei Yisrael* complain to Moshe about the lack of food and water, preferring life in Egypt over their current situation (Bamidbar, chapter 20). God instructs Moshe to speak to a rock, telling him that it will then bring forth water. Moshe takes his staff, says to the people, "Listen, you rebels, shall we get water for you out of this rock?," and hits the rock twice, whereupon water gushed out, providing enough for all to drink. God then informs Moshe and Aharon that they will not be allowed to lead *Bnei Yisrael* into the land, "Because you did not believe in Me to sanctify Me in the eyes of the children of Israel."

Commentators provide dozens of explanations of what Moshe and Aharon did wrong. Famously, Rashi focuses on the fact that Moshe was instructed to speak to the rock but hit it instead. Alternatively, Ramban contends that the problem is highlighted in Moshe's use of the word "we" when saying "shall we get water for you." Instead of capitalizing on an opportunity to demonstrate God's miracles, Moshe insinuated that it was he and Aharon who had the power to bring water from the rock.

Rambam (*Shemonah Perakim*, chapter 4), however, takes a different approach, focusing on the phrase "Listen now you rebels." Embedded in this language, according to Rambam, is anger. Moshe's sin is that he responded in anger towards *Bnei Yisrael*. The angry response was problematic from a character perspective as he should have responded with more patience. Additionally, there was the theological danger that *Bnei Yisrael* might mistakenly think that if Moshe is angry, God is as well, which would have been incorrect.

Rabbi Moshe Feinstein (*Darash Moshe*, p. 127) elaborates on Rashi's approach, according to which Moshe's fault was hitting the rock instead of speaking to it, and offers a powerful educational insight. Rabbi Feinstein suggests that God wanted Moshe to "speak to the rock because he wanted to teach the lesson that one must speak words of Torah and ethics even to those who seem not to comprehend. Repeating and reviewing ultimately results in understanding" (translation by Rabbi Dr. Tzvi Hersh Weinreb, *The Person in the Parsha*, p. 461). As an example, a parent "must never despair of educating his children just because they appear not to understand what he is telling them." It is essential to repeat ideas and provide consistent communication, so that they will eventually understand.

While Rabbi Feinstein builds off Rashi and focuses on the importance of persistence in the face of despair, the message can be amplified if we add Rambam's anger approach to the mix. As a leader and a teacher, Moshe had educational aspirations for *Bnei Yisrael*. He wanted them to be grateful to God for taking them out of Egypt and for providing for them in the desert. Yet, after uprisings, scandals, and incessant complaints they didn't seem to be getting the message. He became angry because the message was not getting through, and he was not achieving his goals. Instead of expressing anger, he should have modeled patience in the face of unfulfilled goals.

When we have important values, traits, or behaviors that we want to teach others, but those around us do not seem to absorb or accept those messages, it may be natural for us to feel frustrated and express anger. Yet we are called upon to choose patience instead. Our best bet is to use clear and consistent communication and hope that the message eventually makes an impact.

Parshat Balak

The Language of Animals

"The human being is the only animal that..." This sentence, Dr. Daniel Gilbert from Harvard University argues, is one which every psychologist, at some point in their career, attempts to complete based on their own line of research. Most of these attempts are later challenged by other psychologists who are looking for their own way to complete the sentence. As one example, many have argued that "The human being is the only animal that can use language," but were forced to retract when chimpanzees were taught to communicate with hand signals. Research with animals using language has its share of controversy, but there seems to be ample evidence that chimps, gorillas, bonobos, dolphins, border collies, and African gray parrots can all acquire the ability to communicate using some form of language.

When Bilaam went with the servants of Moav to Balak, God, angry that Bilaam went, placed an angel on the road to prevent them from passing. While Bilaam was unable to see the sword-wielding angel, his donkey noticed it and veered off the path. Bilaam, frustrated with his animal's behavior, hit it with his stick. The angel repositioned himself and the donkey, again trying to avoid the angel, pressed against a wall, squeezing Bilaam's foot. Bilaam responded by hitting his donkey for the second time. The donkey, still confronted by the angel and with nowhere to go, squatted on the ground. Bilaam, in his anger, hit the donkey once again.

At that point, the strange story became even more bizarre. God opened the donkey's mouth and a conversation ensued between Bilaam and his donkey. The donkey, hurt after being hit three times, asked for an explanation. Bilaam, unphased by a talking donkey, responded that the donkey had made a mockery of him, and that if he had had a sword, he would have killed her. Pleading her case, the donkey asked Bilaam to consider all the years they have been together and whether her behavior was characteristic.

Bilaam acknowledged that it was not, and at that point, God uncovered his eyes and revealed the angel to him. The angel rebuked Bilaam for hitting his donkey three times and explained that the donkey actually saved his life by avoiding the angel.

How are we to understand a talking donkey? The most prevalent explanation is to ascribe it to a Divine miracle. The Mishnah in *Avot* (5:6) lists the talking donkey as one of the ten miracles that God created during twilight of the first Shabbat. A textual problem with such an explanation is that even though a talking donkey is within the purview of God's abilities, it presumably wasn't in the realm of the expected for Bilaam. The fact that he seems to take the talking donkey in stride presents a problem. Another possibility is to follow Rambam's view (*Moreh Nevuchim* 2:41) that anytime anybody in Tanach encountered an angel, it happened in the context of a dream state. If so, the whole episode, including the donkey talking, took place in Bilaam's mind.

A third possibility is presented by Rabbi Samuel David Luzzatto. Rabbi Luzzatto points out that if you look carefully, the text never explicitly states that the donkey speaks (*d-v-r*). He argues that the donkey did not express a full, well-articulated statement, in human language. Rather, the donkey brayed and bellowed as a response to getting hit, *as if to say*, "why are you hitting me?" Bilaam responded to the donkey's cries by saying that she humiliated him, the same as any pet owner may converse with his or her pet. Animals may not be able to talk using speech to formulate sentences in the way humans do, but they can use other forms of language to communicate.

Perhaps, embedded in this strange interaction, is a veiled critique of Bilaam's broader behavior. One of Bilaam's flaws was his inability to hear, understand, and intuit what God really wanted from him. He did not pick up on the subtle cues and listen to the true essence of what was expected of him. It was a case of motivated listening, of hearing what he wanted to hear and acting accordingly. Bilaam's initial impetuous and violent behavior toward his donkey reflected this inability to attend to the not fully-articulated feelings of the other. In contrast, Midrashim abound with descriptions of the empathy and care that great Jewish leaders, such as Moshe and David, exhibited as shepherds towards their flock. The way and extent to which one listens and responds to those who are more vulnerable and who are unable to fully communicate is a litmus test for their true character. A test that Bilaam failed, and one we can aspire to pass – if we listen carefully.

Postive Sleep

Dr. Martin Seligman, known as the founder of the positive psychology movement, writes in his book *Authentic Happiness* that when his children were younger, he did two activities with them as part of their bedtime routine. First, he would have them recount all the positive events of the day, as well as the parts that were not as successful, to show them how the positives generally outweighed the negatives.

Second, right before they went to sleep, he had his children think about one specific positive event to continue thinking about as they fell asleep. He explains his reasoning behind this ritual, writing that "[t]he last thoughts a child has before drifting into sleep are laden with emotion and rich in visual imagery, and these become threads around which dreams are woven" (p. 228). The last thoughts that we think before we go to sleep heavily impact what we will think about while sleeping.

Though Bilaam clearly wanted to curse the Jews, God would not let him. Instead of curses, we read of some of the most beautiful blessings that describe the strong spiritual characteristics that personify *Bnei Yisrael*. "How great are your tents" (Bamidbar 24:5) is understood as referencing the remarkable modesty that *Bnei Yisrael* demonstrated while encamping in the wilderness. Other verses praise their spirituality; "He perceived no iniquity in Yaakov, he saw no perversity in Israel" (Bamidbar 23:21), and "there is no divination in Yaakov and no sorcery in Israel" (Bamidbar 23:23). The blessings then abruptly switch from spiritual praise to physical prowess: "The people will arise like a lion cub and raise itself like a lion; It will not lie down until it consumes prey, and drinks the blood of the slain" (Bamidbar 23:24). There is quite a radical transition from spiritual loftiness to savagely guzzling down the blood of the enemy.

Rashi, following the lead of the Midrash, explains that even this physical praise is a spiritual allusion. Not lying down until consuming prey and drinking its blood refers to the ritual of reciting the *Shema* before going to sleep. The connection requires some elaboration. What does reciting the bedtime *Shema* have anything to do with slaying enemies?

The Talmud (*Berachot* 5a) relates in the name of Rabbi Yitzchak that "anyone who recites *Shema* on his bed, it is as if he holds a double-edged sword" guarding him from evil, and that even the "demons stay away from him." Some understand these demons, known in Aramaic as *mazikin*, to be dangerous metaphysical entities that can physically harm people. Saying the *Shema* in bed protects one from being injured by them. Meiri, however, takes a more psychological approach, explaining that the *mazikin* should be understood as irrational, rebellious thoughts that can entrap people when they are not busy. Since our minds tend to wander into these negative thoughts before bed, it is essential to sanctify and unify our thoughts for spiritual purposes. Reciting the *Shema* at night protects us from harmful thinking patterns.

The thoughts we think right before we go to bed have a profound impact on our sleep. Many people have trouble falling asleep, disturbed by anxious and other disturbing thoughts. By mindfully reciting the *Shema*, we can ward off whatever "*mazikin*" we may have, allowing us to sleep more peacefully. By so doing we can also transform the physical experience of sleep into a deeply spiritual endeavor.

Parshat Pinchas

Social & Emotional Leadership

After processing the news that he will not be leading *Bnei Yisrael* into the land of Canaan, due to his and Aharon's sin at Mei Merivah, Moshe turns to God and asks Him to appoint a successor. In his dialogue with God, Moshe addresses Him with a strange appellation – *Elokei HaRuchot*. Two *pesukim* later, God tells Moshe to take Yehoshua, a man who has *"ruach,"* and appoint him as the leader. The role of *ruach* is clearly essential to the narrative, but it is unclear exactly what it is and why it is so important.

Depending on the context, the term *ruach* can mean several things in Tanach, including wind, breath, spirit, feelings, or will. Rashi understands the term here as a reference to people's dispositions. God is a God of *ruchot*, meaning that the personality of every individual is revealed before Him. He should appoint a leader who will be able to tolerate each person based on his or her own inner makeup. Yehoshua is a man who has *ruach*, meaning, he can conduct himself in a manner that would correspond to every individual.

Rashi's description of the skills required for leadership is striking on two fronts. The first is the care and concern the leader must have for *all* his or her followers. Rashi emphasizes the importance of understanding the innumerable differences between each individual and the duty to adapt accordingly. The leader doesn't just focus on the whole group or prioritize a select few. He or she needs to tend to all members of the flock.

The second aspect of Rashi's gloss that is striking is its seeming parallel to the constructs of social and emotional intelligence. Broadly speaking, emotional intelligence incorporates the ability to read and manage emotions both in the self and in others. Social intelligence encompasses verbal and listening skills, a depth of understanding of social situations, and the capacity to conduct oneself according to context. Rashi's description of *ruach* highlights the need to understand the other's personality and manage oneself and others accordingly. Research in educational and industrial-organizational psychology demonstrates the importance of these skills for leaders and educators. The question then becomes, how can we attain these abilities?

One answer is that possessing this type of *ruach* is simply a gift from God. I either have it or I don't. All I can do is *daven* and hope that God grants me these abilities. In fact, we find precedent for such a notion when God took some of Moshe's *ruach* and placed it upon the elders, who then acquired it (Bamidbar 11:17). However, the Alshich points out, this is not the same procedure that takes place with Yehoshua. Yehoshua apparently already had these traits, so he did not need Divine intervention. That is why, according to Abarbanel, God tells Moshe in reference to Yehoshua *kach lecha*, "*you* take," meaning Divine intervention is not necessary. Yehoshua already has the skills because he spent years observing Moshe's behavior and modeling his own behavior accordingly. The rest is up to Yehoshua and Moshe – hence the word *lecha*.

Most of us, in some form or another, whether at home, work, or school, take on the position of leader. We learn from this narrative that we need to be a person of *ruach* – we need to care and tend to everyone we are guiding, to try to understand their inner psychology by using our emotional and social intelligence, and to deal with each one accordingly. The good news is that this is a skill that can be taught and learned, making it a worthwhile investment of our time and resources if we want to develop into more effective leaders.

Words Can Change Your Brain

In their book *Words Can Change Your Brain*, Drs. Andrew Newberg and Mark Robert Waldman describe research they conducted on the harmful impact that negative words have on our brains. They used an fMRI scanner to record the brain activity of research participants, while these participants were exposed to negative words such as "NO!" They found that stress-producing hormones and neurotransmitters were released by the amygdala and interrupted regular brain activities that assist with logical thinking and effective communication. Even a single negative word or phrase, when focused upon for extended periods of time, can damage key brain structures that regulate memory and emotion. They also argue that verbalizing the negativity causes even more stress chemicals to be released, in both the speaker and the listener. Words and speech can change the structures in our brains, altering how we perceive and relate to ourselves and the world.

Rabbi Tzadok HaKohen of Lublin points out that the three *haftarot* read during the three weeks preceding Tisha b'Av each begin with related, but different words. The first week begins with "*Divrei,*" the second with "*Shim'u,*" and the last with "*Chazon.*" These three words correspond to *dibbur*, *shemi'ah*, and *re'iyah*, namely, speech, hearing, and seeing. Consequently, during each of the three weeks, we should focus on the corresponding concept. The first *haftorah*, the one which focuses on *dibbur*, is read with *Parshat Pinchas*, making it an apt time to highlight the importance of speech and improving how we utilize it in our daily lives.

Bereishit 2:7 states that God blew in man's nostrils, making him a "*nefesh chayah.*" Onkelos famously translates this term as *ruach memamela*, a speaking spirit. According to this approach, speech defines and distinguishes humans from other creatures. Maharal explains further that speech acts as the synthesis of our body and soul. This, Rabbi Akiva Tatz writes (*Worldmask*, p. 129), is why our voice originates in the neck, at the junction of the head (representing the soul) and the rest of the body.

The centrality of speech to our spiritual lives is alluded to in the narrative of *Parshat Pinchas* and its surrounding *parshiyot*. In *Parshat Balak* we read about Bilaam's attempt to curse the Jewish people with words. While that endeavor failed, we are informed in *Parshat Mattot* that Bilaam is the one responsible for influencing the licentious actions described at the end of *Parshat Balak* that leads to Pinchas' act of zealotry, the aftermath of which is presented in this week's reading. As a punishment for his actions, we are told that Bilaam was killed *be-charev* – with a sword. Rashi comments that Bilaam originally came to provoke *Bnei Yisrael* using the tribes' own specialty, that of speech. *Bnei Yisrael* worship God through prayer, and Bilaam had the nerve to try and use the power of negative speech – a curse – to destroy them. As a consequence, Bilaam was killed by *Bnei Yisrael* not with their usual mode of speech, but with the other nations' weapon of choice, namely, a sword.

Toward the end of *Parshat Pinchas* we are presented with details of various sacrifices that were brought in the *Mishkan*. One important function of the sacrifices was that they provided atonement for sins. In a fascinating passage, the Talmud (*Taanit*, 27b) presents a dialogue between Avraham and God, where Avraham is concerned with what would happen if the Jewish people sin. God reassures him that they will not be destroyed like the generation of the flood, because they will have sacrifices to provide atonement. Avraham retorts that sacrifices only work when the Temple is standing, but asks what will happen afterwards. God answers that learning and reciting the passages related to the sacrifices will provide the requisite atonement.

While our words undeniably have the power to change our brains, their significance does not stop there. Speaking words of Torah can provide atonement. Our prayers characterize us as the Jewish people. Our speech defines us as human beings. The first of the three weeks is a worthwhile time to work on improving our speech and utilizing the power of our words for meaningful purposes.

Parshiyot Mattot-Masei

Precommitment Devices

Parshat Mattot begins by introducing the laws of vows and oaths: "When a man makes a vow to God or takes an oath to obligate himself by a pledge, he must not break his word but must do everything he said" (Bamidbar 30:3). Oaths lend extra force to a commitment, making one's word more binding. A person can even decide, the Talmud notes, to take an oath to perform or not to violate a commandment (*Nedarim* 8a), even though the person is already obligated by the Torah. The oath functions to intensify the original biblical law.

In his classic work *Michtav me-Eliyahu* (4:237), Rabbi Eliyahu Dessler elucidates the psychology behind taking an oath to comply with a mitzvah. At times, he writes, we become aware of our own laxness in Torah observance, and we want to improve our own behavior. We often try to fight our desires or weaknesses head on, but when put to the test, the *yetzer hara* is too powerful and we fail. We can handle this by forcing our own hand, and avoiding the battle for self-control at the outset. We need to construct the situation such that we are forced to comply. The classic biblical way to accomplish this is through an oath. People viewed oaths with such awe and trepidation that adding an oath to a desirous behavior was generally a strong enough intervention to force self-compliance.

In later times, the reverence extended to oaths diminished, and Chazal frowned upon and limited their usage. People would make oaths but still fail to keep them. In so doing, they would not only violate the original biblical commandment, but would violate an oath as well. Since we now generally abstain from taking oaths, it is essential that we find other legitimate ways to deepen our commitments. We need to think of ways, Rabbi Dessler suggests, to effectively bind ourselves to our commitments without taking an oath. For example, if someone is struggling to learn Torah, he or she could commit to giving a *shiur* on a topic that requires further research. The pressure to give a powerful presentation will force the person to study.

The psychological literature on self-control calls this concept a "precommitment device." In a 2002 research article, Dan Ariely and Klaus Wertenbroch define such a strategy as the "voluntary imposition of constraints (that are costly to overcome) on one's future choices in a strategic attempt to resist future temptations" (p. 219). The oft-cited paradigm of this technique in Greek mythology is Ulysses, who tied himself to a mast so that he could not be lured by the song of the Sirens.

Precommitment devices can potentially help with many self-control battles including procrastination, unhealthy eating habits, drinking too much alcohol, and over-spending. We can overcome our tendency to spend too much time scrolling through social media instead of working on that important project, by using software programs that block our internet or access to social media for a set period of time. If we know that every time we go to a certain restaurant we will end up choosing an unhealthy option, we could "precommit" to a better choice by going to a different restaurant.

Whether the goal is to improve our self-control, increase the amount of *mitzvot* we accomplish, or decrease the amount of *aveirot* we commit, we can learn from the way in which Torah presents oaths, and conceive of different ways to bind ourselves to improvement by precommitting to progress.

Predicting Emotions

Imagine for a moment that you won the lottery – mazal tov! As you envision that hopeful, future self, you presumably predict that you will be filled with overwhelmingly positive emotions. Excitement and happiness are indeed involved in winning, but research shows that over time, lottery winners are not significantly happier than non-winners. Psychologists Timothy Wilson and Daniel Gilbert identify this common misconception as "affective forecasting." As you imagine that scenario, what you are not considering are the hassles and challenges that accompany lottery winners, which contribute to a host of negative emotions. We tend to mis-predict how we would feel in future situations, predicting that certain outcomes will engender more positive emotions than they actually do when they happen, and assuming that bad situations will make us feel worse than they actually do in reality.

Parshat Mattot begins with a discussion of the concept of vows and oaths – "If a man makes a vow to God … he shall not break his word, he shall do according to all that proceeds out of his mouth (Bamidbar 30:3). While *he* may not break his own word after taking a vow, the Talmud (*Chagigah* 10a) interprets the verse as teaching that *others* can annul his vow. This is the process known as *hatarat nedarim* – annulment of vows – a version of which we practice before Rosh Hashanah and Yom Kippur.

Based on early Talmudic commentators, Rabbi Joseph B. Soloveitchik (*Chumash Mesorat HaRav: Bamidbar*) explains that there are two ways to annul a vow. The first is through a mechanism called a *petach* – an opening – in which the person is released from his vow because the vow was made in error. If there were circumstances of which the person who took the vow was unaware, or was not paying attention to when he made the vow, but had he been aware of them he would not have made the vow, a Sage can annul the vow. For example, if a person vowed to fast for a certain amount of time but did not realize that there was a holiday during that time frame, the Sage asks him if he would have made the vow had he been cognizant of the intervening holiday. If the answer is no, then the Sage has found an opening, and the vow is annulled.

The second way to annul a vow is through *charatah* – remorse. In this case there was no misunderstanding of the facts. Rather, his vow can be released, Rabbi Soloveitchik explains, "on the grounds that his tastes have changed, his feelings, his outlook and criteria are different now from what they were at the time he made his vow. Those things which originally seemed to him to be of ultimate importance now appear to be trivial and foolish." (p. 241). As an example, consider a person who, after being insulted, takes a vow to avenge the slight. Over time his anger subsides, and he no longer feels the same intense negativity towards the perpetrator. In contrast to finding "an opening" to annul the vow, here there is no mistake in the external considerations. Rather, "[w]hat happened is that a radical change occurred in the conscience and will of the person who made the vow." (p. 241).

Even if we are not accustomed to making vows, we are prone to making mistakes in decision-making which are related to both these concepts. First, we make mistakes in logic and judgment. We do not take all the factors of the external reality into account when deciding what to do. We act impetuously, before thinking through the details. Second, we are poor affective forecasters. We make decisions in the present, thinking that we know how the outcomes will make us feel in the future. But we are usually wrong. For example, we think we will always feel this angry, so we do something that we will regret once the anger subsides.

Unfortunately, we aren't always blessed with the opportunity to repent or annul our vows. It would be wiser for us to work on avoiding making poor judgements in the first place. We can do this by starting to be more mindful and becoming better aware of our current emotional states. We can then do a better job of predicting our future emotional states. Finally, we can make better decisions in the present, based on the more accurate future forecasting.

Parshat Devarim

Unconditional Positive Regard

One of the most influential ideas of the prominent humanistic psychologists Carl Rogers is called "unconditional positive regard." Demonstrating unconditional positive regard for someone else means to fully accept the person regardless of what he or she has said or done. This does not necessarily mean completely accepting the person's actions. Yet, even when disagreeing with another's behavior, we can still demonstrate positive regard for the person as a human being. When such conditions exist, there is a healthy space to improve and grow.

Parshat Devarim begins with Moshe recapping some of the highlights of *Bnei Yisrael's* travels and travails in the desert. His summary includes critiques, some of which are explicit, while, according to Rashi and others, many of Moshe's criticisms are merely veiled hints and allusions (see Rashi 1:1).

In a very powerful discourse, Rabbi Chaim Shmulevitz (*Sichot Mussar*) addresses the reason Moshe only hinted at some of *Bnei Yisrael's* more serious sins. Would it not have been more effective to state them explicitly? Rashi explains that Moshe chose this method to preserve the dignity of *Bnei Yisrael*. If he enumerated their sins, they would have been ashamed and embarrassed. The consideration of preserving the dignity of the human being – *kavod ha-beriyot* – demands that he soften the rebuke, even if this means that it would be less effective.

Rabbi Zelig Pliskin (*Growth Through Torah*, p. 380) quotes Rabbi Leibel Eiger, who points out that amidst the critique, Moshe inserts a blessing, saying, "May the Lord, the God of your fathers, increase you, similar to you (*kachem*) a thousandfold" (Devarim 1:11). The word *kachem*, which literally means "similar to you," requires elaboration. Rabbi Eiger explains that in the midst of the rebuke, Moshe wanted to assure *Bnei Yisrael* that he did not think poorly of them. Rather, he wished that they multiply, and that their offspring would be *kachem* – just like them. Despite their past sins and bad behavior, Moshe respected and admired them.

In an essay offering several strategies for providing proper rebuke, Rabbi Baruch Simon (*Imrei Baruch: Devarim*, pp. 19–27)quotes Rabbi Isaiah Horowitz (the *Shelah HaKadosh*), who adds an important insight. Moshe speaks of the "wise, discerning, and known" leaders amongst *Bnei Yisrael* (Devarim 1:13). Rabbi Horowitz argues that while providing the rebuke, Moshe is careful to build up the people's self-esteem and self-respect, so he includes these accolades. The verse in Proverbs (9:8) reads "Do not rebuke a scoffer, for he will hate you; Reprove a wise man, and he will love you." According to Rabbi Horowitz, this verse means that the person doing the rebuking should not consider the other person to be a scoffer, and if he does so, he will not be successful. Rather, if the person giving the rebuke relates to the other person as if they were already wise and discerning, then the rebuke will be effective.

Putting these sources together, it seems that Moshe interacted with *Bnei Yisrael* with unconditional positive regard. There was plenty of room to critique their behavior, but Moshe went out of his way to accept them for who they were. Despite their flaws, he demonstrated respect for them as human beings.

When providing feedback and guidance to others, it is all too easy to cause the recipient to feel rejected or devalued as a person. Not only is such rebuke morally problematic, but it also can cause the recipient to become defensive, instead of receptive. In such situations, we would do well to follow Moshe's lead and use language that demonstrates unconditional positive regard. Not only is it the right thing to do, but it also provides the greatest likelihood that the message will be accepted.

The Courage of Judges

Are we born with courage, or can it be cultivated? Dr. Robert Biswas-Diener, in his book *The Courage Quotient*, contends that we *can* increase our levels of courage, and he also outlines several useful strategies for dealing with fear. As one example, he asserts that at times fear is increased by focusing too much on the self. Meaning, the more we focus on the potential negative consequences that can befall us, the more we tend to be afraid. Consequently, one way to decrease fear, and increase courage, is to promote an outward focus, rather than an inner one. The more we remove our *selves* from the situation, the more we can potentially feel courage.

One of the first topics Moshe elucidates as he commences his farewell address is the laws pertaining to judges. Specifically, the judges must act to promote justice and prevent corruption. In this context, the Torah states, "*lo taguru mipnei ish, ki ha-mishpat l'Elokim hu*" (Devarim 1:17). What does the word *taguru* mean in this verse? Rashi presents two interpretations. The first is that *taguru* means "fear," meaning that judges are commanded to not fear other people. The second explanation, based on the Gemara (*Sanhedrin* 6b), is that *taguru* means "remain silent." The example given concerns a student observing his teacher judge a case between a rich and poor person. If the student discerns an argument for the poor person, he should not withhold his point, even if he is afraid how the teacher, or the rich man, will respond. Even according to this second explanation, the central meaning of the word is fear. Fear of another human being cannot be a factor when pursuing justice.

The commentators differ as to the meaning of the continuation: *ki ha-mishpat l'Elokim hu*, "for judgment is God's." Rashi, based on the Gemara (*Sanhedrin* 8a), explains that if a judge rules falsely, it becomes an inconvenience for God. Since God is just, He will need to "work overtime" to devise a way to return the money to the rightful owner. Ramban, perhaps dissatisfied with that answer, presents a broader theological and moralistic explanation. According to Ramban, judges cannot let fear pervert justice because they stand as representatives of God. They serve as God's messengers to bring justice into the world, and if they distort the truth, they are derelict in their hallowed duty.

Both Rashi and Ramban understand that the phrase "for judgment is God's" functions as a reason why a judge should not pervert judgment. By succumbing to one's fear of man, and not acting courageously, a judge will inconvenience God or pervert his God-given mission.

However, based on the idea from *The Courage Quotient* quoted above, perhaps we can suggest that the phrase does not function as a *reason* why judges should not fear man, but as a *strategy* to decrease this fear. Meaning, the way to decrease fear is to realize that justice belongs to God. If fear of another man is increased by a focus and concern for the harm that person can cause the self, the judges should remove the focus from themselves and direct their attention to the Divine. They should increase their courage by transcending the concerns of person and ego and focusing on their Divine mission.

The message concerns judges, but it can be applied to all of us. There will be times when we will be confronted by a moral dilemma. Sometimes, standing up and doing the right thing requires courage, while concerns of what others will say or do can lead to fear and inaction. Even the generally beneficial goal of preserving peace and acting kindly should not come at the expense of perverting justice. In those moments, may we find the courage by rising above our personal worries and remembering that we too can become emissaries of God's word and will, and bring justice to this world.

Parshat Va'etchanan

Grit or Quit?

Imagine you were pursuing a goal with all your heart and soul for years. There were struggles along the way, but you persevered. You are almost there. You can see the finish line. It is within your grasp. But you stumble one more time, and this time, you can't seem to figure a way out. You try repeatedly, but you keep getting stuck. Do you persist or do you give up?

Dr. Angela Duckworth, a psychologist from the University of Pennsylvania, studies the construct of grit, which is the ability to persevere and persist towards long-term goals despite challenges and setbacks. Those who demonstrate grit tend to be more successful in academic and professional settings. As we have argued in the past, grit is essential to learning Torah and fulfilling *mitzvot*. Yet we may ask: Is grit always the proper response? Can't grit sometimes manifest as unhealthy stubbornness?

In contrast to Dr. Duckworth, Dr. Carsten Wrosch, a psychologist from Concordia University in Montreal, studies the benefits of quitting. He argues that there are certain times when giving up is a better response than persisting. People who let go of unattainable goals tend to have fewer depressive symptoms, less negative affect, lower levels of cortisol, less systemic inflammation, and fewer physical health problems. Moreover, investing time and energy into one goal can prevent us from attempting different, perhaps more attainable or more beneficial, goals.

It is not always easy to identify the line between healthy grit and unhealthy stubbornness. However, perhaps we can learn from Moshe Rabbeinu how to act when an impassioned goal is beyond our reach. Moshe longed to enter the land of Israel, and desired to finish his original mission of bringing *Bnei Yisrael* into the land. He yearned to fulfill the various *mitzvot* that are only pertinent within the physical boundaries of Israel (Talmud, *Sotah* 14a). But he could not reach the finish line. After the rebellion of Mei Merivah, God told him he could not enter.

Moshe did not go down without a fight. He begged and pleaded with God to let him enter the land. The Midrash expounds on the numerical value of the word *va'etchanan* (ואתחנן), and informs us that Moshe articulated 515 supplications to God. Moshe serves as a paradigm for grit in the face of challenges. When faced with an obstacle, we should be determined, tenacious, and persistent.

Yet, taken from a different perspective, Moshe also serves as a paradigm for knowing when to acquiesce. When God told him to stop pleading, he stopped. He put in the effort, but once he realized that the goal was unattainable, he admitted defeat. This acceptance then allowed him to focus on a new task. He put his effort into crafting a farewell message that would influence generations to come in the land of Israel, even though he would not physically be present there.

Within the same narrative, Moshe serves as a role-model for extreme persistence in goal attainment, as well as an example for conceding when the goal is clearly no longer attainable. When confronted with challenges to our own goals, we are also called on to find the balance between persistence and giving up. It is generally beneficial to be gritty in the face of obstacles. However, if we are consistently unsuccessful, it may be strategic to reconsider our original goal, and invest our energies into a different pursuit. May God grant us the wisdom to discern whether to respond with grit or to quit, the strength to persevere if necessary, and the courage to give up when appropriate.

Does Torah Make Us Psychologically Healthier?

Is being religious good for one's mental health? Many psychologists, starting with Freud and continuing to some extent to psychologists working
during the last part of the 20th century, believed that religion was antithetical to mental health. Some therapists even went so far as to challenge their
patients' religious beliefs in order to increase their well-being. However,
increased cultural sensitivities and robust scientific research led the field
to shift its perspective. While certain types of religious beliefs have been
identified as negatively impacting mental health, for the most part, holding
religious beliefs is correlated with increased mental well-being.

In a recent application of this idea, Dr. Steven Pirutinsky, Aaron Cherniak, and Dr. David Rosmarin published an article entitled "COVID-19,
Mental Health, and Religious Coping Among American Orthodox Jews," in
the *Journal of Religion and Mental Health*. Their research indicates that valu-
ing religion, trusting in God, and using faith to facilitate problem-solving
all played a crucial role for many Orthodox Jews in decreasing stress and
adapting well to the challenges of COVID-19.

Parshat Va'etchanan relates the law concerning a person who accidently
kills another, and explains that the manslayer should then flee to a city of
refuge for protection. The Talmud (*Makkot* 10a) provides a fascinating
addition to this law: If a student is forced into exile, his teacher must go
into exile with him. This requirement is based on the verse that states that
the person who kills unintentionally "shall flee to one of these cities and
live" (Devarim 4:22). The simple reading of the verse is that escaping to the
city physically protects the killer from the blood avenger, but the Talmud
understands the word *va-chai*, "and live," as referencing the killer's spiritual
life. For that, he needs his teacher to teach him Torah.

In another use of the word "live," Moshe tells *Bnei Yisrael* to observe all
the laws so "that you may *live* to enter and occupy the land that the Lord,
the God of your fathers, is giving you" (Devarim 4:1). The commentators
are troubled by the word "live" in the verse, which seems to be superfluous.
Ibn Ezra explains that "live" in this verse references physical life: keep the
laws, or you will not survive. However, Rabbi Naftali Tzvi Yehudah Berlin,
the Netziv, disagrees with Ibn Ezra on empirical grounds: plenty of people
do not keep the laws, yet remain alive.

The Netziv offers an alternative explanation. "To live" does not just
mean physical living; rather it means "to flourish." "Life" implies a "full

life, a happy and meaningful life, replete with the delight one experiences with the achievement of spiritual wholeness" (translation from Rabbi Dr. Tzvi Hersh Weinreb, *The Person in the Parsha*, p. 531). The Netziv makes the same point in *Parshat Acharei Mot* (Vayikra 18:5), which states that we should follow the laws *va-chai bahem*, "and live through them." Learning and living a life of Torah is supposed to lead to psychological flourishing and a sense of general well-being.

If done correctly, living a life infused with God and Torah is good for our mental health. The *mitzvot* provide opportunities for creating transcendent experiences, fostering meaningful relationships with others, and establishing a connection to God. Our religious and spiritual ideals are meant to provide support for us during challenging times, guiding us to live lives filled with happiness and meaning. While the psychological literature has been catching up to this idea in recent years, its roots are embedded within the "life" of the Torah.

Parshat Ekev

Grateful Thinking

Dr. Jeffrey Froh, a psychologist at Hofstra University, is one of the leading gratitude researchers. As part of his quest to increase levels of gratitude in students, he designed a curriculum that helps develop the thought processes people have in relation to gratitude. He delineates three "grateful thinking" strategies that can enhance the experience of gratitude. The first is to consider the intent of the benefactor. The second is to recognize the cost incurred by the benefactor. The third is to contemplate the extent of the benefits that he or she accrued. In his research study, middle school students who were taught this curriculum and practiced thinking about these three components experienced increased well-being and exhibited more gratitude behaviors (i.e., they wrote more thank-you cards to their Parent–Teacher Association) than students in a control group.

Over the course of his farewell address to *Bnei Yisrael*, Moshe strove to make them aware of two potential dangers they may face after entering the land of Israel. The first was external: *Bnei Yisrael* should beware the other cultures and nations surrounding them. Those nations' debasement, framed primarily in terms of idol worship, could influence *Bnei Yisrael* to the point where they might even reject God and Torah. The second was internal: Material success could lead to arrogance, and arrogance to forgetting God: "Your heart will become haughty and you will forget (*ve-shachachta*) the Lord, your God, who took you out of Egypt" (Devarim 8:14). This haughtiness in forgetting God will lead to not only forgetting the Exodus from Egypt, but also that God guided and protected the Jews in the desert, and He conducted miracles to provide them with food and water. The remedy for the external dangers is to reject the influence of foreign cultures. Is the antidote for arrogance to reject material wealth?

This solution hardly seems likely, as the promise of the land of Israel has always been framed within the context of material wealth. After all, it is the land that flows with milk and honey. How, then, are *Bnei Yisrael* to prevent the arrogance that seems to flow from economic success? Perhaps the answer is embedded in a reinterpretation of the verse quoted above. The letter *vav* of *ve-shachachta* can mean either *and* or *because*. Instead of reading "Your heart will become haughty *and* you will forget the Lord," we can read, "Your heart will become haughty *because* you will forget the Lord." Forgetting and ingratitude serve as intervening variables that stand between material success and arrogance. Success is not the cause of arrogance, and poverty is not the solution. Rather, arrogance is rooted in forgetting, and forgetting is rooted in ingratitude.

Ibn Ezra elaborates upon the forgotten emotional experience that stands behind these historical events. *Bnei Yisrael* will forget how low their spirits were when they were slaves, before God emancipated them. They will forget the pain and suffering they experienced in the desert, before God provided the miracles to help them cope in the harsh terrain. Rabbi Mordechai Gifter (*Pirkei Emunah*, p. 74) expands on Ibn Ezra's comments and finds an essential lesson which helps deepen our experience of gratitude: When God or another person does something that benefits us, it is insufficient to just thank them. True gratitude requires "grateful thinking" as well: We must contemplate the essence of the good that was bestowed upon us. This means that we are required to reflect on the situation that we were in before receiving the benefit and our situation after receiving the benefit. This is the only way to fully appreciate the depths of the gratitude we owe. Moshe was cautioning *Bnei Yisrael* to not forget the good God has performed, by contemplating the pain and suffering that they endured before being saved.

To protect against the arrogance that material success can bring, we need to be grateful. Yet, we cannot fulfill our obligation of gratitude with a quick and perfunctory thank you. If we want to truly experience gratitude, we need to step back and employ strategies of "grateful thinking." To fully appreciate what we have, we must vividly imagine what life would be like if we had not received all the good. Performing this cognitive exercise can help deepen our thankfulness to God for all He provides, and enhance our gratefulness to those around us who enrich our lives.

Mind over Milkshakes

In a fascinating study conducted at Yale University, participants were each given a 380-calorie milkshake. Though all participants received the same shake, half were told it was a sensible, 140-calorie shake, while the other half were told it was an indulgent, 620-calorie shake. The people in the "indulgent" milkshake group rated themselves as fuller than those in the "sensible" milkshake group, a finding which testifies to the subjective nature of satiety. But the researchers did not just rely on the participants' self-report of how full they felt. They also measured the levels of ghrelin, a gut hormone whose presence is associated with feeling hungry. They found lower levels of ghrelin in the people who thought they were drinking the indulgent shake, even though they had in fact ingested the same number of calories! The researchers conclude that "mindset meaningfully affects physiological responses to food" (p. 424).

In *Parshat Ekev*, Moshe informs *Bnei Yisrael* that when they enter the Land of Israel, they "will eat, be satisfied, and bless God" (Devarim 8:10). This is the source for the commandment of *Birkat HaMazon* –reciting blessings after eating a meal that contains bread. The trigger for being obligated in the commandment is the feeling of satiety. Despite the subjectivity of satiation inherent in the verse, the Rabbis of the Talmud set specific criteria which obligate a person to recite *Birkat HaMazon* (after partaking of either an olive-sized or egg-sized portion of bread).

The Talmud presents an enigmatic Aggadic dialogue between God and the angels, where the angels ask God how He can show favor to the Jewish people (as is implied in the Priestly Blessing), since any bias does not seem to align with fairness and justice. God justifies His decision by pointing to the fact that even though the verse only requires *Birkat HaMazon* after being satiated, *Bnei Yisrael* recite the blessings even after only eating an olive- or egg-sized piece of bread (a far smaller quantity).

This cryptic passage requires explanation. If the Sages wanted to teach the importance of going above and beyond the bare requirements, why choose *Birkat HaMazon* as the example? Additionally, if the biblical obligation is triggered only after being satiated, wouldn't it be problematic to recite the blessings if one is not full? Wouldn't these be considered blessings made in vain?

Perhaps the significance of reciting the blessing on a small piece of bread is not that the Jewish people recite blessings even when they are still hungry. Rather, working on our attitude and changing our mindset impacts our biology. After conscientious training, we can physically feel satiated – both psychologically and biologically – with a smaller amount.

A verse in Proverbs (13:25) states, "a righteous person eats to satisfy his soul." Our ideal is to eat enough to have energy to serve God, not to indulge when there is no physical or spiritual benefit. While we should all consult the relevant health professionals for guidance on what and how much to eat, perhaps the Talmud's message is that we could work on being mindful of our satiation, and adjust our mindset to decrease the amount of food we require in order to become satiated.

Parshat Re'eh

Don't Believe What You See

In what is popularly known as the Invisible Gorilla experiment, Christopher Chabris and Daniel Simons demonstrate the phenomenon known as "selective attention." During the experiment, people are asked to count how many times a basketball is being passed between six participants in a video. Twenty seconds into the video, a person dressed in a gorilla costume conspicuously walks through the people passing the ball, bangs on his chest, and continues walking through the scene. At the end of the video, the participants are asked how many passes they counted. They are then asked if they saw the gorilla, which, shockingly, around 50% of the participants report not noticing. When I have informally showed the video to students in my psychology courses, half the class usually also does not see it.

The experiment reveals that people often miss things that are right in front of their eyes. When focusing attention on one thing (counting the passes), people can miss something extraordinary (a man in a gorilla costume). In their book *The Invisible Gorilla*, Chabris and Simons use this experiment, among others, to make a broader argument about the limits of human perception. In addition to not seeing things that are right in front of us, sometimes we also mistakenly see things that are not there at all. Professor Gustav Kuhn from the University of London investigates the psychology and neuroscience behind magic tricks. One trick that he has studied is the Vanishing Ball Illusion, in which a magician uses misdirection to make people think that they saw a ball vanish in mid-air. In his book *Experiencing the Impossible: The Science of Magic*, Kuhn provides numerous explanations for such illusions, but what is plainly clear is that people really believe they see something that did not actually happen.

Parshat Re'eh, as perhaps its name suggests, is heavily concerned with seeing. The beginning of the *parsha* is startling in its simplicity: See the blessing and the curse in front of you, and choose the blessing. Yet, as the *parsha* continues, vision is anything but black and white. A running theme throughout is that without safeguards, human nature will lean us towards seeing and doing what is correct in our own eyes: *ha-yashar be-einav* (Devarim 12:8). What is necessary, in contrast, is to follow what is correct in the eyes of God: *ha-yashar be-einei Hashem*, as is emphasized three times (Devarim 12:25, 12:28, and 13:19). The message is clear – trust God's eyes and His perspective, not our own.

This lesson is embedded in two other instances in the *parsha*, emphasizing how easily our eyes can be deceived by others. The first concerns the false prophet, who will use signs and wonders – magic tricks, if you will – to try and convince us to follow other gods (Devarim 13:3). But how can we know whether a prophet is false? If his "magic" leads us away from God, it is deception, not reality. Immediately after discussing false prophets, the *pesukim* bring another example where our "eyes" can lead us astray, namely in the case of a relative or friend who tries to convince us to follow other gods. The Torah warns us that not only are we not allowed to listen to or follow him, we cannot even empathize with him: despite our close relationship with that relative or friend, we are commanded that "our *eyes* should not have pity on him" (Devarim 13:9).

As much as we may think we see everything accurately, we often miss important information or see things that are not actually true. The message of *Parshat Re'eh* is to acknowledge the limitations of our own perception, and that instead we should rely on the wisdom and vision of God and His Torah.

There Is No "I" in Happy

If you want to be happy, should you focus on yourself or on others? In a study entitled *Do Unto Others or Treat Yourself? The Effects of Prosocial and Self-Focused Behavior on Psychological Flourishing*, Katherine Nelson and colleagues showed that doing acts of kindness for others, or for the world at large, did more to achieve an elevated mood and increased well-being than doing acts of kindness for oneself. These results align with previous research that indicates that spending money on others increases levels of happiness more than spending money on oneself. These findings stand in contrast to the more popular conception that in order to be happy, one should focus on self-care.

One of my favorite stories concerns Rabbi Jonathan Sacks retelling what he heard about the Lubavitcher Rebbe. Someone had written to the Rebbe, "I am depressed. I am lonely. I keep *mitzvot* but find no peace of mind. I need the Rebbe's help." The Rebbe's only response to the letter was to just circle the first word of every sentence: "I."

The word *simchah*, which can be roughly translated as "happiness" or "joy," appears seven times in *Parshat Re'eh*. Fascinatingly, in each of the seven times, the *simchah* occurs in relation to others. The individual does not rejoice by himself, but with his family, servants, Levites, strangers, orphans, and widows (see Devarim 12:7, 12:12, 12:18, 14:26, 16:11, 16:14, and 16:15). Rabbi Sacks calls this happiness shared, or collective joy (*Covenant and Conversation: Deuteronomy*, pp. 125–129). When we rejoice, it is with others present and others in mind. We share the happiness with these others. There is no "I" in happy and there is no "I" in joy.

Yet there is another pattern among the seven mentions of the word *simchah*. Not only is *simchah* presented in relation to others, but as Rabbi Joseph B. Soloveitchik highlights, it is also connected to being *lifnei Hashem*, before God (see *Nefesh Harav*, pp. 314–315). Being in the presence of God both necessitates and generates feelings of joy. The experience of transcending the self and encountering the Divine provides a framework for true *simchah*.

This explains the commandment to be happy on the Three Festivals when everyone would visit the *Beit HaMikdash*, the place where the Divine Presence rested. It is also the reason why the *Kohen Gadol*, who was in the presence of God every day, had a continuous obligation to be happy. Rabbi Soloveitchik develops the idea further, explaining that there is a commandment to be happy on Rosh Hashanah and Yom Kippur as well, since those are both days where we attain spiritual closeness to God.

It is striking that happiness appears exclusively in the context of the other. Happiness is experienced when we stand before God, and when it is shared with other people. Focusing exclusively on the "I" to boost happiness will inevitably fail to make us happy. Rather, if we want to enhance our experience of *simchah*, we should look for opportunities to help others and strive to become closer to God.

Parshat Shoftim

Better than Average

How would you rate your driving ability? What about your intelligence? Memory? Popularity? Honesty? Personality?

Research on the better-than-average-effect demonstrates that most people rate themselves as being higher than average across a wide-range of skills, intelligence, and personality characteristics (including the ones mentioned in the above questions), even though it is statistically impossible for a majority of people to be above-average in any particular area. Behind these findings is the theory that most of us have a self-enhancement bias, meaning that we are prone to interpret the world in a way that makes us feel better about ourselves, even if it is plainly not true. We even have a bias that assumes that we are less biased than the average person!

While discussing related concepts in his book *The Happiness Hypothesis*, social psychologist Jonathan Haidt uses a metaphor of "the inner lawyer" to describe these tendencies. It is like we each have an attorney inside our heads whose job it is to always defend ourselves against any possibility of fault.

In the Jewish spiritual-ethical Mussar literature, we are called upon to overcome these biased tendencies, which are detrimental to the trait of humility and disregard the values of truth and honesty. They can also negatively impact our relationships with others and with God.

In the beginning of *Parshat Shoftim*, Moshe outlines a robust system of governance to ensure justice: "You shall set up judges and law enforcement officials for yourself in all your cities...and they shall judge the people with righteous judgment" (Devarim 16:18). Some commentators notice a superfluous word in the verse. The Torah could just have commanded us to set up judges and officials in all your cities, but instead it adds the word *lecha*, "for yourself." What added meaning can be deduced from emphasizing that the judges and officials are "for yourself"?

Rabbi Moshe Feinstein suggests that the "for yourself" transforms the message from being one exclusively about governance and community, to a personalized message about the inner life of each individual. We are all called upon to be our own inner judges, to ensure that our actions are proper. We should also be our own law-enforcement officials to make sure that we follow through on the proper course of action.

The subsequent commands that seem to be speaking directly to judges, now apply to all of us personally, when judging ourselves. We should "not judge unfairly," "show favoritism," or "take a bribe" (Devarim 16:19) in the evaluation of our own selves. In a direct reversal of the self-enhancement bias and the above-average effect, Rabbi Feinstein suggests that even if we are in reality Torah scholars or righteous people, we should not assume that what we are doing is virtuous. Rather, we should view ourselves as simple and average people and judge ourselves accordingly.

Our inner lawyers can be very good at their jobs, effectively justifying our self-enhanced beliefs, defending us against seeing our faults, and making us seem better to ourselves than we are in reality. We are called upon to counterbalance the defense attorneys with fair, righteous, and honest judges, who can help us ground our beliefs about ourselves in truth and reality. Doing so will help us stay appropriately self-aware, allowing us to improve and grow, and become more righteous individuals.

Deep Work

In his best-selling book, *Deep Work: Rules for Focused Success in a Distracted World*, Dr. Cal Newport makes a strong case for the essentiality of securing time and energy to focus without distraction on cognitively demanding tasks. He goes so far to call this ability a super-power, as it will make us more productive and impactful in life and at work, as well as provide a sense of meaning and satisfaction. Yet, because of the incessant pull to be distracted, most of us don't prioritize deep work, and instead fill our schedules and routines with busywork that keeps our attention floating on the surface.

In *Parshat Shoftim*, the king is commanded that he should have a copy of the Torah with him and that he should read from it every day in order that he would learn to revere God and observe all the laws of the Torah (Devarim 17:18–19). In a powerful speech delivered in 1971 to the students of the Mirrer Yeshiva in Jerusalem before their summer break, Rabbi Chaim Shmuelevitz uses this verse as a springboard to discuss the importance of deep work and not getting distracted. He quotes Rabbi Moshe Chaim Luzzato, who writes in *Mesillat Yesharim* (chapter 25), that the fact that the king had to carry this Torah with him and read it with him every day "teaches that reverence is only learned by uninterrupted study." Distraction is the enemy of both growth in character as well as success in learning. Rabbi Shmuelevitz laments the plateauing of achievement in the yeshiva and attributes it to the prevalence of distraction which obstructs the possibility of true greatness. If that was true in the Mir in 1971, all the more so 50 years later, with all of the technological advancements that constantly vie for our already depleted attention.

The dangers of distraction are evident in another aspect of *Parshat Shoftim*. Before troops were led into battle, the officials announced (Devarim 20:5), "Who is the man that has built a new house and has not inhabited it? Let him go and return to his house, lest he die in the war and another man inhabit it." And the same instructions were given to those who planted a vineyard and had not redeemed it, and to someone who was engaged, but not yet married. At first glance, these seem to be relatively weak excuses for not being able to fight in the war. Why do these cases warrant exemptions?

Rashi comments that the thought that someone else may finish the task causes psychological anguish. Chizkuni elaborates that his whole heart and desire will be to finish the job that he started, and he will therefore not be able to concentrate appropriately to the task at hand. His distracted self will be a risk during battle and have dramatic consequences for the entire army. Being in battle requires deep work and concentration. Any distraction will have disastrous consequences.

If we want to be successful in our learning, our careers, or our personal growth, we need to learn how to be fully absorbed in the task at hand. If we are consistently distracted and only addressing surface level ideas, we will have a hard time making any meaningful progress. In a reality where many of us have multiple responsibilities driving us in different directions, compounded with even more technological distractions, it has become even more important to carve out time and space for deep work.

Parshat Ki Teitzei

The Ben Franklin Effect

In his autobiography, Benjamin Franklin describes his poor relationship with a rival legislator. Franklin devised what may seem to be a counter-intuitive plan to win him over. Knowing that this rival had a rare book in his library, Franklin sent him a message requesting that the legislator lend him the book for a few days, and returned the book with a thank you note a week later. Subsequently, the man who until then had never spoken to Franklin treated him with great civility, and they kindled a friendship which lasted the rest of their lives. The lesson from this story became known in the psychological literature as the Ben Franklin Effect. First studied in the 1960s by Jon Jecker and David Landry, the Ben Franklin Effect demonstrates that a benefactor who does a favor for another person is likely to increase positive feelings towards the person he is benefiting, even if the benefactor did not initially like the other person.

Psychologists hypothesize that this phenomenon is an example of cognitive dissonance. We tend to dislike having competing conceptions of ourselves in our minds, so we generally try to resolve perceived differences. On the one hand, it does not make sense to help someone I don't like, yet on the other hand, I helped this person who I thought I didn't like. This type of dissonance will lead me to resolve the conflict by reasoning that I actually do like the person.

If we pay close attention to the laws Moshe Rabbeinu repeats in *Sefer Devarim*, we will notice discrepancies between the formulation of these laws in Devarim as compared to previous presentations. In *Parshat Ki Teitzei* the law regarding helping a fallen animal on the road states, "If you see your fellow's donkey or ox fallen on the road, do not ignore it; you must help him raise it" (Devarim 22:4). Yet in *Parshat Mishpatim* the same law reads as follows: "When you see the donkey of your enemy lying under its burden and would refrain from raising it, you must nevertheless raise it with him" (Shemot 23:5). While there is more than one difference between the two sources, the most glaring one, which the commentators address, is the shift from the animal belonging to one's enemy ("*sonaacha*") to belonging to one's fellow ("*achicha*"). Why does the law change the owner of the donkey from enemy to friend?

Rabbi Meir Simcha of Dvinsk, in his commentary *Meshech Chochmah*, suggests a chronological answer. Something significant happened in between the presentation in *Parshat Mishpatim* where it says "enemy" and *Parshat Ki Teitzei* where it says "fellow": namely, the sin of the golden calf. To make his point, Rabbi Meir Simcha first references the Gemara in *Pesachim* (113a) which is bothered by the use of the term *sonaacha*, "enemy" or "hated one," used in *Parshat Mishpatim*. Doesn't the Torah in *Parshat Kedoshim* (Vayikra 19:17) prohibit us from hating each other? The Gemara answers that there is an exception to the rule. One is allowed, and perhaps even obligated, to hate someone who has transgressed a commandment. Rabbi Meir Simcha boldly limits this statement, arguing that it only applied before *Bnei Yisrael* sinned with the golden calf. Afterwards, we all became spiritually flawed and limited. Only someone who is pure and virtuous would be allowed to feel righteous indignation towards those that have sinned. After the sin of the golden calf, nobody could reach such a status; hence everyone should be considered brethren. Therefore, the law in *Parshat Ki Teitzei* switches from speaking of the owner of the donkey as "enemy" to "fellow," because fellow Jews can no longer be termed enemies.

Rabbeinu Bachya suggests a different reason for the transition from enemy to friend. He writes that the Torah is suggesting a strategy to transform someone from an enemy to a friend. If there is someone that you do not like, and you go out of your way to help him, you will come to like him. By doing him a favor, you will become his friend. In other words, the change of words from "enemy" to "fellow" hints at the Ben Franklin Effect.

If we would like to decrease the amount of strife and hatred in our lives, we would do well to internalize these messages. First, we should realize that there is a limited number of acceptable justifications for hating someone. Second, if we have strong negative feelings towards other people, we should consider doing them a favor. By acting kindly towards them, we can alter our own perceptions and repair or enhance the relationship, transforming them from *sonaacha* to *achicha*.

Remembering & Forgetting

In the late 19th century, Hermann Ebbinghaus conducted a pioneering experiment on himself, in which he tracked how well he could memorize nonsense syllables. Based on the results, Ebbinghaus developed what he referred to as the "forgetting curve," which is the rate at which people forget information over time if they make no attempt to retain it. The sharpest decline in memory occurs within the first twenty minutes of acquiring the information, which then continues to decline rapidly over the first hour. More recently, in his book *The Seven Sins of Memory: How the Mind Forgets and Remembers*, Professor Daniel Schacter codifies the forgetting that occurs with the passage of time, which he labels *transience*. One way to overcome transience, or the forgetting curve, is by "spaced learning." By relearning the material after some time has elapsed, the rate of forgetting decreases.

The themes of remembering and forgetting recur throughout *Parshat Ki Teitzei*, perhaps most famously when we are commanded, "Remember what Amalek did to you on your journey, after you left Egypt... Do not forget!" (Devarim 25:17–19). What are the parameters and guidelines for fulfilling this commandment? How should we remember, and how do we ensure we do not forget?

Rambam explains this mitzvah, writing that it is a "positive commandment to constantly remember their evil deeds" (*Hilchot Melachim* 5:5). Notwithstanding Rambam's insertion of the concept of "constantly," *Sefer HaChinuch* (Mitzvah 603) notes that there is no indication in the Torah or the Talmud as to how often one should perform this commandment. In the absence of any such regulation, he suggests fulfilling the mitzvah every one to three years. *Chatam Sofer* suggests that the mitzvah must be fulfilled once a year, because the Talmud indicates that memories generally last for twelve months (see *Berachot* 58a). While the Sages debate the exact details of how frequently we need to fulfil this mitzvah by actively remembering, it is clear that without spaced re-learning, transience will cause us to forget Amalek's acts.

The second of Professor Schacter's "Sins of Memory" is absentmindedness, or a lapse in attention that results in memory failure. We generally regard absentmindedness as something negative, as a "sin" that gets in the way of our goals. It is religiously and morally valuable to remember to perform worthy tasks, such as *mitzvot*, and to be mindful to avoid negative actions.

However, there is a commandment in *Parshat Ki Teitzei* that redeems absentmindedness and forgetfulness – *shechichah*. The verse states, "When you reap the harvest in your field and overlook a sheaf in the field, do not turn back to get it; it shall go to the stranger, the fatherless, and the widow – in order that the Lord your God may bless you in all your undertakings" (Devarim 24:19). Although overcoming failures of memory is generally essential for maintaining a religious lifestyle, there seems to be a value placed here on forgetfulness. How are we to distinguish between when to actively remember and when to forget? Perhaps, absentmindedness and forgetfulness are valued, as they are with *shechichah*, when they decrease meticulousness about one's own possessions and lead to benefiting others. Forgetting our own material goods for the sake of helping others is beneficial. Extrapolating to a similar scenario, perhaps forgiving and forgetting a slight to our ego made by another, can likewise have redemptive value.

For the most part, we are called on to counter transience with spaced learning and repetition, making sure to be mindful of our values, beliefs, and obligations. When our forgetfulness can help others, however, we can allow transience to take its normal course. May we merit to properly use both remembering and forgetting in the service of God and others.

Parshat Ki Tavo

Healthy Happiness

Our emotional experiences sometimes seem to come out of nowhere. When we try to understand what caused a certain emotion, we are sometimes left with more questions than answers. Various theories try to explain how and why we experience emotions. One such approach, which is gaining popularity in the field, is referred to as the "cognitive theory" of emotions. This theory posits that emotions are generally based on appraisals of reality, and are tied to goals: Positive emotions, such as happiness, derive from an assessment, either conscious or unconscious, of moving towards a goal, while negative emotions, such as sadness or regret, arise when a goal is blocked.

Parshat Ki Tavo presents a long list of curses which could befall *Bnei Yisrael*. The Torah tells us that these curses will befall them "Because you did not serve the Lord your God with joy and with goodness of heart when you had an abundance of all" (Devarim 28:47). Rabbeinu Bachya and others understand this as highlighting the essential element of joy that should be present when serving God. Being happy is a vital and necessary component of performing *mitzvot*. This can be understood from a cognitive perspective: being happy when following the Torah signals that our appraisal and goal systems are aligned with God's will.

Yet, there are two strong arguments against such an understanding of the *pasuk*. First, as Rabbi Moshe Alshich contends, it does not accord with the broader explanation for the curses that permeate the chapter. Namely, that *Bnei Yisrael* would be punished for not serving God at all, and not for serving Him with insufficient joy. Second, the portended punishment does not seem to fit the crime. If *Bnei Yisrael* keep all the *mitzvot*, but are just not happy while doing so, do they really deserve such harsh curses?

Rabbi Meir Simcha of Dvinsk understands the issue differently, perhaps because of these questions. The Torah is not indicating that they will be punished for not serving God with joy, as Rabbeinu Bachya insisted. Rather, the punishment will come because they were not serving God at all. Joy is mentioned in the verse not as a qualifier of how they were serving God, but as an explanation for why they were not serving God. Because they were happy and enjoying material wealth, they did not serve God. The *pasuk* is explaining that *Bnei Yisrael*'s abundance of physical good would fill them with joy and happiness, and this abundance would lead them to stop serving God. In a similar vein, Rabbi Yaakov Yitzchak of Peshischa also argues that not only would *Bnei Yisrael* not serve God at all, but they would enjoy not doing so. The fact that they would enjoy a lifestyle not aligned with God's will demonstrates that their goals and appraisals are distorted and misplaced.

Commenting on the joy *Bnei Yisrael* experienced while sinning with the golden calf, Rabbi Moshe Alshich argues that it is one thing to violate commandments, but it is much worse to be happy about it. Ideally, he writes, by referencing the aforementioned *pasuk*, we should serve God with joy. If we sin, the proper emotional response should be sadness and regret. Our goal is to serve God, and when we do, we should experience positive emotions. If we fail in our goal, we should experience a healthy dose of negative emotions, which should motivate us to fix the problem. Someone who is happy when sinning has no chance of repenting.

As we continue to traverse the month of Elul and progress towards the Yamim Noraim, we would do well to reflect on our goals, and make sure they are aligned with what God is asking of us. If they are not, we should feel a healthy amount of sadness and regret that should motivate us to try harder and improve our relationship with God. If they are, we should experience joy and happiness knowing that we are living a life of Torah and *mitzvot*.

Appreciating Blessings

The best strategy to improve one's overall happiness levels is to work on inculcating the trait of gratitude. In the psychological literature, gratitude is consistently correlated with happiness. Additionally, working on gratitude through various interventions, such as actively counting your blessings in a journal, has been shown to boost happiness levels. In addition to merely demonstrating the connection between gratitude and happiness, researchers also seek to understand *why* there is a connection. What is it about gratitude that increases happiness? In one of the most important articles on the subject (*Counting Blessings Versus Burdens*), researchers Robert Emmons and Michael McCullough hypothesize that responding gratefully to life's circumstances allows people to "positively interpret everyday experiences," and that well-being and happiness come from "the ability to notice, appreciate, and savor the elements of one's life" (p. 378).

Moshe describes the blessings we will enjoy if we obey God, and states, "All these blessings will come upon you (*u-vau alecha*) and will reach you (*ve-hisigucha*)" (Devarim 28:2). The seeming redundancy within the verse troubles many commentators. What is the added benefit of a blessing "reaching" someone, if it has already "come upon" them? Rabbi Yissocher Frand, quoting Rabbi Elyakim Schlessinger, explains that blessings might "come upon" us, but we may not realize it. Our lives may be filled with blessings, but if we do not develop an attitude of awareness and appreciation, those blessings may not "reach" us. The blessings are there, we just need to notice them.

One of the reasons that we may have trouble noticing blessings is that there is a human tendency to always want more. The Torah sets forth the confession that accompanies the bringing of the first fruits to the Temple, and then concludes: "You shall rejoice with all the good (*ve-samachta be-chol ha-tov*) that the Lord, your God, gave you and your household" (Devarim 26:11). Rabbi Mordechai Gifter (*Pirkei Torah*) understands the rejoicing not as a description, but as a commandment. We are commanded to be satisfied, appreciate the good, and be happy. We have a natural proclivity to downplay the blessings of the harvest, so we need a religious imperative to motivate us to overcome that tendency.

Subjective interpretation of events does not just apply to blessings, but plays a part in understanding the curses as well. One particularly ominous verse outlines three elements related to fear: "(1) And your life shall hang in doubt before you; (2) and you shall fear night and day, (3) and you shall have no assurance of your life" (Devarim 28:66). The Talmud (*Menachot* 103b) interprets the three parts of this verse as representing three approaches that may lead people to acquire food before they need it: (1) people who buy grain in one year to last them through the next because they are not certain they will find enough grain to eat throughout the year, (2) people who purchase grain every Friday for the entire week, because they are not sure they will have enough money to buy for the rest of the week, and (3) people who rely on the baker to give them bread because they have no grain of their own. Rabbi Chaim Shmuelevitz (*Sichot Mussar*) references this teaching to demonstrate the subjectivity of the experience of the curse and the subsequent accompanying fear and anxiety. If we have enough to satisfy our current need, our worries should be allayed. But if we are obsessed about next week or overly concerned about next year, then we can subjectively create our own curse through self-imposed mental anguish.

Our lives are filled with both blessings and curses, pleasantries and hardships, positive and negative experiences. It is up to us to determine the subjective experience of the blessings and curses. Let us choose to approach what we are given with appreciation and gratitude, counting our blessings and being thankful to God for the good He has bestowed upon us.

Parshiyot
Nitzavim-Vayeilech

Benefit Finding

Moshe Rabbeinu predicts that *Bnei Yisrael* will turn away from God, and consequently they will be punished and exiled. Following this, he pronounces that they will eventually deteriorate to such a degree that they will mend their ways. After hitting rock bottom, *Bnei Yisrael* will repent and be returned to the land. Yet, in introducing this turn of events, Moshe adds a word that seems to contradict his message: "When all these things befall you, the blessing and the curse that I have set before you, and you take them to heart... and you will return to the Lord your God..." (Devarim 30:1–2). The broader context of Moshe's speech is that the curse will serve as catalyst for repentance. If so, why does Moshe mention the blessing as well?

Ktav Sofer, amidst a broader historical analysis of the fate of the Jewish people, suggests that the Torah is offering a deep psychological insight here. The impact of the curse is amplified by the fact that *Bnei Yisrael* had previously experienced blessing. Pain and suffering are intensified when they are preceded by joy and comfort. By referencing the blessing, the Torah is making the curse even harder to bear.

In a more hopeful explanation, *Or HaChaim* suggests that the *pasuk* is presenting alternative options to spark repentance. Ideally, we would strive to improve our ways during times of blessing. If we do not, then the less desirable option, is to repent after experiencing the curses.

Or HaChaim presents another answer, and this one contains deep theological implications. The Mishnah (*Berachot* 9:5) states that a person should recite a blessing when experiencing a calamity, just as he would when enjoying good fortune. Rava explains (*Berachot* 60b) that even though the content of the blessing for positive occurrences is different than the one for negative ones, the general mindset while making both types of blessings should be the same; namely, they should be said with the same resolve. *Or HaChaim* suggests that when Moshe combines the blessings and the curses together, he is teaching us that we should view the curses from the same perspective as the blessings. Malbim adds that the curse is a "gift" just like the blessing, as it causes *Bnei Yisrael* to repent and create an optimal spiritual life in the Land of Israel.

It is not always easy to apply this concept. If someone is experiencing intense pain, whether physical or emotional, it is rarely appropriate or helpful for another person to bluntly suggest that the person who is suffering perceive the situation as a blessing. Yet, tremendous spiritual and psychological benefits can accrue to people who perceive their own anguish in a more positive light, whether through their own introspection or with the help and support of a close friend or therapist. In the psychological literature, the concept of experiencing positive effects after traumatic events is often referred to as "post-traumatic growth" or as "benefit finding." People who have survived traumatic events such as cancer, violence, sexual assault, natural disasters, and chronic pain, can benefit greatly from their ability to find a positive facet of their suffering. This is not to say that it is better to have experienced trauma than to not have, but that there is value in attempting to process the trauma in a way that can lead to psychological growth.

Internalizing this message can be incredibly difficult, and sometimes just as painful and arduous as the actual suffering. Yet, we can attain spiritual and psychological benefits by seeing the blessing within a curse. Ideally, we hope to not have to be confronted with such challenges. May we be blessed with a year of positivity, in which our greatest challenge should be the opportunity to see the blessing within a blessing.

There Is Always Hope

The biggest impediment to change is not believing that change is possible. The first stage in Drs. James Prochaska and Carlos DiClemente's Stages of Change Theory is precontemplation, meaning that the person is not even contemplating the possibility that they should change. People in this stage are actively resistant to change, often as a result of failed attempts to change which resulted in continual disappointments. "Some precontemplators are so demoralized," they write, "that they are resigned to remaining in a situation they consider their 'fate'" (1994, p. 75). Once they give up, their initial problem usually spirals, putting them in an even worse condition than before. Not believing in our ability to change leads us to get trapped in our ways.

The curses that Moshe delineated in *Parshat Ki Tavo* were meant to serve as deterrents to abandoning God and turning to other gods. In *Parshat Nitzavim*, Moshe addresses a subtype of individuals who may hear the threat of curses but react with indifference: "When such a one hears the words of these sanctions, he may fancy himself immune, thinking, 'I shall be safe, though I follow my own willful heart'" (Devarim 29:18). Rabbi Norman Lamm (*Derashot Ledorot: Deuteronomy*, pp. 109–113) identifies two streams of thought within the Aramaic translations of this verse, each pointing to a different possible explanation for why someone would ignore such warnings.

The first stream, which he calls "Immunity Theory," is based on Targum Onkelos, and is elucidated by Rashi. This explanation indicates a person who is obstinate, and confident that he will not be harmed by the curses. He believes he could act immorally and will not get caught. He considers himself above the law, and is thus impervious to its consequences. The second stream – what Rabbi Lamm deems the more common explanation – is based on Targum Yonatan and is what Rabbi Lamm calls "Despair Theory." The person acts not out of arrogance, but out of hopelessness. He does not believe in his own ability to change. The evil inclination has him bound to repeat his behaviors. As is taught by the great Chasidic masters, and later echoed by Prochaska and DiClemente, this despair will lead to even more sin.

The concept of *teshuvah*, which is a recurring motif in *Parshat Nitzavim*, serves as the antidote to this type of despair. Repentance "is not too baffling for you, nor is it beyond reach... it is not in the heavens... [n]either is it beyond the sea...Rather it is very close to you, in your mouth and in your heart, to observe it" (Devarim 30:12–14, according to Ramban). While it is not always easy, *teshuvah* is always an option. Nothing, our Sages tell us, could impede repentance. Even the apostate Elisha ben Avuyah (known as Acher), who heard a Heavenly voice saying that "everyone can return except for Acher," should have realized that even he could still return (*The Rav Speaks*, pp. 193–199). There is always hope.

Rabbi Baruch Simon (*Imrei Baruch: Devarim*, pp. 261–267) locates this idea within the first two verses of the *parsha* as well. Everyone, we are told, stood before God. This included "your tribal heads, your elders and your officials, all the men of Israel, your children, your wives, even the stranger within your camp, from woodchopper to water-drawer" (Devarim 29:9–10). Moshe goes out of his way to describe the different types of individuals present, which highlights the importance of realizing that everyone is unique, and everyone has a role to play. While we should never underestimate what our fellow can accomplish, we should be sure not to minimize our own capabilities either. We should never degrade our own abilities. Even if we have stumbled in the past, Rabbi Simon writes, we are forbidden to lose faith in ourselves. We must always believe in our ability to improve.

The goal of Elul is to help us move from being precontemplators about our flaws to being contemplators. We should minimally be thinking that change is possible and that we could theoretically work on ourselves. To the extent that we have bad habits or behaviors that we have given up on changing, it is imperative that we shake ourselves out of this despair. We must believe that there is always hope. Nothing can stand in the way of repentance.

Parshat Haazinu

Defying Death with Life

In his 1973 Pulitzer Prize winning book *The Denial of Death*, anthropologist Ernest Becker argued that subconsciously, we are so terrified of death, that everything we do, without even necessarily being aware of it, is in some way an attempt to deny the fact that we will eventually die. Based on Becker's work, psychologists Jeff Greenberg, Sheldon Solomon, and Tom Pyszczynski formulated what they call Terror Management Theory (TMT). Their goal was to demonstrate, through research, that we behave differently when reminded, either subtly or explicitly, of death-related concepts. Researchers conducted hundreds of TMT studies, many of which were carried out near funeral homes and cemeteries. One of the primary results of these studies is that when we are reminded of death, we manage the anxiety that comes along with such "terror" by thinking and behaving in ways that build self-esteem and encourage us to invest in our value system.

In *Parshat Haazinu*, Moshe prophesizes the misdeeds that *Bnei Yisrael* are foreseen to commit and the punishment that will ensue. He laments, "if they were to be wise, they would understand this; they would reflect upon their fate [*yavinu acharitam*]" (Devarim 32:29). The simple meaning of this *pasuk* is that if *Bnei Yisrael* would be aware and mindful of the heavy costs their actions will engender, they would choose the course of their behavior more wisely. Rabbi Simcha Zissel Ziv, known as the Alter of Kelm, adds an additional level of interpretation in his work *Chochmah U'Mussar* (1:35). He says that they should reflect upon their ultimate fate (*acharitam*), namely, death. As Rabbi Eliezer (*Shabbat* 153a) recommends we should repent every day, because nobody knows when they will die. Rabbi Ziv implores us to constantly be conscious of our eventual demise.

This can cause us to be more aware of our actions and motivate us to live a life based on our ultimate values.

In a captivating address launching the publication of the *Koren Sacks Sukkot Machzor*, Rabbi Jonathan Sacks suggests that this is the core message of Kohelet. The most prominent word in Kohelet is *hevel*, which Rabbi Sacks translates not as "futile" or "vanity" as do most commentators, but as a "shallow" or "fleeting breath." The theme of the book is that while we may accomplish and accumulate a lot in this world, we are all essentially a breath away from death. The first person to die in Tanach is Hevel, who is killed by his brother Kayin. Kayin's name derives from the concept of acquisition. Many people acquire goods in order to assuage the anxiety brought about by the fragility of life. But material acquisition, Shlomo HaMelech contends, is not the way to confront the existential anxiety. The true way to defeat the terror that comes from the awareness of death is through *simchah* – by living in the moment, and by being mindful of and enjoying what we are given and can experience in the present, despite the transience of the present moment. This coheres, Rabbi Sacks argues, with the message of the holiday of Sukkot as well. A Sukkah, by definition, is a temporary structure. The mitzvah of *simchah* on Sukkot encourages us to rejoice in the temporary and in the insecurity.

When confronted by the inevitability of death, our response should not be to suppress the possibility or to be overly anxious about it. We would be wise to *yavinu acharitam* – reflect upon our eventual fate. This should motivate us to maximize our time, continually improve, and live a life guided by Torah and *mitzvot*. Finally, we should practice being mindful, enjoying the *simchah* that living in the present affords us.

Twisted Thinking

Who is responsible for our pain and suffering? In *Parshat Haazinu* Moshe tells *Bnei Yisrael* that God "is perfect and just. He is without iniquity; He is righteous and upright. Destructiveness does not come from Him. The blemishes belong to His children, who are a warped and twisted generation" (Devarim 32:4–5). Rambam (*Moreh Nevuchim* 3:12), based on these verses, argues that we are responsible for our own suffering;

> Individual persons are exposed to numerous evils, which can be traced to the defects existing in the persons themselves. We complain and seek relief from our own faults: we suffer from the evils which we, by our own free will, inflict on ourselves, and ascribe these evils to God, who is far from being connected with them.

It is true that we do not fully understand God's ways. Sometimes bad things happen to good people, and we cannot explain why. But that does not detract from the fact that there are examples where suffering is both justifiable and explainable, even without the concept of Divine punishment. Often there are natural, negative consequences to our actions for which we cannot blame God, as they fall squarely within our own responsibility.

Rabbi Dr. Abraham J. Twerski (*Twerski on Chumash*, p. 438) connects the concept of a "warped and twisted generation" to the warped and twisted thinking he often encountered in his work with alcoholics. While alcoholics often think they are being logical, there are so many holes and distortions within their thinking that lead to harmful behaviors. For instance, an alcoholic can refuse to go to an Alcoholics Anonymous meeting because he is afraid to be exposed as an alcoholic, but has no problem drinking, becoming intoxicated, and acting foolishly in public.

This kind of thinking is not just endemic to alcoholics. We all have warped and twisted thinking at times. Cognitive therapists have identified many cognitive distortions and thinking errors that cause mental distress and lead to harmful behaviors. For example, "control fallacies" can manifest as the belief that we have absolutely no control over our lives, which is not accurate. Perhaps these verses allude to the subset of people who claim they have no control over their troubles, placing the burden directly in God's hands. Moshe's message is that we have more control than we think. We bear the burden and responsibility of changing our fate.

Another cognitive distortion that is related to these verses is termed "labeling," which is the tendency to reduce ourselves or others to a single negative characteristic or description. The Netziv assumes that the "warped and twisted generation" is referencing the people who lived at the time of the destruction of the Second Temple. These people were learned and driven by holy causes, yet their actions were perverted. Their perverseness stemmed from the fact that they judged anyone who transgressed to be a Sadducee, traitor, or heretic. By engaging in this act of "labeling," seemingly righteous people were led to de-humanize those around them which they used to justify "bloodshed for the sake of heaven." This type of stereotyping and behavior stands in stark contrast to our Patriarchs' behavior which was straight and upright, not warped or twisted. They were able to treat even idolaters with favor and love.

While we will not always understand God's ways, if we reflect on our actions and are honest with ourselves, we will recognize that there are things that go wrong in our lives and communities which can be traced back to our own thoughts and behaviors. If we can identify and change our warped and twisted approaches, we can hopefully progress toward more happy, fulfilling, and spiritual lives.

Parshat Vezot Haberachah

Buying Happiness

Can money buy happiness? Psychologists and economists have conducted many studies to answer this complex question, and the answer, in short, is maybe. More precisely, it depends how we define "money," "buy," and "happiness." In a 2010 landmark study, Drs. Daniel Kahneman and Angus Deaton distinguished between everyday experiences of happiness and a broader evaluation of life satisfaction, and found that in terms of broader life satisfaction, money was – up to a point – positively correlated with satisfaction. Beyond an annual income of around $75,000, there was no connection between money and happiness. A more recent (2021) study by Dr. Matthew Killingsworth utilized technological advances to design a more robust study, and found, in contrast to Kahneman and Deaton, that even above the $75,000 threshold, everyday happiness increased with the amount of money earned.

Drs. Elizabeth Dunn, Daniel Gilbert, and Timothy Wilson focused, not on how much people earn, but on how people spend their money. Their findings show that money is more likely to buy happiness if: (1) it is spent on experiences rather than on material goods, and (2) if it is used to benefit others, rather than oneself.

A comprehensive analysis of the nuances of the Torah's approach to money and happiness would require an extensive study of excerpts from Mishlei, Kohelet, *Pirkei Avot*, the Talmud, and later commentaries. In brief, these sources suggest that the unabashed pursuit of money for its own sake would have an adverse effect on both our spiritual and psychological lives. Given the above, there is a verse in *Parshat Vezot HaBerachah* that requires some further analysis. As part of his final address to *Bnei Yisrael*, Moshe bestows a unique blessing on each of the tribes. The tribe of Zevulun, who is known for business pursuits, is told to "Rejoice Zevulun in your departures" (Devarim 33:18). What aspect of their business activities is Moshe encouraging them to enjoy?

One answer could be that Moshe is speaking of the happiness that comes from the way in which they spent their money, and not of the intrinsic enjoyment of earning a livelihood. The Midrash (*Bereishit Rabbah* 99:9), quoted by Rashi, asserts that the people of Zevulun would share their profits with Yissachar, affording Yissachar the opportunity to learn Torah. Thus, *Or HaChaim* contends, their joy stems from the knowledge that their money is spent in support of Torah study. Furthering this theme, that joy is connected to the way in which they spend their money, the next verse states that "[t]hey invite people to the mountain, where they will offer sacrifices of success" (Devarim 33:19). One could argue that happiness is directly tied to hosting guests, especially in the context of bringing sacrifices to God. Happiness comes by spending money on spiritual experiences, specifically ones that benefit others.

Abarbanel offers an explanation which may illuminate an additional path to happiness. First, unlike the Midrash, Abarbanel contends that according to the basic reading of the verses, the tribes of Yissachar and Zevulun were both in business together. Zevulun would sail across the seas and import goods, while Yissachar would be "tent-to-tent" salespeople, selling the goods on land. Consequently, the rejoicing which Moshe mentions cannot be interpreted as referring to strictly spiritual pursuits. Rather, according to Abarbanel, Moshe is telling each tribe to rejoice in their distinct business roles, each one befitting their particular personalities. They should each be happy and content with their business pursuits.

Abarbanel's approach is very powerful because he legitimizes the pursuit of a career as a path to spiritually acceptable happiness, without adding the caveat that happiness can only come if the money is used to support Torah. Happiness can and should come through spending money for spiritual experiences and helping others, but one can also feel happy by "enjoying the fruits of your labor" (Tehillim 128:2).

While we may be unable to determine whether money can always buy happiness, these studies and commentaries provide a basic blueprint for approaching the question. Earning money through a profession that provides meaning and matches our personalities and skill sets, along with spending money on spiritual experiences that specifically benefit others, are paths that lead us to relate to money in a psychologically and spiritually healthy way.

Social Comparisons

Most of us tend to compare ourselves with others. In the mid-1950s, psychologist Leon Festinger proposed the "social comparison theory" which maintains that the purpose of this tendency is to provide more accurate self-evaluations, which can then lead to self-enhancement. Sometimes we make downward social comparisons, comparing ourselves to someone who we judge as being less advanced than us in a particular area. At other times we make upward social comparisons, measuring ourselves against people who exceed our own levels. For the most part, we compare ourselves to people who have characteristics similar to our own. If the other person was too far removed from us, the comparison would not provide any meaningful information.

One interesting manifestation of this concept is associated with the ways in which we relate to the stories of our great religious leaders. One approach is to emphasize their transcendent and pristine status, which in turn should garner awe and reverence. In an important passage, Rabbi Samson Raphael Hirsch disagrees with this approach, one which deliberately ignores the flaws of the patriarchs and matriarchs. He writes (Bereishit 12:10) that "The Torah never hides from us the faults, errors, and weaknesses of our great people." This does not diminish from their greatness, but rather, renders them "greater and more instructive." If they were perfect, without struggles of their own, then they would not serve as effective models for us to emulate. In other words, upward social comparison would not be beneficial if we could not relate to our role models.

Yet, there is one context where the Torah explicitly tells us that no comparison can be made. After Moshe's death, the Torah states that "Never again did there arise in Israel a prophet like Moshe, whom God knew face to face" (Devarim 34:10). Moshe cannot serve as a model for those seeking to become prophets, and therefore, the comparison itself is likely to be unhelpful.

Moshe's prophetic status precludes him from being the target of social comparison, which makes the following statement of the Rambam even more powerful. Rambam explains that the concept of free will is crucial, and writes that God does not decree in utero whether a person will be righteous or wicked. Rather, everyone has the capability to shape his or her personality to be good or evil (*Hilchot Teshuva* 5:2). To emphasize this point, he writes that "[e]very person is capable of being as righteous as Moshe Rabbeinu or as wicked as Jeroboam." Remarkably, this formulation is not made explicit in previous Rabbinic literature, and Rambam could have made the same point without invoking Moshe. There seems to be a contradiction between Rambam mentioning Moshe, and the verse which indicates Moshe is beyond comparison.

Rabbi Elchanan Wasserman explains that Rambam must be distinguishing between prophecy, in which we cannot possibly attain the status of Moshe, and righteousness, where every person can reach Moshe's level (*Kovetz Maamarim*, p. 56). While no one can attain Moshe's prophetic status, Rambam deems Moshe a viable option for upward social comparison in terms of righteousness.

Yet, as Rabbi Wasserman notes, it is still rather baffling to say that everyone can be as righteous as Moshe. It seems too high a level to attain. To make the concept slightly more practical and relatable, he notes that Moshe is known as an *eved Hashem*, "a servant of God" (Devarim 34:5). Radak (Yehoshua 1:1) explains that *eved Hashem* means that all his efforts, motivations, and actions were dedicated to God. While this level is difficult to achieve, Rabbi Wasserman contends that anyone can attain it. Rambam did not necessarily mean that everyone can accomplish the same as Moshe, but that everyone could maximize their own moral and spiritual potential by being a servant of God, just as Moshe did on his level.

What emerges from this analysis is that while comparisons can and should be inspirational, it is essential for people to recognize their limits. Not everyone can achieve the same as others in every area of life. We may not have Moshe's potential, but we do have the ability to maximize our own potential. We can view others as role models, but we also need to be firmly rooted in our own self-awareness. Our goals should be aspirational, yet realistic, as we continually strive to improve ourselves. The ultimate goal is to become a servant of God by actualizing our own potential, not by comparing ourselves unrealistically to the accomplishments of others.

Further Reading

Parshat Bereishit

THE ORIGINAL MARSHMALLOW TEST

Ma, F., Zeng, D., Xu, F., Compton, B.J., & Heyman, G.D. (2020). Delay of gratification as reputation management. *Psychological Science, 31*(9), 1174–1182. https://doi.org/10.1177/0956797620939940

Mischel, W., Ebbesen, E.B., & Raskoff Zeiss, A. (1972). Cognitive and attentional mechanisms in delay of gratification. *Journal of Personality and Social Psychology, 21*(2), 204.

Mischel, W. (2014). *The Marshmallow Test: Mastering self-control*. Little, Brown and Co.

Schlam, T.R., Wilson, N.L., Shoda, Y., Mischel, W., & Ayduk, O. (2013). Preschoolers' delay of gratification predicts their body mass 30 years later. *The Journal of Pediatrics, 162*(1), 90–93.

HEALTHY & UNHEALTHY EMOTIONS

Graton, A., & Ric, F. (2017). How guilt leads to reparation? Exploring the processes underlying the effects of guilt. *Motivation & Emotion, 41*(3), 343–352. https://doi.org/10.1007/s11031-017-9612-z

Kashdan, T.B., & Biswas-Diener, R. (2014). *The upside of your dark side: Why being your whole self – not just your "good" self – drives success and fulfillment*. Penguin.

Lickel, B., Kushlev, K., Savalei, V., Matta, S., & Schmader, T. (2014). Shame and the motivation to change the self. *Emotion, 14*(6), 1049–1061. https://doi.org/10.1037/a0038235

Opriş, D., & Macavei, B. (2005). The distinction between functional and dysfunctional negative emotions: An empirical analysis. *Journal of Cognitive & Behavioral Psychotherapies, 5*(2), 181–195.

Parshat Noach

LIVING MERCIFULLY

Hilbrand, S., Coall, D.A., Gerstorf, D., & Hertwig, R. (2017). Caregiving within and beyond the family is associated with lower mortality for the caregiver: A prospective study. *Evolution and Human Behavior, 38*(3), 397–403. https://doi.org/10.1016/j.evolhumbehav.2016.11.010

Hui, B.P.H., Ng, J.C.K., Berzaghi, E., Cunningham-Amos, L.A., & Kogan, A. (2020). Rewards of kindness? A meta-analysis of the link between prosociality and well-being. *Psychological Bulletin, 146*(12), 1084–1116. https://doi.org/10.1037/bul0000298.supp

Kramer, C.K., Mehmood, S., & Suen, R.S. (2019). Dog ownership and survival: A systematic review and meta-analysis. *Circulation: Cardiovascular Quality and Outcomes, 12*(10).

Roth, D.L., Haley, W.E., Hovater, M., Perkins, M., Wadley, V.G., & Judd, S. (2013). Family caregiving and all-cause mortality: Findings from a population-based propensity-matched analysis. *American Journal of Epidemiology, 178*(10), 1571–1578.

THE RIGHT KIND OF PRAISE

Brummelman, E., Crocker, J., & Bushman, B.J. (2016). The praise paradox: When and why praise backfires in children with low self-esteem. *Child Development Perspectives, 10*(2), 111. https://doi.org/10.1111/cdep.12171

Brummelman, E. (Ed.). (2020). *Psychological perspectives on praise.* Routledge. https://doi.org/10.4324/9780429327667

Parshat Lech Lecha

SPIRITUAL GRATITUDE

Emmons, R.A. (2007). *Thanks!: How the new science of gratitude can make you happier.* Houghton Mifflin Harcourt.

Rosmarin, D., Pirutinsky, S., Cohen, A., Galler, Y., & Krumrei, E. (2011). Grateful to God or just plain grateful? A comparison of religious and general gratitude. *Journal of Positive Psychology, 6*(5), 389–396. https://doi.org/10.1080/17439760.2011.596557

Rosmarin, D.H., Pirutinsky, S., Greer, D., & Korbman, M. (2016). Maintaining a grateful disposition in the face of distress: The role of religious coping. *Psychology of Religion and Spirituality, 8*(2), 134–140. https:// yulib002.mc.yu.edu:3180/10.1037/rel0000021

Schimmel, S. (2004). Gratitude in Judaism. In R.A. Emmons & M.E. McCullough (Eds.), *The psychology of gratitude.* (pp. 37–57). Oxford University Press. https://yulib002.mc.yu.edu:3180/10.1093/acprof:oso /9780195150100.003.0003

Schnall, E., Schiffman, M., & Cherniak, A. (2014). Virtues that transcend: Positive psychology in Jewish texts and tradition. In C. Kim-Prieto (Ed.), *Religion and spirituality across cultures.* (Vol. 9, pp. 21–45). Springer Science + Business Media.

RESOLVING CONFLICTS

Gottman, J.M., Coan, J., Carrere, S., & Swanson, C. (1998). Predicting marital happiness and stability from newlywed interactions. *Journal of Marriage and the Family,* 5–22.

Gottman, J.M., & Silver, N. (2015). *The seven principles for making marriage work: A practical guide from the country's foremost relationship expert.* Harmony.

Parshat Vayeira

HEALED BY KINDNESS

Ballard, P.J., Daniel, S.S., Anderson, G., Nicolotti, L., Caballero Quinones, E., Lee, M., & Koehler, A.N. (2021). Incorporating *volunteering into treatment for depression among adolescents: Developmental and clinical considerations. Frontiers in Psychology,* 12, 1581

Kim, E.S., Whillans, A.V., Lee, M.T., Chen, Y., & VanderWeele, T.J. (2020). Volunteering and subsequent health and well-being in older adults: An outcome-wide longitudinal approach. *American Journal of Preventive Medicine,* 59(2), 176–186

Musick, M.A., & Wilson, J. (2003). Volunteering and depression: The role of psychological and social resources in different age groups. *Social Science & Medicine,* 56(2), 259–269. https://doi.org/10.1016/S0277 -9536(02)00025-4

Sneed, R.S., & Cohen, S. (2013). A prospective study of volunteerism and hypertension risk in older adults. *Psychology and Aging,* 28(2), 578–586. https://doi.org/10.1037/a0032718

WORST THINGS FIRST

Ariely, D., & Wertenbroch, K. (2002). Procrastination, deadlines, and performance: Self-control by precommitment. *Psychological Science, 13*(3), 219–224.

Newby-Clark, I. (2010, October 26). *Worst Things First: Three Reasons to Do the Toughest Thing Right Away.* Psychology Today. https://www .psychologytoday.com/za/blog/creatures-habit/201010/worst-things -first-three-reasons-do-the-toughest-thing-right-away?amp

Steel, P. (2007). The nature of procrastination: A meta-analytic and theoretical review of quintessential self-regulatory failure. *Psychological Bulletin, 133*(1), 65.

Steel, P. (2010). *The procrastination equation: How to stop putting things off and start getting stuff done.* Random House Canada.

Parshat Chayei Sarah

SMART CHESED

Conte, E., Grazzani, I., & Pepe, A. (2018). Social cognition, language, and prosocial behaviors: A multitrait mixed-methods study in early childhood. *Early Education and Development, 29*(6), 814–830. https://doi -org.ezproxy.yu.edu/10.1080/10409289.2018.1475820

Eisenberg, N., & Mussen, P. (1989). Cognition, role taking, interpersonal problem solving, and moral judgment. In *The roots of prosocial behavior in children* (Cambridge Studies in Social and Emotional Development, pp. 108–129). Cambridge University Press. doi:10.1017 /CBO9780511571121.009

Eisenberg, N., & Fabes, R.A. (1998). Prosocial development. In W. Damon & N. Eisenberg (Ed.), *Handbook of child psychology: Social, emotional, and personality development* (pp. 701–778). John Wiley & Sons, Inc.

Guo, Q., Sun, P., Cai, M., Zhang, X., & Song, K. (2019). Why are smarter individuals more prosocial? A study on the mediating roles of empathy and moral identity. *Intelligence, 75*, 1–8.

INTELLECT & EMOTION

Bechara, A., Damasio, A.R., Damasio, H., & Anderson, S.W. (1994). Insensitivity to future consequences following damage to human prefrontal cortex. *Cognition, 50*(1–3), 7–15.

Damasio, A.R. (2006). *Descartes' error*. Random House.

Sacks, J. (2015, September 16). *Torah as song (Vayelech 5775)*. https://rabbisacks.org/torah-as-song-vayelech-5775/

Sacks, J. (2017, June 26). *Descartes' error (Chukat 5777)*. https://rabbisacks.org/descartes-error-chukat-5777/

Sacks, J. (2019, April 15). *Thinking fast and slow (Acharei Mot 5779)*. https://rabbisacks.org/thinking-fast-and-slow-acharei-mot-5779/

Parshat Toldot

THE SPACE TO GROW

Bowen, M. (1976). Theory in the practice of psychotherapy. *Family Therapy: Therapy: Theory and Practice*, 4(1), 2–90.

Bowen, M. (1993). *Family therapy in clinical practice*. Jason Aronson.

THE TRUTH ABOUT HONESTY

Ariely, D., & Jones, S. (2012). *The (honest) truth about dishonesty*. New York: Harper Collins Publishers.

Association for Psychological Science. (2016, July 29). *The truth about lying*. https://www.psychologicalscience.org/observer/the-truth-about-lying

Knowledge@Wharton. (2014, September 14). Is every lie 'a sin'? Maybe not. https://knowledge.wharton.upenn.edu/article/when-lying-is-ethical/

Levine, E.E., & Schweitzer, M.E. (2014). Are liars ethical? On the tension between benevolence and honesty. *Journal of Experimental Social Psychology*, 53, 107–117.

Parshat Vayeitzei

BELIEVING IN OUR ABILITIES

Bandura, A. (1982). Self-efficacy mechanism in human agency. *American Psychologist*, 37(2), 122.

Bandura, A. (1997). *Self-efficacy: The exercise of control*. W H Freeman/ Times Books/ Henry Holt & Co.

MAKING TIME FLY

Campbell, L.A., & Bryant, R.A. (2007). How time flies: A study of novice skydivers. *Behaviour Research and Therapy*, 45(6), 1389–1392.

Gable, P.A., & Poole, B.D. (2012). Time flies when you're having approach-motivated fun: Effects of motivational intensity on time perception. *Psychological Science, 23*(8), 879–886.

Wittmann, M. (2016). *Felt time: The psychology of how we perceive time.* Mit Press.

Parshat Vayishlach

WHO IS IN CONTROL?

Lefcourt, H.M. (2014). *Locus of control: Current trends in theory & research.* Psychology Press.

Rotter, J.B. (1966). Generalized expectancies for internal versus external control of reinforcement. *Psychological Monographs: General and Applied, 80*(1), 1–28. https://doi.org/10.1037/h0092976

HEALTHY ANXIETY

Moran, D.J., Bach, P.A., & Batten, S.V. (2018). *Committed action in practice: A clinician's guide to assessing, planning, and supporting change in your client.* New Harbinger Publications.

Myers, D.G. (2004). *Exploring psychology.* Macmillan.

Stein, D.J., & Nesse, R.M. (2015). Normal and abnormal anxiety in the age of DSM-5 and ICD-11. *Emotion Review, 7*(3), 223–229.

Parshat Vayeishev

INFLUENCE TECHNIQUES

Cialdini, R.B., & Goldstein, N.J. (2004). Social influence: Compliance and conformity. *Annual Review of Psychology, 55,* 591–621. https://doi-org.ezproxy.yu.edu/10.1146/annurev.psych.55.090902.142015

Cialdini, R.B. (2021). Influence: The psychology of persuasion (4th edition). *New York: William Morrow.*

Langer, E.J., Blank, A., & Chanowitz, B. (1978). The mindlessness of ostensibly thoughtful action: The role of "placebic" information in interpersonal interaction. *Journal of Personality and Social Psychology, 36*(6), 635.

JEWISH MINDFULNESS

Grossman, P., Niemann, L., Schmidt, S., & Walach, H. (2004). Mindfulness-based stress reduction and health benefits: A meta-analysis. *Journal of Psychosomatic Research* 57(1), 35–43.

Hayes, S.C., Follette, V.M., & Linehan, M. (Eds.). (2004). *Mindfulness and acceptance: Expanding the cognitive-behavioral tradition.* Guilford Press.

Kabat-Zinn, J. (2003). Mindfulness-based interventions in context: Past, present, and future. *Clinical Psychology: Science and Practice,* 10(2), 144–156. https://doi-org.ezproxy.yu.edu/10.1093/clipsy.bpg016

Kabat-Zinn, J. (2009). *Wherever you go, there you are: Mindfulness meditation in everyday life.* Hachette Books.

Parshat Mikeitz

NEED FOR APPROVAL

Harter, S., Stocker, C., & Robinson, N.S. (1996). The perceived directionality of the link between approval and self-worth: The liabilities of a looking glass self-orientation among young adolescents. *Journal of Research on Adolescence.*

Rudolph, K.D., Caldwell, M.S., & Conley, C.S. (2005). Need for approval and children's well-being. *Child Development,* 76(2), 309–323. https://doi.org/10.1111/j.1467–8624.2005.00847_a.x

FREEZING EMOTIONS

McKay, M., Wood, J.C., & Brantley, J. (2019). *The dialectical behavior therapy skills workbook: Practical DBT exercises for learning mindfulness, interpersonal effectiveness, emotion regulation, and distress tolerance.* New Harbinger Publications.

Parshat Vayigash

PERSPECTIVES OF THE PAST

Drake, L., Duncan, E., Sutherland, F., Abernethy, C., & Henry, C. (2008). Time perspective and correlates of wellbeing. *Time & Society,* 17(1), 47–61.

Stolarski, M., Fieulaine, N., & Van Beek, W. (Eds.). (2015). *Time perspective theory: Review, research and application.* Springer International Publishing.

Zimbardo, P., & Boyd, J. (2008). *The time paradox: The new psychology of time that will change your life.* Simon and Schuster.

CONTRADICTORY EMOTIONS

Linehan, M.M. (2018). *Cognitive-behavioral treatment of borderline personality disorder.* Guilford Publications.

McKay, M., Wood, J.C., & Brantley, J. (2019). *The dialectical behavior therapy skills workbook: Practical DBT exercises for learning mindfulness, interpersonal effectiveness, emotion regulation, and distress tolerance.* New Harbinger Publications.

Parshat Vayechi

ELEMENTS OF RESILIENCE

Cohen, J.A., Mannarino, A.P., & Deblinger, E. (Eds.). (2012). *Trauma-focused CBT for children and adolescents: Treatment applications.* Guilford Press.

Cohen, J.A., Mannarino, A.P., & Deblinger, E. (2016). *Treating trauma and traumatic grief in children and adolescents.* Guilford Publications.

Murray, H., Merritt, C., & Grey, N. (2015). Returning to the scene of the trauma in PTSD treatment–why, how and when?. *The Cognitive Behaviour Therapist, 8.*

Murray, H., Merritt, C., & Grey, N. (2016). Clients' experiences of returning to the trauma site during PTSD treatment: an exploratory study. *Behavioural and Cognitive Psychotherapy, 44*(4), 420–430.

THE BIRTH ORDER EFFECT

Sulloway, F.J. (1996). *Born to rebel: Birth order, family dynamics, and creative lives.* Pantheon Books.

Sulloway, F.J., & Zweigenhaft, R.L. (2010). Birth order and risk taking in athletics: A meta-analysis and study of major league baseball. *Personality and Social Psychology Review, 14*(4), 402–416.

Parshat Shemot

BYSTANDER EFFECT

Darley, J.M., & Latané, B. (1968). Bystander intervention in emergencies: Diffusion of responsibility. *Journal of Personality and Social Psychology, 8*(4, Pt. 1), 377–383. https://doi-org.ezproxy.yu.edu/10.1037/h0025589

Fischer, P., Krueger, J.I., Greitemeyer, T., Vogrincic, C., Kastenmüller, A., Frey, D., Heene, M., Wicher, M., & Kainbacher, M. (2011). The bystander-effect: A meta-analytic review on bystander intervention in dangerous and non-dangerous emergencies. *Psychological Bulletin, 137*(4), 517–537. https://doi.org/10.1037/a0023304

Gansberg, M. (1964, March 27). *37 who saw murder didn't call the police.* New York Times. https://www.nytimes.com/1964/03/27/archives/37-who-saw-murder-didnt-call-the-police-apathy-at-stabbing-of.html

Kassin, S.M. (2017). The killing of Kitty Genovese: What else does this case tell us?. *Perspectives on Psychological Science, 12*(3), 374–381.

Polanin, J.R., Espelage, D.L., & Pigott, T.D. (2012). A meta-analysis of school-based bullying prevention programs' effects on bystander intervention behavior. *School Psychology Review, 41*(1), 47–65.

COMPASSIONATE EMPATHY

Ekman, P. (2007). *Emotions revealed: Recognizing faces and feelings to improve communication and emotional life (2nd edition)*. Henry Holt and Company.

Goetz, J.L., Keltner, D., & Simon-Thomas, E. (2010). Compassion: an evolutionary analysis and empirical review. *Psychological Bulletin, 136*(3), 351.

Shamay-Tsoory, S.G., Aharon-Peretz, J., & Perry, D. (2009). Two systems for empathy: A double dissociation between emotional and cognitive empathy in inferior frontal gyrus versus ventromedial prefrontal lesions. *Brain, 132*(3), 617–627.

DEEP BREATHS

Hopper, S.I., Murray, S.L., Ferrara, L.R., & Singleton, J.K. (2019). Effectiveness of diaphragmatic breathing for reducing physiological and psychological stress in adults: a quantitative systematic review. *JBI Evidence Synthesis, 17*(9), 1855–1876.

Ma, X., Yue, Z.Q., Gong, Z.Q., Zhang, H., Duan, N.Y., Shi, Y.T., Wei, G.X.,

& Li, Y.F. (2017). The effect of diaphragmatic breathing on attention, negative affect and stress in healthy adults. *Frontiers in Psychology, 8*, 874. https://doi.org/10.3389/fpsyg.2017.00874

Nestor, J. (2020). *Breath: The new science of a lost art.* Penguin UK.

Zaccaro, A., Piarulli, A., Laurino, M., Garbella, E., Menicucci, D., Neri, B., & Gemignani, A. (2018). How breath-control can change your life: A systematic review on psycho-physiological correlates of slow breathing. *Frontiers in Human Neuroscience, 12*, 353. https://doi.org/10.3389/fnhum.2018.00353

CONFIRMATION BIAS

Lord, C.G., Ross, L., & Lepper, M.R. (1979). Biased assimilation and attitude polarization: The effects of prior theories on subsequently considered evidence. *Journal of Personality and Social Psychology, 37*(11), 2098–2109. https://doi-org.ezproxy.yu.edu/10.1037/0022-3514.37.11.2098

Oswald, M.E., & Grosjean, S. (2004). Confirmation bias. In R.F. Pohl (Ed.), *Cognitive illusions: A handbook on fallacies and biases in thinking, judgement and memory* (pp. 79–96). Psychology Press.

Nickerson, R.S. (1998). Confirmation bias: A ubiquitous phenomenon in many guises. *Review of General Psychology, 2*(2), 175–220.

Tavris, C., & Aronson, E. (2020). *Mistakes were made (but not by me): Why we justify foolish beliefs, bad decisions, and hurtful acts (3rd edition).* Houghton Mifflin Harcourt.

Parshat Bo

FAKE IT TILL YOU BECOME IT

Carney, D.R., Cuddy, A.J., & Yap, A.J. (2010). Power posing: Brief nonverbal displays affect neuroendocrine levels and risk tolerance. *Psychological Science, 21*(10), 1363–1368.

Cuddy, A. (2012, June). *Your body language may shape who you are* [Video]. TED Conferences. https://www.ted.com/talks/amy_cuddy_your_body_language_shapes_who_you_are

Cuddy, A. (2015). *Presence: Bringing your boldest self to your biggest challenges.* Hachette UK.

LEARNING BY TEACHING

Bargh, J.A., & Schul, Y. (1980). On the cognitive benefits of teaching. *Journal of Educational Psychology, 72*(5), 593.

Chase, C.C., Chin, D.B., Oppezzo, M.A., & Schwartz, D.L. (2009). Teachable agents and the protégé effect: Increasing the effort towards learning. *Journal of Science Education and Technology, 18*(4), 334–352.

Parshat Beshalach

FEED YOUR BRAIN

Barnes, J.N., & Joyner, M.J. (2012). Sugar highs and lows: The impact of diet on cognitive function. *The Journal of Physiology, 590*(12), 2831–2831.

Cordner, Z.A., & Tamashiro, K.L. (2015). Effects of high-fat diet exposure on learning & memory. *Physiology & Behavior, 152*, 363–371.

Reichelt, A.C., Westbrook, R.F., & Morris, M.J. (2017). Editorial: Impact of diet on learning, memory and cognition. *Frontiers in Behavioral Neuroscience, 11*, 96. https://doi.org/10.3389/fnbeh.2017.00096

Rogers, P.J. (2001). A healthy body, a healthy mind: Long-term impact of diet on mood and cognitive function. *Proceedings of the Nutrition Society, 60*(1), 135–143

Spencer, S.J., Korosi, A., Layé, S., Shukitt-Hale, B., & Barrientos, R.M. (2017). Food for thought: How nutrition impacts cognition and emotion. *npj Science of Food, 1*(1), 1–8.

ACTIVE HOPE

Cheavens, J.S., Michael, S.T., & Snyder, C.R. (2005). The correlates of hope: Psychological and physiological benefits. *Interdisciplinary Perspectives on Hope*, 119–132.

Ciarrochi, J., Parker, P., Kashdan, T.B., Heaven, P.C., & Barkus, E. (2015). Hope and emotional well-being: A six-year study to distinguish antecedents, correlates, and consequences. *The Journal of Positive Psychology, 10*(6), 520–532.

Lee, J.Y., & Gallagher, M.W. (2018). Hope and well-being. In M.W. Gallagher & S.J. Lopez (Eds.), *The Oxford handbook of hope* (pp. 287–298). Oxford University Press.

Lopez, S.J. (2013). *Making hope happen: Create the future you want for yourself and others*. Simon and Schuster.

Pleeging, E., Burger, M., & van Exel, J. (2021). The relations between hope and subjective well-being: A literature overview and empirical analysis. *Applied Research in Quality of Life, 16*(3), 1019–1041.

Parshat Yitro

EMOTIONAL RESPONSIBILITY

Barrett, L.F. (2017). *How emotions are made: The secret life of the brain*. Houghton Mifflin Harcourt.

Power, M., & Dalgleish, T. (2015). *Cognition and emotion: From order to disorder* (2nd edition). Psychology Press.

EFFECTIVE FEEDBACK

Stone, D., & Heen, S. (2015). *Thanks for the feedback: The science and art of receiving feedback well (even when it is off base, unfair, poorly delivered, and frankly, you're not in the mood)*. Penguin.

Parshat Mishpatim

THE DANGERS OF GROUPTHINK

Janis, I.L. (1972). *Victims of groupthink: A psychological study of foreign-policy decisions and fiascoes*. Houghton Mifflin.

Janis, I.L. (2008). Groupthink. *IEEE Engineering Management Review, 36*(1), 36.

Schnall, E., & Greenberg, M.J. (2012). Groupthink and the Sanhedrin: An analysis of the ancient court of Israel through the lens of modern social psychology. *Journal of Management History, 18*, 285–294.

VERBAL SENSITIVITY

Johnson, J.G., Cohen, P., Smailes, E.M., Skodol, A.E., Brown, J., & Oldham, J.M. (2001). Childhood verbal abuse and risk for personality disorders during adolescence and early adulthood. *Comprehensive Psychiatry, 42*(1), 16–23. https://doi-org.ezproxy.yu.edu/10.1053/comp.2001.19755

Teicher, M.H., Samson, J.A., Polcari, A., & McGreenery, C.E. (2006).

Sticks, stones, and hurtful words: Relative effects of various forms of childhood maltreatment. *American Journal of Psychiatry, 163*(6), 993–1000.

Parshat Teruma

KNOWING NOTHING

Ames, C. (1995). Achievement goals, motivational climate, and motivational processes. In G.C. Roberts (Ed.), *Motivation in sport and exercise* (pp. 161–176). Human Kinetics Books.

Valentini, N.C., & Rudisill, M.E. (2006). Goal orientation and mastery climate: A review of contemporary research and insights to intervention. *Estudos de Psicologia (Campinas), 23,* 159–171.

THE LIMITS OF AUTHENTICITY

Sheldon, K.M., Ryan, R.M., Rawsthorne, L.J., & Ilardi, B. (1997). Trait self and true self: Cross-role variation in the Big-Five personality traits and its relations with psychological authenticity and subjective well-being. *Journal of Personality and Social Psychology, 73*(6), 1380.

Sutton, A. (2020). Living the good life: A meta-analysis of authenticity, well-being and engagement. *Personality and Individual Differences, 153,* 109645.

Parshat Tetzaveh

APPRECIATING BEAUTY

Martínez-Martí, M.L., Hernández-Lloreda, M.J., & Avia, M.D. (2016). Appreciation of beauty and excellence: Relationship with personality, prosociality and well-being. *Journal of Happiness Studies, 17*(6), 2613–2634.

Peterson, C., & Seligman, M.E. (2004). *Character strengths and virtues: A handbook and classification.* Oxford University Press.

MULTIPLE INTELLIGENCES

Gardner, H.E. (2008). *Multiple intelligences: New horizons in theory and practice.* Basic books.

Gardner, H.E. (2020, July 8). A Resurgence of Interest in Existential Intelligence: Why Now? Howard Gardner. https://www.howardgardner .com/howards-blog/a-resurgence-of-interest-in-existential-intelligence -why-now

Parshat Ki Tisa

THE DANGERS OF RIGIDITY

Hayes, S. (2016, February 22). *Psychological flexibility: How love turns pain into purpose* [Video]. Youtube. https://www.youtube.com/watch?v= 079_gmO5ppg

Kashdan, T.B., Rottenberg, J. (2010). Psychological flexibility as a fundamental aspect of health. Clinical Psychology Review, 30, 865–878. doi:10 .1016/j.cpr.2010.03.001

Lydia Morris, & Warren Mansell. (2018). A systematic review of the relationship between rigidity/flexibility and transdiagnostic cognitive and behavioral processes that maintain psychopathology. *Journal of Experimental Psychopathology, 9*(3). https://doi.org/10.1177 /2043808718779431

DIGNITY CULTURE

Leung, A.K.Y., & Cohen, D. (2011). Within-and between-culture variation: Individual differences and the cultural logics of honor, face, and dignity cultures. *Journal of Personality and Social Psychology 100*(3), 507.

Parshiyot Vayakhel-Pekudei

MOMENTS RIPE FOR ANGER

Beck, R., & Fernandez, E. (1998). Cognitive-behavioral therapy in the treatment of anger: A meta-analysis. *Cognitive Therapy and Research, 22*(1), 63–74.

Schiffman, M. (2016). Incorporating Jewish texts with REBT in the treatment of clinical anger. *Journal of Rational-Emotive & Cognitive-Behavior Therapy, 34*(3), 225–239.

THE BENEFITS AND DETRIMENTS OF HUMOR

Martin, R., & Kuiper, N.A. (2016). Three decades investigating humor and laughter: An interview with Professor Rod Martin. *Europe's Journal of Psychology*, 12(3), 498–512. https://doi.org/10.5964/ejop.v12i3.1119

Martin, R.A., & Ford, T. (2018). *The psychology of humor: An integrative approach* (2nd edition). Academic press.

Parshat Vayikra

MISTAKES WERE MADE

Tavris, C., & Aronson, E. (2020). *Mistakes were made (but not by me): Why we justify foolish beliefs, bad decisions, and hurtful acts* (3rd edition). Houghton Mifflin Harcourt.

FEARLESS SACRIFICES

Edmondson, A. (1999). Psychological safety and learning behavior in work teams. *Administrative Science Quarterly*, 44(2), 350–383. https://doi.org/10.2307/2666999

Edmondson, A.C. (2018). *The fearless organization: Creating psychological safety in the workplace for learning, innovation, and growth.* John Wiley & Sons.

Parshat Tzav

THE FRESH START EFFECT

Dai, H., Milkman, K.L., & Riis, J. (2014). The fresh start effect: Temporal landmarks motivate aspirational behavior. *Management Science*, 60(10), 2563–2582.

Milkman, K., & Milkman, K.L. (2021). *How to change: The science of getting from where you are to where you want to be.* Penguin.

PAY IT FORWARD

Bartlett, M.Y., & DeSteno, D. (2006). Gratitude and prosocial behavior: Helping when it costs you. *Psychological Science*, 17(4), 319–325.

DeSteno, D. (2018). *Emotional success: The power of gratitude, compassion, and pride.* Houghton Mifflin Harcourt.

Parshat Shemini

MISTAKEN ANGER

Beck, A.T., & Deffenbacher, J.L. (2000). Prisoners of hate: The cognitive basis of anger, hostility and violence. HarperCollins.

Ellis, A., & Tafrate, R.C. (1998). *How to control your anger before it controls you.* Citadel Press.

Martin, R.C., & Dahlen, E.R. (2004). Irrational beliefs and the experience and expression of anger. *Journal of Rational-Emotive and Cognitive-Behavior Therapy, 22*(1), 3–20.

AHARON'S SILENCE

Pelcovitz, D. (2013, February 25). *The psychology of death and mourning in Judaism* [Audio]. Yutorah. https://www.yutorah.org/sidebar/lecture.cfm/791991/dr-david-pelcovitz/the-psychology-of-death-and-mourning-in-judaism/

Van der Kolk, B.A., Roth, S., Pelcovitz, D., Sunday, S., & Spinazzola, J. (2005). Disorders of extreme stress: The empirical foundation of a complex adaptation to trauma. *Journal of Traumatic Stress: Official Publication of the International Society for Traumatic Stress Studies, 18*(5), 389–399.

Van der Kolk, B.A. (2015). *The body keeps the score: Brain, mind, and body in the healing of trauma.* Penguin Books.

Parshiyot Tazria-Metzora

BIASES OF THE SELF

Forsyth, D.R. (2008). Self-Serving Bias. In W.A. Darity (Ed.), *International encyclopedia of the social sciences* (2nd edition) (p. 429). Macmillan Reference.

Pronin, E., Lin, D.Y., & Ross, L. (2002). The bias blind spot: Perceptions of bias in self versus others. *Personality and Social Psychology Bulletin, 28*(3), 369–381.

HEDGING FOR HUMILITY

Pennebaker, J.W., Mehl, M.R., & Niederhoffer, K.G. (2003). Psychological aspects of natural language use: Our words, our selves. *Annual Review of Psychology, 54*(1), 547–577.

Pennebaker, J.W. (2013). *The secret life of pronouns: What our words say about us.* Bloomsbury Publishing USA.

SEARCHING FOR MEANING

Frankl, V.E. (1985). *Man's search for meaning.* Simon and Schuster.

Frankl, V.E. (2014). *The will to meaning: Foundations and applications of logotherapy.* Penguin.

Parshat Acharei-Mot

THE POWER OF CONFESSION

Murray-Swank, A.B., McConnell, K.M., & Pargament, K.I. (2007). Understanding spiritual confession: A review and theoretical synthesis. *Mental Health, Religion and Culture, 10*(3), 275–291.

THE LIMITS OF RESPONSIBILITY

Hazleden, B. (2014). Whose fault is it? Exoneration and allocation of personal responsibility in relationship manuals. *Journal of Sociology, 50*(4), 422–436.

Overholser, J.C. (2005). Contemporary psychotherapy: Promoting personal responsibility for therapeutic change. *Journal of Contemporary Psychotherapy, 35*(4), 369–376.

Rimke, H., & Brock, D. (2012). The culture of therapy: Psychocentrism in everyday life. *Power and Everyday Practices,* 182–202.

Parshat Kedoshim

ASSERTIVENESS TRAINING

Ellis, A., & Tafrate, R.C. (1998). *How to control your anger before it controls you.* Citadel Press.

Speed, B.C., Goldstein, B.L., & Goldfried, M.R. (2018). Assertiveness training: A forgotten evidence-based treatment. *Clinical Psychology: Science and Practice, 25*(1), e12216.

EXPANSION OF THE SELF

Aron, A., Aron, E.N., Tudor, M., & Nelson, G. (1991). Close relationships as including other in the self. *Journal of Personality and Social Psychology, 60*(2), 241.

Aron, A., & Aron, E.N. (1997). Self-expansion motivation and including other in the self. In S. Duck (Ed.), *Handbook of personal relationships: Theory, research and interventions* (pp. 251–270). John Wiley & Sons Inc.

Parshat Emor

SEFIRAT HAOMER: PROCESS AND OUTCOME

Freund, A.M., Hennecke, M., & Mustafić, M. (2012). On gains and losses, means and ends: Goal orientation and goal focus across adulthood. In R.M. Ryan (Ed.), *The Oxford handbook of human motivation* (pp. 280–300). Oxford University Press.

Freund, A.M., & Hennecke, M. (2015). On means and ends: The role of goal focus in successful goal pursuit. *Current Directions in Psychological Science, 24*(2), 149–153.

HAPPINESS & WHOLENESS

Adler, J.M., & Hershfield, H.E. (2012). Mixed emotional experience is associated with and precedes improvements in psychological well-being. *ONE, 7*(4). https://doi-org.ezproxy.yu.edu/10.1371/journal.pone .0035633

Kashdan, T.B., & Biswas-Diener, R. (2014). *The upside of your dark side: Why being your whole self – not just your" good" self – drives success and fulfillment.* Penguin.

Parshiyot Behar-Bechukotai

PORTION CONTROL

Rolls, B.J. (2018). The role of portion size, energy density, and variety in obesity and weight management. In T.A. Wadden & G.A. Bray (Eds.), *Handbook of obesity treatment., 2nd ed.* (pp. 93–104). The Guilford Press.

Rolls, B.J., Morris, E.L., & Roe, L.S. (2002). Portion size of food affects energy intake in normal-weight and overweight men and women. *The American Journal of Clinical Nutrition, 76*(6), 1207–1213.

INDIVIDUALISM VS. COLLECTIVISM

Hofstede, G., Hofstede, G.J., & Minkov, M. (2005). *Cultures and organizations: Software of the mind.* New York: Mcgraw-hill.

Sacks, Y. (1990). Individualism and Collectivism: A Torah Perspective. *The Torah U-Madda Journal, 2,* 70–75.

GRITTY TORAH

Duckworth, A.L., Peterson, C., Matthews, M.D., & Kelly, D.R. (2007). Grit: Perseverance and passion for long-term goals. *Journal of Personality and Social Psychology, 92*(6), 1087–1101. https://doi.org/10.1037/0022 -3514.92.6.1087

Duckworth, A. (2016). *Grit: The power of passion and perseverance.* Scribner/ Simon & Schuster.

Parshat Bamidbar

UNIFIED DIVERSITY

University of Oklahoma. Institute of Group Relations, & Sherif, M. (1961). *Intergroup conflict and cooperation: The Robbers Cave experiment* (Vol. 10, pp. 150–198). Norman, OK: University Book Exchange.

INTELLECTUAL HUMILITY

Krumrei-Mancuso, E.J. (2017). Intellectual humility and prosocial values: Direct and mediated effects. *The Journal of Positive Psychology, 12*(1), 13–28.

Krumrei-Mancuso, E.J., Haggard, M.C., LaBouff, J.P., & Rowatt, W.C. (2020). Links between intellectual humility and acquiring knowledge. *The Journal of Positive Psychology, 15*(2), 155–170.

Parshat Naso

SITUATIONAL CONTROL

Duckworth, A.L., Gendler, T.S., & Gross, J.J. (2016). Situational strategies for self-control. *Perspectives on Psychological Science, 11*(1), 35–55.

HIERARCHY OF NEEDS

Bridgman, T., Cummings, S., & Ballard, J. (2019). Who built Maslow's pyramid? A history of the creation of management studies' most famous symbol and its implications for management education. *Academy of Management Learning & Education, 18*(1), 81–98.

Kaufman, S.B. (2021). *Transcend: The new science of self-actualization.* Penguin.

Maslow, A.H. (1943). A theory of human motivation. *Psychological review, 50*(4), 370.

Parshat Behaalotcha

VARIETY EFFECT

Embling, R., Pink, A.E., Gatzemeier, J., Price, M., D Lee, M., & Wilkinson, L.L. (2021). Effect of food variety on intake of a meal: A systematic review and meta-analysis. *The American Journal of Clinical Nutrition, 113*(3), 716–741.

Rolls, B.J., Rowe, E.A., Rolls, E.T., Kingston, B., Megson, A., & Gunary, R. (1981). Variety in a meal enhances food intake in man. *Physiology & Behavior, 26*(2), 215–221.

THE LIMITS OF CONSCIENTIOUSNESS

Boyce, C.J., Wood, A.M., & Brown, G.D. (2010). The dark side of conscientiousness: Conscientious people experience greater drops in life satisfaction following unemployment. *Journal of Research in Personality, 44*(4), 535–539.

Friedman, H.S., & Kern, M.L. (2014). Personality, well-being, and health. *Annual Review of Psychology, 65,* 719–742.

Hayes, N., & Joseph, S. (2003). Big 5 correlates of three measures of subjective well-being. *Personality and Individual differences, 34*(4), 723–727.

Widiger, T.A. (Ed.). (2017). *The Oxford handbook of the five factor model.* Oxford University Press.

Parshat Shelach

THE COLOR OF TZITZIT

Elliot, A.J., & Maier, M.A. (2007). Color and psychological functioning. *Current Directions in Psychological Science, 16*(5), 250–254.

Elliot, A.J., & Maier, M.A. (2014). Color psychology: Effects of perceiving color on psychological functioning in humans. *Annual Review of Psychology, 65,* 95–120.

THE SELF-ESTEEM OF THE SPIES

Donnellan, M.B., Trzesniewski, K.H., & Robins, R.W. (2011). Self-esteem: Enduring issues and controversies. In T. Chamorro-Premuzic, S. von Stumm, & A. Furnham (Eds.), *The Wiley-Blackwell handbook of individual differences* (pp. 718–746). Wiley Blackwell.

Twerski, A.J. (1987). *Let us make man: Self-esteem through Jewishness.* Traditional Press.

Parshat Korach

UNHEALTHY CONFLICT

Coleman, P.T., Deutsch, M., & Marcus, E.C. (Eds.). (2014). *The handbook of conflict resolution: Theory and practice.* John Wiley & Sons.

Kaminsky, H. (2017). *Fundamentals of Jewish conflict resolution.* Academic Studies Press.

Parshat Chukat

SELF-MONITORING

Cohen, J.S., Edmunds, J.M., Brodman, D.M., Benjamin, C.L., & Kendall, P.C. (2013). Using self-monitoring: Implementation of collaborative empiricism in cognitive-behavioral therapy. *Cognitive and Behavioral Practice, 20*(4), 419–428.

BLOCKED GOAL ANGER

Lewis, M. (2010). The development of anger. In *International handbook of anger* (pp. 177–191). Springer, New York, NY.

Schmitt, A., Gielnik, M.M., & Seibel, S. (2019). When and how does anger during goal pursuit relate to goal achievement? The roles of persistence and action planning. *Motivation and Emotion, 43*(2), 205–217.

Parshat Balak

THE LANGUAGE OF ANIMALS

Beecher, M. (2020). Animal communication. In *Oxford Research Encyclopedia of Psychology*. https://oxfordre.com/psychology/view/10.1093/acrefore/9780190236557.001.0001/acrefore-9780190236557-e-646.

Gilbert, D. (2009). *Stumbling on happiness*. Vintage Canada.

Pepperberg, I.M. (2017). Animal language studies: What happened?. *Psychonomic Bulletin & Review, 24*(1), 181–185.

POSITIVE SLEEP

Seligman, M.E. (2002). *Authentic happiness: Using the new positive psychology to realize your potential for lasting fulfillment*. Simon and Schuster.

Parshat Pinchas

SOCIAL & EMOTIONAL LEADERSHIP

Caruso, D.R., Mayer, J.D., & Salovey, P. (2002). Emotional intelligence and emotional leadership. In R.E. Riggio, S.E. Murphy, & F.J. Pirozzolo (Eds.), *Multiple intelligences and leadership* (pp. 55–74). Lawrence Erlbaum Associates Publishers.

Riggio, R.E., & Reichard, R.J. (2008). The emotional and social intelligences of effective leadership: An emotional and social skill approach. *Journal of Managerial Psychology, 23*(2), 169–185. https://doi-org.ezproxy.yu.edu/10.1108/02683940810850808

WORDS CAN CHANGE YOUR BRAIN

Newberg, A.B., & Waldman, M.R. (2013). *Words can change your brain: 12 conversation strategies to build trust, resolve conflict, and increase intimacy.* Penguin.

Parshiyot Mattot-Masei

PRECOMMITMENT DEVICES

Ariely, D., & Wertenbroch, K. (2002). Procrastination, deadlines, and performance: Self-control by precommitment. *Psychological Science, 13*(3), 219–224.

PREDICTING EMOTIONS

Wilson, T.D., & Gilbert, D.T. (2003). Affective forecasting. In M.P. Zanna (Ed.), *Advances in experimental social psychology,* Vol. 35, (pp. 345–411). Elsevier Academic Press. https://doi.org/10.1016/S0065-2601(03)01006-2

Wilson, T.D., & Gilbert, D.T. (2005). Affective forecasting: Knowing what to want. *Current Driections in Psychological Science, 14*(3), 131–134.

Parshat Devarim

THE COURAGE OF JUDGES

Biswas-Diener, R. (2012). *The courage quotient: How science can make you braver.* John Wiley & Sons.

Hannah, S.T., Sweeney, P.J., & Lester, P.B. (2007). Toward a courageous mindset: The subjective act and experience of courage. *The Journal of Positive Psychology, 2*(2), 129–135.

UNCONDITIONAL POSITIVE REGARD

Bozarth, J.D. (2013). Unconditional positive regard. In M. Cooper, M. O'Hara, P.F. Schmid, & A.C. Bohart (Eds.), *The handbook of person-centred psychotherapy and counselling., 2nd ed.* (pp. 180–192). Palgrave Macmillan/Springer Nature. https://doi-org.ezproxy.yu.edu/10.1007/978-1-137-32900-4_12

Rogers, C.R. (1957). The necessary and sufficient conditions of therapeutic personality change. *Journal of Consulting Psychology, 21*(2), 95.

Parshat Va'etchanan

GRIT OR QUIT?

Duckworth, A.L., Peterson, C., Matthews, M.D., & Kelly, D.R. (2007). Grit: perseverance and passion for long-term goals. *Journal of Personality and Social Psychology, 92*(6), 1087.

Wrosch, C., Scheier, M.F., Miller, G.E., Schulz, R., & Carver, C.S. (2003). Adaptive self-regulation of unattainable goals: Goal disengagement, goal reengagement, and subjective well-being. *Personality and Social Psychology Bulletin, 29*(12), 1494–1508.

TORAH & MENTAL HEALTH

Koenig, H., Koenig, H.G., King, D., & Carson, V.B. (2012). *Handbook of religion and health.* Oxford University Press.

Pirutinsky, S., Cherniak, A.D., & Rosmarin, D.H. (2020). COVID-19, mental health, and religious coping among American Orthodox Jews. *Journal of Religion and Health, 59*(5), 2288–2301.

Parshat Ekev

GRATEFUL THINKING

Froh, J., & Bono, G. (2014). *Making grateful kids: The science of building character.* Templeton Foundation Press.

Froh, J.J., Bono, G., Jinyan Fan, Emmons, R.A., Henderson, K., Harris, C., Leggio, H., & Wood, A.M. (2014). Nice thinking! An educational intervention that teaches children to think gratefully. *School Psychology Review, 43*(2), 132–152. https://doi.org/10.1080/02796015.2014.12087440

MIND OVER MILKSHAKES

Crum, A.J., Corbin, W.R., Brownell, K.D., & Salovey, P. (2011). Mind over milkshakes: Mindsets, not just nutrients, determine ghrelin response. *Health Psychology, 30*(4), 424.

Parshat Re'eh

DON'T BELIEVE WHAT YOU SEE

Chabris, C.F., & Simons, D.J. (2010). *The invisible gorilla: And other ways our intuitions deceive us.* Harmony.

Kuhn, G., Amlani, A.A., & Rensink, R.A. (2008). Towards a science of magic. *Trends in Cognitive Sciences, 12*(9), 349–354.

Kuhn, G. (2019). *Experiencing the impossible: The science of magic.* MIT Press.

Simons, D.J., & Chabris, C.F. (1999). Gorillas in our midst: Sustained inattentional blindness for dynamic events. *Perception, 28*(9), 1059–1074.

THERE IS NO "I" IN HAPPY

Nelson, S.K., Layous, K., Cole, S.W., & Lyubomirsky, S. (2016). Do unto others or treat yourself? The effects of prosocial and self-focused behavior on psychological flourishing. *Emotion, 16*(6), 850.

Parshat Shoftim

BETTER THAN AVERAGE

Alicke, M.D., Klotz, M.L., Breitenbecher, D.L., Yurak, T.J., & Vredenburg, D.S. (1995). Personal contact, individuation, and the better-than-average effect. *Journal of Personality and Social Psychology, 68*(5), 804.

Haidt, J. (2006). *The happiness hypothesis: Finding modern truth in ancient wisdom.* Basic books.

DEEP WORK

Goleman, D. (2013). *Focus: The hidden driver of excellence.* HarperCollins Publishers.

Newport, C. (2016). *Deep work: Rules for focused success in a distracted world.* Hachette UK.

Parshat Ki Teitzei

THE BEN FRANKLIN EFFECT

Jecker, J., & Landy, D. (1969). Liking a person as a function of doing him a favour. *Human Relations, 22*(4), 371–378.

Niiya, Y. (2016). Does a favor request increase liking toward the requester?. *The Journal of Social Psychoiogy, 156*(2), 211–221.

REMEMBERING AND FORGETTING

Ebbinghaus, H. (2013). Memory: A contribution to experimental psychology. *Annals of Neurosciences, 20*(4), 155.

Schacter, D.L. (2002). *The seven sins of memory: How the mind forgets and remembers.* HMH.

Parshat Ki Tavo

HEALTHY HAPPINESS

Izard, C.E. (2009). Emotion theory and research: Highlights, unanswered questions, and emerging issues. *Annual Review of Psychology, 60*, 1–25.

APPRECIATING BLESSINGS

Emmons, R.A. (2007). *Thanks!: How the new science of gratitude can make you happier.* Houghton Mifflin Harcourt.

McCullough, M.E., Emmons, R.A., & Tsang, J.A. (2002). The grateful disposition: A conceptual and empirical topography. *Journal of Personality and Social Psychology, 82*(1), 112.

Wood, A.M., Froh, J.J., & Geraghty, A.W. (2010). Gratitude and well-being: A review and theoretical integration. *Clinical Psychology Review, 30*(7), 890–905.

Parshiyot Nitzavim-Vayeilech

BENEFIT FINDING

Helgeson, V.S., Reynolds, K.A., & Tomich, P.L. (2006). A meta-analytic review of benefit finding and growth. *Journal of Consulting and Clinical Psychology, 74*(5), 797.

Tedeschi, R.G., & Calhoun, L.G. (2004). Posttraumatic growth: conceptual foundations and empirical evidence *Psychological Inquiry*, 15(1), 1–18.

Tedeschi, R.G., & Moore, B.A. (2016). *The posttraumatic growth workbook: Coming through trauma wiser, stronger, and more resilient.* New Harbinger Publications.

Tedeschi, R.G., Shakespeare-Finch, J., Taku, K., & Calhoun, L.G. (2018). *Posttraumatic growth: Theory, research, and applications.* Routledge.

THERE IS ALWAYS HOPE

Prochaska, J.O., Norcross, J.C., & DiClemente, C.C. (1994). *Changing for good.* Avon Books.

Prochaska, J.O., & DiClemente, C.C. (1983). Stages and processes of self-change of smoking: Toward an integrative model of change. *Journal of Consulting and Clinical Psychology, 51*(3), 390.

Prochaska, J.O., Redding, C.A., & Evers, K.E. (2015). The transtheoretical model and stages of change. In K. Glanz, B.K. Rimer, & K.V. Viswanath (Eds.), *Health behavior: Theory, research, and practice* (pp. 125–148). Jossey-Bass/Wiley.

Parshat Haazinu

DEFYING DEATH WITH LIFE

Becker, E. (1997). *The denial of death.* Simon and Schuster.

Solomon, S., Greenberg, J., & Pyszczynski, T. (1991). A terror management theory of social behavior: The psychological functions of self-esteem and cultural worldviews. *Advances in Experimental Social Psychology, 24,* 93–159.

Solomon, S., Greenberg, J., & Pyszczynski, T. (2015). *The worm at the core: On the role of death in life.* Random House.

TWISTED THINKING

Twerski, A.J. (2009). *Addictive thinking: Understanding self-deception.* Simon and Schuster.

Yurica, C.L., & DiTomasso, R.A. (2005). Cognitive distortions. In A. Freeman (Ed.), *Encyclopedia of cognitive behavior therapy* (pp. 117–122). Springer.

Parshat Vezot Ha-Beracha

BUYING HAPPINESS

Dunn, E.W., Gilbert, D.T., & Wilson, T.D. (2011). If money doesn't make you happy, then you probably aren't spending it right. *Journal of Consumer Psychology, 21*(2), 115–125.

Kahneman, D., & Deaton, A. (2010). High income improves evaluation of life but not emotional well-being. *Proceedings of the National Academy of Sciences, 107*(38), 16489–16493.

Killingsworth, M.A. (2021). Experienced well-being rises with income, even above $75,000 per year. *Proceedings of the National Academy of Sciences, 118*(4).

SOCIAL COMPARISONS

Collins, R.L. (1996). For better or worse: The impact of upward social comparison on self-evaluations. *Psychological Bulletin, 119*(1), 51.

Festinger, L. (1957). Social comparison theory. *Selective Exposure Theory,* 16.

Gibbons, F.X., & Gerrard, M. (1989). Effects of upward and downward social comparison on mood states. *Journal of Social and Clinical Psychology, 8*(1), 14–31.

In Praise of PSYCHED *for* TORAH

"Rabbi Dr. Mordechai Schiffman has done a masterful job of showing how Torah values and psychological insights can be woven together to become an integral part of our religious lives. This is a powerful book that will no doubt deepen your appreciation of Torah while simultaneously providing new perspectives on your own life and sense of self."　　　**Rabbi Dr. Ari Berman, President, Yeshiva University**

"Dr. Schiffman's exploration of psychological factors through the lens of Torah is inspired and inspiring. With his deep understanding of both realms, Dr. Schiffman invites the reader to a deeper understanding of ancient wisdom for today's times."
Dr. Rona Novick, Dean, Azrieli Graduate School, Yeshiva University

"Rabbi Dr. Schiffman is a clear and methodical thinker who has supplemented his years of rabbinical studies with the highest level of training with some of the leading experts in psychology. The wisdom and practical guidance that emerges from these two streams of insight will enrich the lives of readers, helping them to achieve depth and integration in their weekly review of the Torah reading."
Dr. David Pelcovitz, Straus Chair in Psychology, Yeshiva University

"Dr. Mordechai Schiffman offers us nuggets of wisdom on every page that integrate psychology and the weekly parsha, distilling ideas into accessible and relevant ways to reframe our understanding of the ancient stories that serve as the touchstone of a Torah life and offers us insights into ourselves along the way."
Dr. Erica Brown, Vice Provost and Director of Sacks Center, Yeshiva University

"Mordechai Schiffman has written an important book that bridges ancient wisdom and modern research, theory and practice, religion and psychology. This is a powerful guide that can help you gain a deeper, more nuanced understanding of the Torah--as well as lead a happier and more fulfilling life."
Dr. Tal Ben-Shahar, Founder of Happiness Studies Academy

Rabbi Dr. Mordechai Schiffman is an Assistant Professor at Yeshiva University's Azrieli Graduate School, and an instructor at RIETS, Wurzweiler School of Social Work, and the Straus Center for Torah and Western Thought. He received his MS from Azrieli, rabbinic ordination from RIETS, and a doctorate in psychology from St. John's University. Rabbi Dr. Schiffman has been on the rabbinic staff of Kingsway Jewish Center in Brooklyn, NY, since 2011 and practices as a licensed psychologist. His academic and popular articles, as well as many of his lectures, are accessible on www.PsychedForTorah.com.

ISBN 9781947857766

90000

9 781947 857766